VAMPIRES AND ZOMBIES

VAMPIRE

AND

ZOI

IRES
BIES

TRANSCULTURAL MIGRATIONS AND
TRANSNATIONAL INTERPRETATIONS

Edited by

Dorothea Fischer-Hornung and Monika Mueller

UNIVERSITY PRESS OF MISSISSIPPI † JACKSON

www.upress.state.ms.us

Designed by Peter D. Halverson

The University Press of Mississippi is a member of the Association of American University Presses.

First printing 2016

∞

Library of Congress Cataloging-in-Publication Data

Vampires and zombies : transcultural migrations and transnational interpretations / edited by Dorothea Fischer-Hornung, Monika Mueller.
pages cm
Includes bibliographical references and index.
ISBN 978-1-4968-0474-7 (hardback) —
ISBN (invalid) 978-1-4968-0475-4 (ebook) 1. Vampires in mass media.
I. Fischer-Hornung, Dorothea, 1949– editor. II. Mueller, Monika, 1960– editor.
P96.V35V36 2016
398ʼ.45—dc23
2015020155

British Library Cataloging-in-Publication Data available

CONTENTS

PART 3: CULTURAL ANXIETIES

PART 4: CIRCULATING TECHNOLOGIES

VAMPIRES AND ZOMBIES

INTRODUCTION

DOROTHEA FISCHER-HORNUNG AND MONIKA MUELLER

Monsters loom large in the cultural imaginary. From folktales to splatter movies, from the Bible to computer games, from birth to death, monsters such as devils, werewolves, dragons, ghosts, cyborgs, zombies, and vampires inundate our imagination. Monsters, which can be understood as symbols of human vulnerability, can, however, also help us to imagine triumphing over danger. As Stephen T. Asma points out, they are "beneficial foes" that are "imaginative foils for thinking about our own responses to menace" (2009, online).

In his "Monster Culture (Seven Theses)," Jeffrey Jerome Cohen notes that monsters are "difference made flesh" (1996, 7), that they appear in times of crisis, and often reflect political or ideological difference (see 6–8). Their embodiment of otherness, however, also makes them an ideal vehicle for the representation of deviance, which is similarly susceptible to monsterization (see 9). Boundaries of submission and resistance, race and sex, nation and national identity—life and death itself—are challenged. This makes monsters simultaneously attractive and repulsive, and, in Cohen's reading, this may account for their continued cultural popularity (see 17).

Currently, of all these monsters, vampires and zombies seem to be the most trendy—the most humanly embodied of the undead and the most frequently paired monsters in the media and popular culture.[1] Moreover, both figures have experienced radical reinterpretation in the context of contemporary cultural concerns. If in the past vampires were evil, bloodsucking exploiters and zombies were brainless victims, they now have metamorphosed into kinder, gentler vampires and crueler, flesh-eating zombies.[2]

Vampires originally hailed from Transylvania and zombies originated in Haiti. They soon surfaced elsewhere and both—each in their own way—became a global metaphor for the exploited masses. The appeal of both vampires and zombies can, perhaps, initially be attributed to the seemingly clear-cut binary opposition of perpetrator and victim. However, their transspacial and transtemporal distributions have revealed them to be highly variable signifiers. Contemporary vampires can be both perpetrators and, more recently, victims; zombies have gone from enslaved victims of a *bokor*, the zombie master, to flesh-eating, brainless, and insatiably out-of-control devouring monsters. Further, they have simultaneously contracted and expanded gender, race, and class roles, at once confirming and deconstructing these concepts. Although the portrayal of both vampires and zombies can be traced to specific regions and predates mass media, the introduction of mass distribution through film and game technologies has served to significantly modify their depiction over time and in various locations. This volume—authored by scholars from different national and cultural backgrounds—explores some of these transformations the vampire and zombie figures have experienced in literature and media.

The historical vampire figure, Dracula, of whom the Transylvanian Vlad Tepes is a prototype, originates in Europe. In these early manifestations, he is part of Eastern European culture and is ultimately subdued by the rituals of Christianity. Bram Stoker's genre-initiating novel *Dracula* (1897) represents Eastern Europeans as dangerous, atavistic others, who threaten the more advanced, democratic social order of nineteenth-century Britain. Khair and Höglund note that "[t]he publication of *Dracula*, a narrative where many of the folkloristic elements converge, marks the institutionalization of the authoritative European vampire" (2013, 2). As early as 1966, Richard Wasson had already called attention to the vampiric cultural politics of Stoker's novel. He argued that Stoker's nineteenth-century Western European readers perceived Romania as a "culture-free zone": "While the rest of Europe ha[d] been free to develop a culture, this area [remained] a bloody battle ground" (24). In a more recent article, Diane Long Hoeveler has added ethnicity and race to the discussion of the presentation of demonic otherness in *Dracula*. She writes that "[f]ears of Eastern Europeans, dark others, and the earlier, atavistic forms of race and religion mark the text and are finally eradicated in a rabidly neo-Christian phantasmagoria that concludes the novel" (2006, online). Both analyses focus on transcultural aspects of the Eastern European Dracula vampire myth in relation to Western Europe, yet as this volume shows, vampires and their local manifestations also have many non-European variants and perhaps even origins.

In an early reading, Ernest Jones has added the vampire's psychological motivation to the figure's cultural significance. According to Jones, the vampire is "a social or political tyrant who sucks the life from the people [and] an irresistible lover who sucks away energy, ambition, or even life for selfish reasons" ([1931] 2006, 151). The vampire's individual obsession with power and dominance also has immediate social repercussions. S/he becomes a prime example not only of the tyrannical landowning European gentry, but also of the slave-master and the colonizer, as evidenced in two works discussed in this volume: Herbert George de Lisser's *The White Witch of Rosehall* and Octavia Butler's *Fledgling*.

Over the years, the figure has been transformed from an exploitative European aristocrat into a captivating cosmopolitan everyman. The TV series *Buffy the Vampire Slayer*, for example, was part of a trend in the 1990s to "undemonize" vampire characters. The series gave them human emotions in order to save them from being "an inferior, entirely different race ... [the] Other personified" (Money 2002, 105). This trend is also reflected in Poppy Z. Brite's novel *Lost Souls*, whose vampires are "everymen" who work as musicians and bartenders. However, Brite's vampires also conform to the stereotype of the vampire as an irresistible murderous lover. This alluring, seductively desirous, yet destructive vampire still figures large in the imaginary of current popular culture. S/he is portrayed as polyamorous and practicing everything from heterosexual to homosexual to incestuous sex.

In some of his or her recent incarnations, the twenty-first-century vampire no longer even appears particularly dangerous or exploitative. In the popular, globally broadcast US television show *True Blood*, for example, the vampires are more or less ordinary citizens of a small Southern town. Due to the invention of synthetic blood—"Tru Blood" by Japanese Yellow-Peril scientists—they do not have to feed on human blood anymore. Quite to the contrary, they sometimes have to be protected from ordinary human citizens. Thus, in the show's first episode, Sookie Stackhouse, the primary protagonist, succeeds in saving a vampire from a human couple that tries to get at his blood for its propensities as a drug used by humans. Yet there are clearly larger and changing cultural issues at stake: in his review of *True Blood*, Ken Tucker suggests that in this show, "vampire rights stand for gay rights" (2009, online).

The physical manifestations of the vampire are still rather clear-cut. S/he mostly appears as a bloodsucking human with fangs, but sometimes also as a vampire bat or another beast that can be the result of his/her shape-shifting abilities. The vampire customarily functions—by bloodsucking definition— as a perpetrator, whereas traditionally the will-less zombie is the prototypical victim. However, present-day media zombies, in contrast to the original Haitian zombie, are most often portrayed as aggressors, as people-eating ghouls. The most often quoted, if sometimes tendentious, discussion of the classical Haitian zombie can be found in Wade Davis's *Passage of Darkness: The Ethnobiology of the Haitian Zombie*. Davis informs his readers that in addition to the "spirit zombies" there are the more well-known "living dead" zombies who are:

> *innocent victims raised in a comatose trance from their graves by ma-*
> *levolent sorcerers, led away under cover of night to distant farms or*
> *villages where they must toil indefinitely as slaves. . . . According to folk*
> *belief, these sad individuals may be recognized by their docile natures,*
> *their glassy, empty eyes, the nasal twang to their voices . . . and by the*
> *absence of will, memory, and emotion.* (1988, 60)

From this description it is clear that the "living dead" are indeed perfect victims and that they seem to be quite the opposite of the flesh-eating monsters of globalized zombie splatter movies.

But how did this metamorphosis of the zombie come about? As Davis already noted, the "subject of the Haitian zombie is one that has fascinated—indeed titillated—foreign observers for decades" (56). The first flurry of US zombie movies, such as *White Zombie* and *I Walked with a Zombie,* was already produced in the 1940s—in the decade after the US occupation of Haiti between 1915 and 1934. These films, through cultural circulation, initiated significant changes in the traditional zombie figure, in particular moving it out of the African Caribbean tradition by "whitening" both the zombie and the zombie master.

Zombies seem to be particularly scary because they speak to an array of human fears, such as the ur-fear of death, in particular, of being turned into an enslaved zombie despite being "innocent" (Larkin 2006, 26). Kyle Bishop has pointed out that the postoccupation imperialist discourse of the 1940s movies produced in the United States expressed generalized and rampant racist fears of miscegenation and hybridity, "of black and white intermingling, the terror of black [male] bodies dominating whites" (2010, 69). Moreover, as the location of the only successful slave revolution in history and the first independent black republic, Haiti is not only a site of African enslavement, but also a site of successful African resistance. The Haitian zombie is thus coded as simultaneously eminently powerless and frightfully powerful.

The zombies of today's popular culture—as a number of contributions in this volume suggest—are no longer only found in Haiti, but have become a truly transnational and transcultural phenomenon. Zombies of the obsessional cannibal variety have been popularized by George A. Romero's *Living Dead* movie series. As our contributor Richard Hand illustrates, Romero's monsters in turn were inspired by the living dead of earlier horror comics, which evoked a generally apocalyptic atmosphere.

Shawn McIntosh suggests that the term zombie that came to describe Romero's creation might actually be a misnomer: "Romero essentially conflated the zombie with the ghoul, a cannibalistic monster type that never became very popular" (2008, 8). The idea that Romero's monsters might actually be ghouls rather than zombies once more suggests that—like the vampire—the will-less zombie has become a hybrid, an empty signifier to be filled with meaning at will:

Zombies are an amalgam of life in death, death in life. . . . [W]e are not thinking subjects divorced from the eviscerated object, but an entanglement of subject and object, death held at bay by the thinnest thread of electrical impulse. The zombie stumbling toward you, arms outstretched and moaning, should not just make you run but think about your own hybridity. (Coleman and Trevatt, online)

In *Capital: A Critique of Political Economy* (1867), Karl Marx referred to the vampire's "thirst for the living blood of labour" (online, 172) and the capitalist exploitation of the proletariat: "Capital is dead labor, which, vampire-like, lives only by sucking living labor, and lives the more, the more labor it sucks" (online, 160). More recently, zombies, rather than vampires, have become the global metaphor for the breakdown of neoliberal capitalism.[3] The Occupy (Wall Street) Movement has taken the victimized yet flesh-eating zombie rather than the bloodsucking vampire as its signifier of robber-baron finance capitalism. In a post-Fordian culture, labor and consumerism are redefined in Rob Latham's *Consuming Youth: Vampires, Zombies, and the Culture of Consumption*, which describes consumerism as "objectified cultural labor" (2002, 4). David Punter, in a review of Erik Butler's *Metamorphoses of the Vampire in Literature and Film*, notes that an increase in the visibility of the predatory and eventually terminal processes of capitalism has given the figure of the vampire—and the same could be said of the zombie—a new lease on life (see 2011, 757).

In her article "Zombies: Their Caribbean Heritage and Transnational Journey to Wall Street," Andrea Shaw describes an Occupy Wall Street zombie protest: "With faces whitened to look lifeless and blood stains painted around their mouths, activists lumbered through Manhattan's financial district with fake money stuffed in their mouths to portray the ravenous, monstrous, and even cannibalistic greed propelling America's financial bandits" (2011, online). Zombie walk protests powerfully reflect the universalizing globalized migration of cultural tropes and metaphors across regions and national borders.[4]

In the context of such globalizing processes, the terms *transcultural* and *transnational* have seen unprecedented growth in contemporary discourse. As Arif Dirlik points out, these concepts bode potential for forging new identities and raising further questions about identity politics "when a population is dispersed broadly spatially, following different historical trajectories in different locations" (quoted in Fluck 2011, 375). Winfried Fluck maintains that there is also the potential for an "aesthetic transnationalism," which "focuses on the rich diversity of new and interesting objects that is produced by transnational encounters and exchange" (2011, 368). With Fluck, we think it is essential to "recover a world of cultural cross-fertilization that holds the promise of fuller, more meaningful experiences" (368). Ultimately, this collection of essays—discussing a wide range of fictional, film, comic book, and game representations—is firmly based on the conviction that transcultural and transnational imaginaries have shaped and altered the zombie and vampire tropes, fundamentally affecting their representation based on their movement through time and space. Thus, Nina Auerbach's observation that "every age embraces the vampire it needs" (1995, 145) could be modified to read "every age *and culture* creates the vampire *and zombie* it needs."

MIGRATORY TRANSFORMATIONS

This volume opens with a provocative question: How does a filmmaker address the challenge of introducing and incorporating the well-known zombie trope into a culture where such figures are unknown? In her contribution, Katarzyna Ancuta explores the nonexistence of zombies in Thai film. As she points out, in a country that customarily cremates its dead, this absence cannot be particularly surprising in a culture lacking the accoutrements of caskets and full-body burial. She explores the question of how contemporary Thai filmmakers meet the challenge of popularizing the profit-generating zombie movie genre in a society that dedicates its horror films almost exclusively to ghosts and ghouls. As a result, Thai horror movies deal with monsters that the Thai consider imaginable and therefore "real" figures. Zombies, however, who are seen as unimaginable creatures, are not as frightening, and, therefore, zombie movies do not seem as attractive and potentially profitable to investors.

Because zombies simply do not exist in the Thai concept of what is physically or metaphysically possible, the very few Thai zombie films that have been produced have achieved a degree of success only by dramatically altering the understanding of what a zombie is. To make zombie creations more palatable to the Thai audience, zombification is explained in terms of an infection with a virus, transmitted by white foreigners—White-Peril anxiety, an inversion of Yellow-Peril anxiety discussed by Timothy R. Fox in this volume. Anxieties about foreigners and the westernization of Thailand and the conflicts that arise with the contemporary migration of Burmese workers, for example, are also reflected in Thai film zombies, who are portrayed as invasive border-crossing foreign elements.

Looking further back in time, Sabine Metzger likewise explores the insertion of a monster figure—the vampire—into the tradition of a country— Japan—where no such figure previously existed. Lafcadio Hearn, writing about geographical, national, cultural, and generic border crossings in "The Story of Chūgōrō" (1902), systematically avoided any intrusions of Western culture into his retelling of a story from ancient Japan. As Metzger argues, Hearn, himself not Japanese, consciously decided not to take recourse to the European Gothic tradition and its iconography because there was no Japanese Gothic tradition. He could do so because he sensed that his turn-of-the-century readers would not be enthralled by the fact that the protagonist of his story might fall prey to a blood-loving seductress. Rather, he thought they would be more likely to be beguiled by the appeal of Japanese culture by and of itself—the exotic per se. The story points to the tension between sameness and difference, making the bloodthirsty female a mediator between cultures. With her similarity to the Western vampire, the Japanese female vampire proves to be a familiar figure in the midst of the unfamiliar—a figure partaking of what Metzger terms the *transcultural supernatural.*

Like Metzger, who discusses the absence of the vampire in Japanese culture, Timothy M. Robinson identifies the relative absence of the vampire figure in African American fiction. He explores how speculative fiction can provide a space wherein cultural cross-fertilization can be experimentally projected onto alternative realities. He argues that Octavia Butler's novel *Fledgling*, a tale of transcultural and transracial migration, is, however, also deeply embedded in the African American literary tradition of the neo-slave narrative. Moreover, according to Robinson, Butler expands the genre through her use of the vampire trope.

Butler's *Fledgling* signifies upon both the vampire figure and the slave narrative by examining relationships between the vampire clan, the Ina, and its symbionts, the people upon whom they feed. The economic and social relations between the two groups reveal complex dynamics of domination and dependence, manipulation and free will. Robinson views the migratory movements and interactions between Ina and symbionts as transcultural and transracial exchanges that reflect relations between migrants and indigenous residents. Xenophobia and fear of miscegenation are significant as the novel is particularly concerned with "blood purity" and the traumatic consequences of species mixing. *Fledgling* examines "race" and transcultural "identities" as social constructs by drawing on nineteenth-century African American slave narrative tropes, which are utilized to reflect upon oppressive forces in contemporary society. Butler ultimately exposes the archetypal vampire tale as white, patriarchal, heterosexist, and authoritarian. She rewrites the genre partially as a utopian vampire tale that is female centered, omnisexual, and firmly grounded in black cultural traditions.

NON/NORMATIVE SEXUALITIES

With every culture and age creating the vampire and zombie it needs, these figures easily vacillate not only between acting as perpetrator and victim but also between challenging and affirming gender roles. Vampires and zombies reveal the temporal and cultural situatedness of gender. Anna Silver, for instance, calls attention to reactionary contemporary gender politics expressed in Stephenie Meyer's recent, immensely popular *Twilight* series. She points out that the gender politics of the male protagonist, who was born in 1901, are "frozen in time." In the story, he is only seventeen—young and attractive, but old enough to have developed the patriarchal self-image prevalent in his day. Silver views the novels' presentation of gender as detrimental to young readers because the "gender ideology is ultimately and unapologetically patriarchal" (2010, 122).

Vampire and zombie literature has been a widely accepted way to introduce transgressive representations of sexualities into the cultural imaginary. Rasmus R. Simonsen explores what happens when a hybrid being like a zombie that is ontologically "neither this nor that" becomes embodied as a(n) (un)defining element of (sexual) existence. Simonsen explores how the uncertain ontological status that induces dread in the victim grows out of confrontation with the abject. As the "queerest" of movie monsters, the zombie represents the disruption of categories, the destruction of boundaries, and the existence of impurities. While Romero's zombies still stagger slowly and display minimal powers of reasoning, these newly undead—in their incessant craving for human flesh—are not made, as tradition would have it, susceptible to the machinations of an evil puppet master. At the moment of zombification, Simonsen argues, the gender of the newly deceased body is inevitably undefined, thereby interfering with the status quo and the established sexual order. The dead parade around in the uncanny guise of the living—mercilessly intervening in the performative structure of heterosexuality. For Simonsen, the Toronto-based filmmaker Bruce LaBruce's 2008 movie *Otto; or, Up with Dead People* exemplifies the contemporary (sometimes playful) portrayal of queer as zombie. In contrast to Romero's zombies, Otto is blatantly and uncompromisingly sexualized. In Simonsen's reading, the zombie in its undefinedness is queer, always already sexualized in its queerness.

Danielle Borgia discusses gender dynamics in three recent Mexican vampire novels. In the first two novels she focuses on, the trope of a bisexual, promiscuous vampire couple with a network of corrupt allies must be destroyed in order for the heterosexual monogamous love of the protagonists to prevail. However, in the third and later novel, the vampire love triangle portrayed explores bisexuality and polyamory in ways that deliberately blur the binaries solidified in many mass-market novels. Borgia indicates that, for example, Carolina Andújar's vampire novels, like Meyer's, depict young women who discover that fulfillment consists of relinquishing control to male partners through marriage. However, as Borgia argues, in Mexico there is also a growing contemporary acceptance of alternative sexual identities, evidenced by avant-garde vampire narratives.

The vampire's immortality and blood drinking in Adriana Diaz de Enciso's 2001 novel, for example, signal not just sexual and gender transgressions, but also nonnormative emotional states. The protagonists, both human and vampire, are deeply haunted by their inability to connect emotionally with others, thereby giving their "thirst" and mental disturbance, as Borgia argues, an almost spiritual component. By depicting the desires of the vampires as part of the cultural imaginary, this novel acknowledges the growing public visibility of Mexico's queer community and reflects public discourse about nontraditional sexualities.

As in the works discussed by Simonsen and Borgia, undead love is already queered and gender negotiated in Herbert G. de Lisser's 1929 novel *The White Witch of Rosehall*. It presents the historical Annie Palmer as a "white witch" who instrumentalizes both Haitian voodoo and European vampirism in order to dominate—and in some cases also to kill—people who happened to cross her path. Monika Mueller argues that de Lisser relies on Haitian voodoo combined with European vampirism to present Annie—who draws on both traditions—as an emblem of gender transgression and abuse of power. In addition to being imbued with extraordinary, supernatural female power, Annie Palmer is cast as a European Jamaican Creole. She is bolstered in her evil machinations both by the social status bestowed upon her by her white heritage and by her acquired knowledge of African

Caribbean culture. Thus, she also becomes a larger symbol of the colonial presence in the Caribbean. In the context of the period the novel was written in and based on the author's own perceptions, his main protagonist's fusion of cultural traditions results in an evil hybridity. Annie cleverly draws on what can be seen as the worst of two worlds: an "African" susceptibility to a belief in sorcery and a "European" ability to use rationality as a key ingredient in her manipulation of the appropriated African belief system. Whereas the voodoo tropes are evident, the connections to the European vampire tradition are not as immediately apparent. However, the transcultural exchange between Le Fanu's novella "Carmilla" (1872) and other female vampire characters from European lore clearly served as a major source of de Lisser's inspiration as well.

CULTURAL ANXIETIES

Anxieties about invasions and the transgression of personal or national borders, as suggested by Simonsen, are often expressed through the figures of the vampire and zombie. Carmen Serrano's discussion of Mexican vampire movies—some of the more than one hundred films in Spanish made by Hollywood studios in the early 1930s—provides salient examples. With film sets identical to those used to produce versions in English, the Spanish film crew would begin filming at night, using the same script and shot list used during the day, but with Spanish-speaking actors. In her discussion of *El vampiro*, Serrano illustrates that, like the vampire figure, the filmic image itself is reborn, parodied, abused, and killed, only to resurrect again. Serrano argues that the film medium itself is vampiric in its effect on the viewer.

It was, however, as Serrano illustrates, not just a one-way street from North to South, from Hollywood to Mexico. The specific Mexican articulation of the vampire also had an influence on the European vampire image. Within the process of transnational recirculation, the vampire bat alters European vampire folklore as well. Later, when the monster is reappropriated in twentieth-century Latin American texts and films, it has lost its original autochthonous pre-Columbian associations. Furthermore, these Mexican vampire films express anxieties concerning national boundaries and citizenship at specific social and political crossroads. Much like the zombie in Thai films, discussed by Ancuta, the vampire monster is interpreted as a subversive intruder that infects and reproduces itself, threatening national borders from the outside. And, as Mueller shows, a similar circulation of the vampire and the zombie took place in the late 1920s when de Lisser's *The White Witch of Rosehall* investigated the presence of both figures in a colonial setting. Historical, national, and cultural contextualization also helps us to understand how Max Brooks's novel *World War Z* slashed its way into the 2006 *New York Times* top-ten best-seller list, making history as the first zombie novel ever to do so. It also "made" history insofar as it did not avail itself of the traditional novel format. Instead, it presented the reader with a "historical document," a compilation of reportage on the fictional postapocalyptic scenario of viral zombies overrunning the world and the human effort required to repulse this global plague. Timothy R. Fox focuses on these fictional first-person accounts of dozens of individual characters who live through a viral plague that begins in China and spreads worldwide. Though Brooks is successful in giving voice and identities to his multiple "narrators," the novel, as Fox argues, also betrays a number of negative traits easily identified as modern variants of traditional Yellow-Peril thinking. Thus the novel's theme reflects current anti-Asian anxiety in the West. In the Yellow-Peril tradition of Sax Rohmer's highly successful Fu Manchu novels of the 1930s and 1940s, Brooks's novel represents more than just a nationalistic response to the rising global power of China; it also reveals an undercurrent of racially and sexually motivated antagonism. Like Simonsen's gay zombie, Fox's zombie of Asian origin is also always already "queer" and, like the closeted gay individual, he is inevitably seen as a potential transmitter of alien viral disaster. And, much like Serrano's vampire monster, the zombie is seen as a source of alien intrusion.

CIRCULATING TECHNOLOGIES

Contemporary media have circulated the vampire and zombie figures across time and space, enabling cultures to conceive of their own "everymonster." A number of contributors to this volume discuss the impact of media: Serrano illustrates how technology—even such a simple thing as the utilization of double sets for audiences on both side of the US-Mexican border—facilitated migrations and transformations of the vampire trope. Further, Fox demonstrates how faux historiographic fiction can be instrumentalized to circulate Yellow-Peril anxieties in the West. And Ancuta illustrates how media can make transcultural identification with a foreign filmic zombie palatable for Thai moviegoers and profitable for Thai filmmakers. The contributors to the final section of this volume focus on the inevitable changes in media culture effected by the transition from one medium to another: from book and comics to film, from film to video game and vice versa.

Cultural transformations in media can take many forms. Johannes Weber discusses a very early example of filmic representation in Carl Theodor Dreyer's film *Vampyr* (1931) by returning—as other contributors to this volume also do—to Le Fanu's 1872 tale of a lesbian vampire, "Carmilla." Weber argues that the film is less an adaptation of this Gothic tale than a transcultural and transmedial appropriation of certain modes of narrative representation associated with earlier depictions of vampires. While viewing Dreyer's film, the audience is often confused by its expressionist style, with its intentional radical disruption of the filmic spatiotemporal continuum. Very early in the film, viewers have the impression of following the film's protagonist, Gray, into a dreamworld where nothing can be taken for real. Designed to be disquieting, *Vampyr* disturbs by subverting all conventions that usually serve to make it easier to comprehend cinematic representation.

In accordance with recent film theory, Weber argues that watching a film is a physical experience well before it becomes a mental process.[5] Thus, while the protagonist lives through the primal fear of being buried alive, the film viewer is forced to identify with him and his experience with great immediacy. The film technique locates the vampiric not only in the filmic character but in the film technology itself. In the context of this volume, the transition from print medium to film is far more significant than the fact that the Danish filmmaker Dreyer based his film on English pretexts taken from outside his own culture. With great mimetic force, as Weber argues, film in Dreyer's production becomes a vampiric medium feeding on its textual predecessor, thus altering our medial perception.

Not only filmic and fictional precursors, but also early horror comics had a profound impact on the work of many artists, such as filmmaker George Romero and novelist Stephen King. For young readers in the 1940s, as Richard J. Hand elucidates, horror comics were read similarly to proscribed pornography—exploring the twin taboos of death (blatantly) and sexuality (latently). These comics reflected concerns with the Red Peril (anti-Communism) and the dangers of the atomic age (technopohobia) and had an almost forensic textbook verisimilitude. During their childhood or adolescence, horror-genre icons like Romero and King devoured explicit tales of graphic terror—only to have them vanish, almost overnight, with the introduction of the Comics Code in 1954. With its implementation, censorship reduced explicit comic-book horror, which had been more graphic than anything Hollywood or television of the 1950s would have dared to display. Hand reads the zombie portrayed in comics more as a reflection of Hollywood than rooted in its Haitian ethnographic origins, which are presented as purely fantastic. The zombie becomes a potentially revolutionary symbol, an undead everyman or everymonster, setting right the injustices of mortal power structures. The curious mixture of terror and comfort while reading zombie comics remains important to this day—the culture of graphic stills further influences content and form of pictures in motion.

Various media can effect the displacement of horror; in the computer age, horror video games often serve this purpose. But in comparison with the "true" undead of cinema, video-game zombies are, according to Ewan Kirkland, often treated as lesser creatures, a monstrous aberration. Whenever games like *Resident Evil* are cited in zombie studies, the films inspired by the games are referenced more often than the original games themselves. In contrast to other horror archetypes such as vampires or werewolves, Kirkland shows, video-game zombies have been a frequent presence, suggesting a comfortable fit between the zombie and the video game. Video-game zombies shuffle unflinchingly into gunfire, stumble around in pointless circles, and bump into walls, and their bumbling mindlessness can easily be attributed to their rotting gray matter and corroding faculties.

In *Resident Evil*, the avatar is structurally closely related to the zombie: it has little independent movement beyond the player's prompting, which it performs with unthinking diligence. The zombies of *Forbidden Siren*, a video-game series that moves to the setting of the Japanese village of Hanuda, are markedly different creatures than the zombies of US-located *Resident Evil*. But no matter where the game is geographically situated or culturally circulated, the fear of becoming a zombie oneself and the loss of potential interactivity, agency, and control are deeply rooted in these games, making the zombie a potentially useful metaphor in understanding the processes of video-game play as such. The avatar could, Kirkland argues, be understood as a zombie in its original Haitian voodoo sense, as a human possessed or controlled by an outside intelligence—the game medium therefore determines the universalized cultural performance of zombiehood. This brings the zombie culturally full circle.

Catalyzed by various media, the figures of the zombie and the vampire have been significantly modified in their migration through space and time, as this volume demonstrates. Unmistakably, this is reflected in distinct cultural contexts and productions; for example, changes that the vampire bat as well as Count Dracula experience in their travels throughout the world. Similarly, the Haitian zombie also resurfaces globally in zombie horror movies and video games. Anxieties about invasions and transgressions are often expressed through these figures' deviant sexualities, gender roles, and shape-shifting embodiment. As products of the human imagination, vampires and zombies are limitless in their expression of human experience—they are as diverse their human creators.

NOTES

1. According to Joel Stein and Michael White in a recent article, vampires and zombies rank in popularity above Harry Potter, downloaded songs, Moscato wine, and Michele Bachmann (see "Zombies vs. Vampires: Who's Bigger," *Bloomberg Business Week*, August 11, 2011). In an Internet search it was evident that the figures of the vampire and zombie are very frequently paired and studied together. Sasha Levine, for example, explores the current obsession with both figures ("Why Are We So Obsessed with Vampires and Zombies?," *Lifestyle Mirror*, March 14, 2013).

2. As Sarah Juliet Lauro and Karen Embry note in their "Zombie Manifesto," "it is always at the mouth that the zombie feeds, and it is where the physical boundary between zombie and not-zombie is effaced, through its bite" (2008, 99). This would hold equally true for the vampire.

3. There is a plethora of international books on the contemporary global economic crisis with "zombie" in their title—for example, Jessica Irvine, *Zombies, Bananas and Why There Are no Economists in Heaven* (2012); David McNally, *Monsters of the Market: Zombies, Vampires and Global Capitalism* (2011); and John Quiggin, *Zombie Economics: How Dead Ideas Still Walk among Us* (2010).

4. The *Guardian* has been tracking the global Occupy Movement, providing an interactive list: "Occupy Protests around the World: Full List Visualized." For an example of an Easter Sunday zombie walk in Tokyo, see the video posted by the *Guardian* ("Japan's Zombies: The Walking Dead of Tokyo," *Guardian*, March 31, 2013).

5. See, for example, Stacey Abbott (2004) and Marina Warner (2006).

WORKS CITED

Abbott, Stacey. 2004. "Spectral Vampires: *Nosferatu* in the Light of New Technology." In *Horror Film: Creating and Marketing Fear*, edited by Steffen Hantke, 3–20. Jackson: University Press of Mississippi.

Asma, Stephen T. 2009. "Monsters and the Moral Imagination." *The Chronicle of Higher Education*. Accessed May 17, 2013. http://chronicle.com/article/Monstersthe-Moral/48886/.

Auerbach, Nina. 1995. *Our Vampires, Ourselves*. Chicago: University of Chicago Press.

Bishop, Kyle William. 2010. *American Zombie Gothic: The Rise and Fall (and Rise) of the Walking Dead in Popular Culture*. Jefferson, NC: McFarland.

Cohen, Jeffrey Jerome. 1996. "Monster Culture (Seven Theses)." In *Monster Theory: Reading Culture*, edited by Jeffrey Jerome Cohen, 3–25. Minneapolis: University of Minnesota Press.

Coleman, Caryn, and Tom Trevatt. "Editorial—Living On: Zombies." In vol. 3 of *Incognitum Hactenus*. Accessed September 14, 2014. http://incognitumhactenus.com/ editorial-living-on-zombies/.

Davis, Wade. 1988. *Passage of Darkness: The Ethnobiology of the Haitian Zombie*. Chapel Hill: University of North Carolina Press.

Fluck, Winfried. 2011. "A New Beginning? Transnationalisms." *New Literary History* 42:365–84.

Hoeveler, Diane Long. 2006. "Objectifying Anxieties: Scientific Ideologies in Bram Stoker's *Dracula* and *The Lair of the White Worm*." *Romanticism on the Net* 44. Accessed March 1, 2013. http://id.erudit.org/iderudit/014003ar. doi:10.7202/014003ar.

Irvine, Jessica. 2012. *Zombies, Bananas and Why There Are No Economists in Heaven*. Sydney: Allen and Unwin.

Jones, Ernest. [1931] 2006. *On the Nightmare: The Significant Story of Witchery and Religion*. New York: Kessinger Publishing.

Khair, Tabish, and Johnathan Höglund, eds. 2013. "Introduction: Transnational and Postcolonial Vampires." In *Transnational and Postcolonial Vampires: Dark Blood*, 1–10. London: Palgrave.

Larkin, William S. 2006. "Res Corporealis: Persons, Bodies, and Zombies." In *Zombies, Vampires, and Philosophy: New Life for the Undead*, edited by Richard Greene and K. Silem Mohammed, 15–26. Chicago: Open Court.

Latham, Rob. 2002. *Consuming Youth: Vampires, Zombies, and the Culture of Consumption*. Chicago: University of Chicago Press.

Lauro, Sarah Juliet, and Karen Embry. 2008. "A Zombie Manifesto: The Nonhuman Condition in the Era of Advanced Capitalism." *Boundary 2* 35 (1): 85–108.

Marx, Karl. [1887] 2010. *Capital: A Critique of Political Economy*. Vol. I. Book One: *The Process of Production of Capital*. Translated by Samuel Moore and Edward Aveling. Edited by Frederick Engels. Accessed March 13, 2013. http://www.marxists.org/archive/ marx/works/ download/pdf/Capital-Volume-I.pdf.

McIntosh, Shawn. 2008. "The Evolution of the Zombie: The Monster That Keeps Coming Back." In *Zombie Culture: Autopsies of the Living Dead*, edited by Shawn McIntosh and David Leverette, 1–17. Lanham, MD: Scarecrow Press.

McNally, David. 2011. *Monsters of the Market: Zombies, Vampires and Global Capitalism*. Leiden: Koninklijke Brill.

Money, Mary Alice. 2002. "The Undemonization of Supporting Characters in *Buffy*." In *Fighting the Forces: What's at Stake in Buffy the Vampire Slayer?*, edited by Rhonda V. Wilcox and David Lavery, 98–107. New York: Rowman and Littlefield.

"Occupy Protests around the World: Full List Visualized." 2013. Accessed March 31, 2013. http://www.guardian.co.uk/news/datablog/2011/oct/17/occupy-protests-world-list-map.

Punter, David. 2011. "Review of *Metamorphoses of the Vampire in Literature and Film: Cultural Transformations in Europe, 1732-1933* by Erik Butler." *Victorian Studies* 53 (4): 756–58.

Quiggin, John. 2010. *Zombie Economics: How Dead Ideas Still Walk among Us*. Princeton, NJ: Princeton University Press.

Shaw, Andrea. 2011. "Zombies: Their Caribbean Heritage and Transnational Journey to Wall Street." Accessed March 12, 2013. http://www.jamaicans.com/articles/primearticles/zombieswallstreet.shtml#ixzz2PW3o8mwa.

Silver, Anna. 2010. "Twilight Is Not Good for Maidens: Gender, Sexuality, and the Family in Stephenie Meyer's *Twilight* Series." *Studies in the Novel* 42 (1/2): 121–38.

Tucker, Ken. 2009. "*True Blood* Reviewed." Accessed March 8, 2013. http://www.ew.com/ew/article/0,,20284276,00.html.

Warner, Marina. 2006. *Phantasmagoria: Spirit Visions, Metaphors, and Media into the Twenty-First Century.* Oxford: Oxford University Press.

Wasson, Richard. 1966. "The Politics of Dracula." *English Literature in Transition, 1880–1920* 9 (1): 24–27.

PART 1

MIGRATORY
TRANSFORMATIONS

THE SMILING DEAD; OR, ON THE EMPIRICAL IMPOSSIBILITY OF THAI ZOMBIES

KATARZYNA ANCUTA

Although originating in Haitian vodou[1] culture, zombies have truly made their mark on the popular imaginary courtesy of the North American film industry. It is in their George Romero–inspired representation as slow-moving, instinct-driven, brain-eating corpses, rather than soulless (dead or alive) beings controlled by a *bokor* (a vodou priest) for the purpose of slave labor, that they continue to inspire filmmakers around the globe toward producing their own versions of the violently hungry (un)dead for local audiences. Thailand seems an exception here because, taking into consideration that horror remains one of the strongest Thai cinematic genres, it is significant to note the relative absence of Thai zombie movies from its repertoire. Only five out of all theatrically released Thai horror films up to 2014 can be said to feature zombies at all and even then the identity of the creatures in question is not always consistent with what the international horror audiences have come to expect of a zombie icon.

As far as horror monsters are concerned, whether raised from the dead by Haitian voodoo priests, resurrected by accidental chemical spills, or created from scratch through medical experimentation, zombies rely heavily on their corporeality. If, for the sake of simplicity, we could define a zombie as a reanimated corpse driven by instincts in the absence of the higher intellectual powers of the brain, then faced with a culture that customarily cremates its dead we would not expect it to be particularly threatened by a vision of a zombie apocalypse. And, indeed, while zombie-themed films from North America have spurred similar productions from filmmakers in places as distant from each other as Cuba and Australia, Spain and Korea, the Thai horror film industry continues to display a peculiar hesitancy to invest in homegrown zombie films, even as Hollywood productions such as the *Resident Evil* franchise do astonishingly well in drawing crowds to movie houses.[2]

This begs the question as to why filmmakers in Thailand refuse to see zombie films as particularly frightening fantasies worthy of investment. It cannot be said that the local horror-film industry is diffident toward the monstrous or the uncanny, as indeed the typical horror film is almost completely dedicated to supernatural plots. Nor can it be said that the larger Thai film industry has but a small regard for the horror genre, as the Thai movie audience's almost insatiable love of horror has convinced financial backers that horror films are a safe investment. Why, then, are Western-style zombies so rarely able to shuffle their way into the pantheon of Thai cinematic monsters?

THE SUPERNATURAL IN THE THAI FILM WORLD

Part of the problem lies in the very understanding of what a zombie is, and how the essential nature of the zombie displaces it from the Thai concept of what is seen as the essence of horror. Investors see the zombie as a risky monster around which to shape a film, the sense of risk arising from an awareness that such creatures cannot possibly exist in the real world. The argument thus extends to the Thai belief that impossible creatures (for example, zombies) are not as frightening, and therefore for investors not nearly as potentially profitable, as creatures that are either familiar in Thai society or viewed by traditional belief systems as possibly being real (for example, ghosts). In this respect, the rules of Thai horror fiction are rather different from those of the West.

Within multicultural Thailand there exists a great tolerance for the supernatural. This belief in the supernatural originates in the animistic practices of both urban and rural populations, as well as the spiritual beliefs of various migrant communities that have contributed historically to the shaping of contemporary Thai culture and society. Prevalent throughout Thailand is a belief in the coexistence of the material and the spiritual realms, the latter of which is populated with ghosts, angels, guardian spirits, spirits of nature, ancestor spirits, Buddhist demons, Indian wise men, Hindu gods, spirits of past kings, monks and teachers, Chinese mythological figures, and angry spirits of the violently dead. These inhabitants of the spiritual realm are well known for their tendency to meddle in the affairs of the living (Guelden 1995, 14–15). The existence of ghosts and spirits is verified not only through urban legends and office gossip, but also through the media and national institutions. *Thairath*, the most popular Thai daily newspaper, carries stories of magic, haunting, and spiritual possession on the front page almost every day; influential politicians are known to employ fortune-tellers and mediums to help them run the country; shamanistic practices and curses are commonly part of political protests[3]; dead relatives are expected to offer up lucky lottery numbers; and magic tattoos as well as amulets are among the most prized possessions. These and many other examples from everyday life illustrate that when it comes to cinematic ghosts and spirits, no suspension of disbelief is necessary. Ghost stories are successful with Thai audiences because they are seen as authentic and realistic; they are frightening because they portray possible situations that can happen to anyone.

Zombies simply do not exist in the Thai concept of what is physically or supernaturally possible. The Thai language does not even have an original word or phrase to describe the rambling undead, although there are dozens of specific terms for every spirit imaginable. The phrase most typically used to identify a zombie is *phi dip*,[4] roughly translated as a "raw" (uncooked) ghost; the term also refers to an uncremated corpse. Unlike other categories of ghosts and spirits, *phi dip* is not connected to any specific set of beliefs, nor is it a legitimate member of the spirit realm. The *phi dip* is seen rather as an imaginary and impossible monster, quite unlike ghosts that are accepted as a part of everyday existence.

Indeed, domestically produced horror films are known in Thai as *nang phi*, or "ghost movies."[5] Almost every Thai horror film follows a narrow ghost-story formula.[6] Breaking away from this pattern is difficult because Thai horror fans have rather fixed expectations when it comes to the horror genre. And although the steady demand for horror films allows for moderate experimentation as far as film technologies are concerned, the same cannot be said about the plot or the creation of characters. Pakphum Wongjinda,[7] the director of such horror movies as *Scared/Rap Nawng Sayawng Khwan* (2005), *Video Clip* (2007), and *Who R U?/Krai . . . Nai Hong* (2010), recalls the problems he encountered trying to justify a relatively uncomplicated slasher film plot with investors:

> *If you want to talk about, let's say, serial killers you're going to hear that we don't have serial killers in Thailand. It's simply impossible to make people believe that serial killers could actually exist here. You cannot even say that this or that guy is sick and he's running around killing people. Thai people would deny it—no, there is no one like that in Thailand. It's simply impossible. . . . But in Thailand most crimes are seen as motivated by personal revenge. People believe there has to be a*

reason to kill; cause and effect. And so the only way to show killing out-side that cause-and-effect pattern is to involve black magic. And that's something the audience will easily believe here. (Wonjinda 2008, 125–26)

Zombies, like serial killers, seem acceptable to Thai audiences solely as imports, favored only as long as they feature in foreign, preferably Western, films. Thai audiences have different expectations for domestic horror films. Domestic horror films are easily seen as scary, with the fear arising from the social and cultural belief in the possibility that the cinematic source of horror has full potential for actual manifestation in the everyday lives of the viewers. Foreign horror films, both Asian and Western, on the other hand, are generally accepted as entertaining but are only seen as frightening if they tap into the same cultural reservoir of fear the domestic films rely on. In practice, this means that foreign horror movies featuring vengeful spirits, black magic, and other horror figures that have a local Thai equivalent will likely be seen as more frightening than those involving zombies, werewolves, beasts and monsters, serial killers, or nature-gone-wild plots.

This does not mean that zombies are completely alien to Thai cinema. Spurred on perhaps by recognition of the contemporary Western obsession with the zombie, a number of Thai filmmakers have attempted to introduce the pop icon into the domestic horror-film industry. Of the several such attempts, if we exclude straight-to-DVD production frequently with erotic content, only five "zombie" films have been released theatrically, all of which were made in the past decade (2004–14). Four of these films are analyzed in this essay: *Formalin Man/Rak Ter Tau Fa* (2004) by Pakphum Wongjinda, *Curse of the Sun/Suriyakhaat* (2004) by Kittipong Panyataweesap and Anat Yuangnhern, *Sars Wars/Khun Krabii Hiiroh* (2004) by Taweewat Wantha, and *Backpackers* (a segment of *Phobia 2/Ha Phraeng*, 2009) by Songyos Sugmanakan. The fifth and latest production, *Gancore Gud* (dir. Apisit Opasaimlikit, 2011), despite the director's early promises,[8] ended up being a hip-hop zombie comedy very similar to *Sars Wars* and therefore does not add anything new to the discussion here. While the first two films struggle with the conceptualization of zombies as an existential or philosophical category, the remaining two productions of the four analyzed here engage more openly with the conventions of a zombie movie. *Sars Wars* can easily be seen as a direct descendant of classic 1980s zombie comedies, such as *The Return of the Living Dead* (dir. Dan O'Bannon, 1985), while *Backpackers* is clearly a tribute to Danny Boyle's zombie-like rage-infected creatures from *28 Days Later* (2002). At the same time, as this analysis suggests, these four films achieved a degree of success by dramatically altering the definition or understanding of what a zombie is and, thus, making their "zombies" more palatable to the Thai audience.

To win over their audiences, the filmmakers resorted to a number of strategies aimed at justifying the existence of zombie characters in the plot and boosting the culturally defined elements of realism in the stories. All four films engaged in a discussion of zombies as an existential category, as well as a generic one, derived from Hollywood-based zombie-film narratives. Zombies were "explained" in terms of ghosts inhabiting the dead body, black magic, possession by a shaman, or foreign disease. In one instance, the zombie became a metaphor of racial oppression. Each of the films also refrained from using the word *zombie,* referring to the zombies as *phi* (ghosts) or refusing to categorize them altogether.

The appearance of zombies in Thai horror films is a relatively new theme. The latest productions engage more directly with the zombie-film genre, ignoring both the incompatibility of the creatures with the local supernatural lore and the preset condition that all Thai horror films must relate to entities and phenomena accepted as "real" or "possible" by its audiences. Chances are we will see more Thai celluloid zombies in the future. This chapter analyzes a number of zombie validation strategies used in the four discussed movies, such as the presentation of the zombie as a variation of a ghost or a lifeless body reanimated by black magic. It questions the influence of the Western zombie genre on the appearance of new figures of fear in contemporary Thai horror movies and argues the (im)possibility of integrating zombies into the fabric of Thai horror culture.

FORMALIN MAN (2004): THE LIVING DEAD GHOST

The Thai title of Pakphum Wongjinda's first film, *Rak Ter Tau Fa,* can roughly be translated as "I love you like the sky" and comes from one of the songs used in the film.[9] This in itself already suggests that we are not dealing with a typical horror production. Indeed, although the film is based on a supernatural concept, it remains a rather straightforward musical comedy throughout. The plot revolves around the struggle of a Thai *lukthung*[10] singer to keep his band together and save his musicians from falling into the hands of an unscrupulous gangster who would stop at nothing to exploit their talents. Interestingly, the main character, Chatthong, is actually dead and oblivious to the fact that his body continues to decompose throughout the film despite an injection of formalin. Chatthong's death is a result of a car accident and his almost instant resurrection is initially unnoticed by

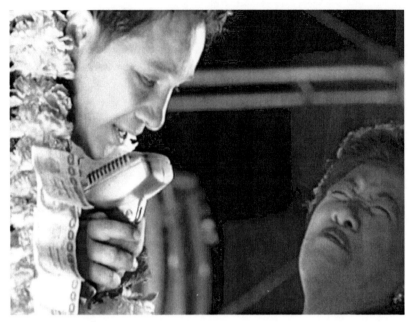

1.1 *FORMALIN MAN,* 2004

everyone, including himself. Contrary to viewer expectations, the undead Chatthong does not turn into a flesh-eating monster and retains his humanity (exemplified through empathy, fair judgment, honesty, and so on) until the end, the only indicators of his abnormality being his lack of appetite, constant insomnia, his decaying body, and his ability to survive all the accidents and assassination attempts that befall him in the course of the film. His supernatural condition is known only to dogs that howl in his presence, a wise monk who offers advice on the rites of passage, and the ghost of a young girl who identifies herself as the most devoted fan of the band (figure 1.1).

The monk describes Chatthong as a ghost that clings to his own body, and this was, indeed, the design of the movie, as confirmed by the director, who explains:

> *I wanted to do something different. So, I thought, how about if the guy dies but he doesn't want to leave his body. It's like you're already dead but you don't know it and you still want to do something in this body, even though the body is decomposing. But the conscience is still there. Only it doesn't want to know that it's dead. (Wonjinda 2008, 135)*

Identified as a "conscience" tied to a body, Chatthong can easily be seen in terms of a Thai ghost, especially since in Thai cinema ghosts are customarily anthropomorphized and portrayed as indistinguishable from the living. But if this is the case, why would the director insist that his approach to the theme was in any way different or innovative? The difference lies in the fact that although Thai cinematic ghosts are by and large material creatures, they are not bound by the materiality of their bodies: they do not rot, grow old and unsightly, or lose body parts in an undignified manner. Even when dealing with the ghosts of the violently dead, or *phi tai hong*, although audiences may be faced with a hideously deformed spirit, the physical condition of the spirit will not deteriorate any further; quite the contrary, once appeased, *phi tai hong* frequently return to their primary human form. This, as we know, is not the case with post-Romero zombies, which by the end of many films are often reduced to oozing fragments of human flesh. It is therefore not difficult to conclude that the "unusual" ghost created for the purpose of Wongjinda's film is actually a zombie, although it is never referred to as such.

Wongjinda explains that like many Thai movies, *Formalin Man* resonates with Buddhist teachings: "We're talking about the body that's not going to last forever. About impermanence. Fame, money, everything will be gone. The only thing that counts is love, whatever love you give to the people who surround you" (2008, 134). The choice of a zombie motif to portray this spiritual tenet is understandable. What better way to portray the impermanence of the body? At the same time, however, zombies known to Thai audiences from foreign movies are usually bloodthirsty creatures driven by murderous instincts, and it is quite possible that such a depiction might have overshadowed the spiritual message of the film. Furthermore, the fact that Western-style cannibalistic zombies feature in the Thai imagination only as figures of momentary entertainment means the pop icon can hardly be expected to pass on life-changing wisdom. On the other hand, ghosts easily function as a force of karmic retribution. By masquerading as a ghost, therefore, the zombie Chatthong is much more acceptable to a Thai viewer, who would otherwise find discomfort in having to question the expected logical premise of the typical horror/ghost film.

The iconic quality of Thai spirits, both the ones appearing on film and those apparently manifesting in real life, links them with the Western concept of the revenant, known from medieval ballads and romantic novels as an animated corpse returning from the grave because it has a mission to fulfill. While the mission in question may entail teaching a valuable lesson to the living, comforting loved ones, revealing a cause of death, or identifying its hitherto unknown burial site, the corporeality of the uneasy spirit—frequently portrayed as bursting through the coffin and clawing its way out of the grave—makes it a prototype of the zombie. Chatthong is no different in this respect. His mission of bringing peace of mind to his small community of musicians can be fulfilled thanks to the spirit's embracing of its bodily attributes. Despite the director's claim that the body is insignificant and only love counts in the end, Chatthong must rely on the physicality of the body, and his singing voice in particular, to achieve his goals. Without the body, apparently, the show cannot go on, and, indeed, the director's intention to portray the Buddhist concept of impermanence can best be executed through bringing the bodies of the protagonists into the foreground. And while the choice of a performance troupe as a backdrop to the plot demands paying a great deal of attention to the way bodies are created and promoted on stage through makeup, elaborate costumes, and dance routines, at the same time, we are also shown that the tricks of the (theatrical) trade are employed to hide the impermanence of the aging and decaying physical form, therefore giving substance to the otherwise impermanent quality of music.

Defined through the attachment to his decaying body, Chatthong can be seen as a budding Thai zombie but he remains acceptable to Thai audiences only as long as he is identified as a ghost. This method of legitimizing zombies in Thai cinema is certainly the easiest, but it makes it difficult to find a relevant point of distinction between the two supernatural categories. The second example discussed below takes a step in the direction of formulaic authenticity but fails when it cannot resist employing a further "rationalizing" existential explanation: spiritual possession.

CURSE OF THE SUN (2004): THE POSSESSED DEAD

The plot of *Curse of the Sun* does not seem to be very coherent, but the main story line is built around a number of assassination attempts on the life of a young woman, Jira, carried out by a murderous zombie that used to be her boyfriend, Tot. Killed in a car crash, Tot becomes a pitiful ghost trapped on this earth while in horror he watches his body being abused as a vessel for evil deeds by a Khmer shaman. The shaman, working for a powerful gangster, uses the dead to commit crimes because, as he puts it, "The dead don't talk." Acting on a perverse impulse, he decides to use Tot's corpse to accomplish his latest mission, which involves killing Jira. The shaman gains control over the corpse by projecting his mind into it and turning the body into a deadly weapon. Impervious to pain and resistant to damage, Tot kills with guns and knives. Seemingly indestructible, zombie-Tot can only be

1.2 *CURSE OF THE SUN,* 2004

killed after the shaman accidentally gets blown to pieces during a shootout between the gangsters and the police (figure 1.2).

In one sense, the reanimated corpse in *Curse of the Sun* fits the standard understanding of what we would expect of a zombie. He moves with the stiffness of a corpse affected by rigor mortis, progressively decomposes from one sighting to another, and is remarkably hard to kill. At the same time, however, we are also told the body is being animated by the will of the controlling shaman—similar to the *bokor* in Haitian vodou—who inhabits it on a temporary basis. The presence of the shaman in the movie legitimizes the appearance of the zombie, as the Thai audience is reassured that they are not dealing with an unfamiliar imaginary creature but rather with an entirely believable case of black magic, making the story line much more acceptable and terrifying. Indeed, daily life throughout Thailand testifies to a prevailing belief in magic, or *saiyasat*. Spirit doctors, shamans, and sorcerers—known in Thai mostly as *mo phi*—are consulted when the Thais feel in need of advice or want to check their fortune, ask for money, find relief from illness, win someone's heart in love, or harm their enemy. Those in search of love and death spells frequently choose to follow the path of Khmer black magic, for Cambodians are seen in Thailand as the primary ethnic group with the knowledge of powerful magical symbols and rituals (Guelden 1995, 113). And although most Khmer black magic involves utilizing the supernatural power of materials obtained from corpses, throwing invisible missiles, and planting harmful objects inside people's bodies, if anybody could make the dead walk, it would most likely be a Khmer sorcerer.

Not surprisingly then, the walking corpse in *Curse of the Sun* is never really referred to as a zombie apart from a single use of the word in the English subtitles, and even then the Thai term that is presumably being translated is *phi farang*, a foreign ghost (or the ghost of a foreigner), where *foreign* indicates a white Caucasian. Other than that, the monster is addressed as Tot,[11] or simply called a ghost (*phi*). To distinguish between the possessed corpse and an actual ghost, the film splits the dead Tot in two: the ghost Tot and the zombie Tot. Because in Thai beliefs ghosts are expected to retain their anthropomorphic attributes, there is very little difference between the two Tots in the film, apart from the fact that unlike the zombie, the ghostly Tot does not deteriorate, and at times appears slightly more transparent. As the ghost of Tot contributes little to the plot, it can be safely assumed that its presence in the movie serves only to justify and, by comparison, highlight the misbehavior of its corporeal counterpart. If the ghost can be understood in terms of soul, mind, consciousness, and conscience, then quite obviously the corporeal revenant is soulless, mindless, and lacking in both consciousness and conscience, which is why it is capable of committing the most heinous deed of all: murdering his own true love. The Khmer sorcerer taking possession of the body can be compared to a malevolent essence, or pure evil rushing through the dried-up veins in Tot's body. The ghost, representing all the love and goodness of the living Tot, is powerless against such potent magic and can only watch without intercession.

Ghosts and black magic are the two most conventional explanations for any inexplicable phenomenon in Thai cinema, serving as they do as a common narrative strategy employed in a variety of film genres. More often than not, ghosts and sorcerers are called on to fill in logical gaps in film scripts because if all else fails, the directors can always count on the audience's reluctance to argue with the supernatural. At the same time, passing zombies off as ghosts or possessed corpses makes it difficult, if not impossible, to view them as zombies at all, since such depictions interfere with the category on a more existential level. The following two films discussed here introduce a viable alternative that allows the filmmakers to relate to the zombie concept on a more acceptable generic level, relating them directly to the characters known from foreign zombie movies. The additional appeal of this approach is that it provides the Thai audience with exactly what it wants to see in a zombie film: foreigners.

SARS WARS (2004): THE FOREIGN DISEASE

Released in 2004, *Sars Wars*[12] is probably the most recognizable Thai zombie film, even though neither the English nor the original Thai title (*Khun Krabii Hiiroh*, roughly translated as "a sword-fighting hero") reveals much of its content. It is also the most straightforward example of a Thai horror film that directly engages with the Western zombie genre and its conventions, even if, once again, the zombies in the film remain an unnamed threat. The zombies in *Sars Wars* do not differ much from their Hollywood prototypes, but their apparent foreignness is more than just a tribute to their North American filmic cousins. Indeed, zombification is explained in the movie in terms of an infection with a foreign virus, patient zero actually being a white foreigner. Interestingly, the role of this first zombie was given to Andrew Biggs, an Australian expat journalist and television celebrity famous in Thailand mostly for his work in promoting English Language Teaching (ELT) (figure 1.3).[13] Still, although the film was marketed with a promotional music video called "Zombie," and the word is used several times in the English subtitles, the Thai-language dialogue once again refrains from categorizing the monsters as zombies or domesticating them in any way, referring to them instead as "it"(*man*), "ghost" (*phi*), or "infected people" (*phu tit chuea*).

    Sars Wars can best be described as a slapstick comedy–horror film. Its rather convoluted plot focuses on an attempt to recover the teenage daughter of a rich man who was kidnapped for ransom by a motley crew of gangsters. Hoping to get his daughter back, the man hires a local hero and his young assistant, who locate the girl and the gang in a Bangkok condominium. The same condominium accidentally becomes the site of a zombie invasion, and all hell breaks loose. This gives the filmmakers an opportunity to slap together a medley of zombies, gangsters, superheroes, schoolgirls in Japanese uniforms, politicians, transvestites, scientists in PVC vinyl shorts and fishnet stockings, zombie babies, and a very large snake, all of which amounts to pretty much everything that was available to the director at the time of production.

    Although *Sars Wars* satisfies horror fans' expectations for guts and gore, it must be kept in mind that the film is first and foremost a comedy, which means that, like most Thai comedies, it relies almost entirely on slapstick gags, local comedians, and media insider jokes understood only by a select circle. If the result appears rather bizarre, this merely emphasizes the tendency of many Thai comedies to challenge both logic and tastefulness. Although zombies seem to play an important part in the story, it is obvious that they function merely as one more comic element. At the end of the film,

1.3 *SARS WARS*, 2004

it is difficult to tell whether the audience laughs more at the sight of the gangsters being chased by the zombies or at discovering that the gangster boss is in fact a transsexual (transsexuals, or *kathoei*, are a major object of ridicule in Thai comedies). As many Thai comedies, *Sars Wars* is an explosive concoction of stereotypes and portrays reality in an overtly simplified way. In fact, at the very beginning of the film, the characters actually transform into animated caricatures of themselves. And as if all this was not enough, the intentions of the filmmakers are made explicit through metafilmic allusions, when the actors address the audience directly and predict which elements of the movie will likely contribute to its success at the box office.

At the same time, like many other Thai films, *Sars Wars* can be read as a commentary on everyday dilemmas of contemporary Thais trapped between the local and the global, with the latter defined largely as "foreign" or "non-Thai." Deadly viruses and the zombie infection are clearly negative examples of such foreign influence. It is also no coincidence that the infection spreads through a Western-style decadent nightclub and into a modern Western-style condominium inhabited by middle-class Thais whose lifestyle is far from traditional. The film's "zombie zero," a *farang* (white foreigner), turns into a cannibalistic monster while still alive as the result of an infection with the SARS virus carried by a large bug of African origin. Although the bug originally lands on a map carried by two foreign tourists, instead of infecting the travelers, whose money is a welcome contribution to the Thai economy, it chooses to bite an obnoxious white expat and it does so at the exact moment when the man happens to scold a lowly Thai *tuk-tuk* driver.

Even though the Thai driver was indeed guilty of a traffic violation, there is no doubt that the sympathy of the filmmakers lies with him rather than with the rich foreigner, who to many Thais represents a rather unwelcome proof of Thai economic dependence on foreign countries.

From this foreign source, the infection spreads in a typical zombie fashion with half-chewed victims rising from the dead to chew on others and wreaking havoc all around. But as the zombies inevitably turn on the westernized Thais, in a somewhat twisted way they become defenders of Thai values, which we are shown will stand triumphant even if they have to be resurrected from the dead. Like many contemporary Thai films, on some level *Sars Wars* can also be read as a commentary on the recent rise of Thai nationalism. In a symbolic gesture of zombie resurrection, the victims die foreign to their own culture only to rise again as pure-blooded Thai monsters ready to defend their newly regained national identity at all costs. Having said that, however, if the foreign way of life is seen as the cause of trouble, foreign knowledge and expertise is also presented as the key to ultimate Thai success. While this may seem a contradiction, such an attitude seems to reflect the complex relationship of Thailand with the West (as well as with the economically significant non-Western countries) relatively well,[14] which is why, at the end of the day, there is nothing strange in the filmmakers' choice to equip the Thai hero with a samurai sword as a weapon or in their decision to educate the sexy Thai scientist at the rather dubiously named African University of Hollywood—nonetheless, a foreign institution.

Overall, although *Sars Wars* introduces full-fledged zombies[15] into Thai cinema, it uses them only as figures of ridicule, never allowing them to reach their horror potential. The creatures in question may be zombies based on their design, and they may be Thai judging by their behavior, but these two characteristics do not necessarily form a coherent whole. By placing these Thai zombies in a slapstick comedy, the filmmakers do not need to worry about the audience's support—after all, comedies can accommodate all types of odd characters and are rarely criticized for not adhering to reality. At the same time, such a portrayal has little chance of changing Thai audiences' attitude toward zombies as such; in order to do so, they would have to be taken more seriously.

BACKPACKERS (2009): THE REPRESSED OPPRESSED

Unlike the three films discussed previously, *Backpackers*, the third episode of a highly successful five-part *Phobia 2/Ha Phraeng*, is a short film inspired by true events (the suffocation of fifty-four illegal Burmese migrants in a Thai truck) that, although never formally acknowledged by the filmmakers, are easily recognizable to anyone familiar with recent Thai history. The plot is rather simple: two Japanese backpackers hitch a ride in a truck that is smuggling Burmese migrants into Thailand. The illegal immigrants have additionally been forced to swallow bags of drugs, but the bad packaging skills of the gangsters result in the deaths of the entire human cargo. For some unexplained reason, the dead return, devouring the guilty and innocent alike, taking revenge on their tormentors and, by extension, on the entire Thai nation. The final shot of the film shows a Burmese zombie child throwing himself onto a Thai Buddhist monk, thereby attacking the respected symbol of righteousness for a society that hypocritically turns a blind eye to the exploitation of those who are most in need of compassion and protection.

The rocky relationship between Thailand and Burma (Myanmar) has been a subject of much international criticism in recent years. The 2009 release of the film coincided with a wave of protests against the mistreatment of the Rohingya ethnic minority from Western Burma who were set adrift with almost no provisions on engineless barges by the Thai military, resulting in the deaths of more than five hundred refugees.[16] The number of Burmese workers living in Thailand today is estimated at over two million, although the exact figure will likely never be known. According to Human Rights Watch, more than 80 percent of all the migrant workers in Thailand come from Myanmar. They are also the most likely to be exploited since the current political and economic situation in Myanmar makes them particularly unwilling to return to their home country.[17] Assessing the plight of Burmese migrant workers in Thailand, Bryant Yuan Fu Yang pointed out that although Thais are willing to acknowledge the enormous contribution of the Burmese labor force to the Thai economy, they also feel that Burmese migrants, willing to work for minimum pay, are a threat to Thai workers. It does not help that the media demonize the immigrants, describing them as a demoralizing criminal element, providing justification for potential mistreatment (Yang 2007, 4).[18] The concerns voiced by human rights organizations confirm that the situation is certainly precarious for migrant workers in Thailand.[19]

Songyos Sugmanakan's *Backpackers* is the third episode in a five-part horror omnibus, *Phobia 2*. It is also the only short film in the collection that does not have a Thai title, which suggests that the choice of the English title was a conscious decision of the director rather than just a result of translation. On the surface, the title refers to the two characters introduced to the viewers at the beginning of the film: the two teenage Japanese tourists loaded down with large backpacks, hitchhiking on a lonely Thai road. As the story progresses, much of what these characters say is left in Japanese, not translated into Thai or English, and so it becomes obvious that they are not the focus of the film. Indeed, the word *backpackers* as used in this film has much more ominous connotations. The two obvious metaphorical interpretations refer to the human cargo *packed* into the *back* of the smuggler's truck and to the use of the immigrants as biological bags (similar to backpacks) for the smuggling of drugs across borders—the Thai gangsters who *packed* the migrants with amphetamines and stuffed them into the *back* of their truck are a different breed of *backpackers* altogether.

The English title of the episode also reflects the focus of the film on foreignness and the tensions between what is local (Thai) and what is not. It is no coincidence that the initial tourist couple is Japanese, as the Japanese are among the most admired ethnic groups in Thailand because of the strong hold that Japanese pop culture has especially over the younger Thai population. But while the Japanese characters are allowed to communicate in their language and are depicted as relatively active and independent (the couple is hitchhiking alone through a foreign country, the boy manages to grab hold of the gun in a critical situation, and so on), the much larger group of migrants represents an unnamed Southeast Asian ethnic minority, and it is this group that is treated like cattle. These human "backpacks" are not allowed to utter even a single word throughout the film, their expressions being limited to tearstained, painfully contorted faces and defensive body postures.

The transformation of this second group into bloodthirsty zombies is compelling, as it portrays the rise of the oppressed. The choice of the filmmakers to follow in the footsteps of Danny Boyle's *28 Days Later* in their rendering of the zombies as fueled by rage rather than hunger is also significant. The fully mobile and extremely fast murderous creatures are in contrast to the traditional depictions of zombies as awkward, slow-moving, and potentially retarded remnants of human beings (figure 1.4). Such a choice, however, is fully understandable insofar as the transformation presented in *Backpackers* does not make zombies out of humans but rather changes one type of zombie into another. The common racial stereotype of Burmese migrant workers in Thailand portrays them as vulnerable, uneducated, and naive people driven by hope of a better life offered by employment in a more economically developed Thailand. They are portrayed as easily manipulated and taken advantage of by anybody, and desperate enough to accept their fate without much protest.[20] This in itself describes a life of zombiehood[21] and the film's representation of the group as mute, passive, and easily controlled only strengthens the image. Transformation of the enslaved into

1.4 *BACKPACKERS*, 2009

anything but hyperactive, forceful, and unstoppable monsters would have been futile.

Just as the zombies remain silent throughout the film, they are also never named, thereby avoiding an opportunity to introduce a convincing zombie figure to Thai horror vocabulary. Because the cause of their deaths is attributed to the spillage of drugs transported in their guts, the Thais (gangsters) are seen as responsible, and the Thais (the larger society) will be the ones who ultimately pay the price. Although the zombies in *Backpackers* are still a foreign element (the zombies in the film do not seem to turn their victims into other zombies; they simply kill), they are effective because they feed on the guilt of the nation, the guilt of those who have turned a blind eye to the crimes committed by their compatriots for too long. The Burmese zombies serve as the executors of karmic justice, but they also bring into question the notion of monstrosity, leaving the audience shocked by the violent images and unnerved by the silent accusation that everyone is potentially an accomplice in the blatant exploitation of one ethnic group by another. This portrayal of the foreign import as a metaphorical representation of domestic guilt enables the acceptability of zombies, a tolerability that is further enhanced by the use of zombies that are more akin to the raving "infected" of Boyle's *28 Days Later*. Therefore, they are not seen as interfering in any way with the overall "realism" of the movie.

All of the films analyzed here make use of the concept of the zombie while simultaneously hiding that fact from viewers. Zombies are rationalized and "explained" in terms of ghosts and Khmer magic, ridiculed as a foreign plague, or morphed into a symbol of national guilt, but few attempts are made to integrate them into the actual Thai belief system. This in itself is not an impossible task. After all, just as Thai audiences apply a "reality check" to the domestic horror imaginary, so too the opposite phenomenon in which the imaginary has influenced what is perceived as reality.[22]

One example of this is the contemporary and increasingly popular lore of the ghost of Mae Nak, a legendary figure for whom a shrine has been erected near the Wat Mahabute temple in Phra Khanong. According to one version of the story, a woman named Nak died in childbirth while her husband was at war. Upon the husband's return, Nak's ghost resumed her wifely duties, at the same time terrorizing the villagers to keep them from revealing the truth about her real nature to her unsuspecting partner. The spectral wife was finally subdued by a famous monk, who turned part of her skull into a potent talisman and entombed her in a clay pot. However, her spirit lives on, resurrected in a multiplicity of narratives. Mae Nak's shrine is said to be located in the neighborhood where the celebrated woman lived and died, this despite the fact that there is absolutely no evidence Mae Nak ever existed outside the pages of the books and the dozens of films devoted to her. Another example of the influence of the imaginary is the modern shift in meaning for the term *phi ta bo*, originally signifying a plain skeleton, and now referring to a ghost without eyeballs, as popularized by Thai ghost films. Even though there is no mention of such an apparition in Thai ghost beliefs, after a handful of ghost films achieved popularity, reports of actual sightings of eyeless ghosts started springing up in the news media. And yet, while fictional figures and eyeless ghosts can find their way into the pantheon of Thai supernatural beings, actual zombies have yet to gain pantheon membership in the minds of modern Thai cinemagoers. For the time being, the uncanny monster that has become a favorite pop icon in the West will remain, in the minds of Thai viewers, a uniquely foreign figure. Thai filmmakers who have found the zombie interesting enough to warrant cinematic attention will likely continue to alter the monster in ways that will make it acceptable and perhaps appropriately frightening to local audiences. These alterations, as noted in this essay, have effectively turned the zombie into a ghost or a puppet, or isolated the zombie as a border-crossing foreign element. Will this situation ever change? Perhaps, but only if a creative team of filmmakers can twist the zombie into a shape that allows it to retain some essential qualities that define zombiism in the West while achieving, in the eyes of Thai viewers, the ability to be seen as capable of existing in the real world outside the cinema.

NOTES

1. Here, I use the Creole spelling of the word (*vodou*) to distinguish between the actual religious ritual and its simplistic cinematic portrayal as used in Hollywood/Thai films (*voodoo*).

2. In 2010, *Resident Evil: Afterlife* (dir. Paul W. S. Anderson) became the fifth-highest-grossing film in Thailand and the highest-grossing horror movie of the year earning 3.4 million USD (US dollars) at the box office. In comparison, the highest-grossing Thai horror film in 2010, *My Ex 2: Haunted Lover/Fan Mai* (dir. Piyapan Choopetch) ranked as number forty-four. In 2012, *Resident Evil: Retribution* (dir. Paul W. S. Anderson) ranked as eighth, earning roughly the same amount, and a year later *World War Z* (dir. Marc Forster) came in seventh, making 3.3 million USD. No Thai zombie film has ever came close to these figures, although in 2011, a ghost film, *Ladda Land* (dir. Sopon Sukdapisit), grossed well over 3.8 million USD, and in 2013, a ghost comedy, *Pee Mak Phrakanong* (dir. Banjong Pisanthanakun), made a whopping 18 million USD in Thailand alone and became the highest-grossing Thai production ever and the highest-grossing film ever released in Thailand (Thailand Yearly Box Office 2011).

3. On March 17, 2010, the *Bangkok Post* newspaper reported on the recent developments in the antigovernment UDD (United Front for Democracy against Dictatorship) protests in Bangkok: "Sakrapee Promchart, who was dressed as a Brahmin priest, dipped his hand in a pool of blood and stamped it on one of the concrete columns at the entrance. He said he had laid a curse on the seat of power but did not name anyone in particular. . . . Wama Thapmunee, the royal palace's chief Brahmin priest, denounced the rite and said Brahmin rites were normally performed on auspicious occasions" ("Government 'Cursed' as UDD Protest Turns Bloody" 2010). Magic seems to be used by every political faction, as demonstrated by the previous antigovernmental PAD (Peoples' Alliance for Democracy) protests. As the BBC reported on March 18, 2010: "More dramatically, analysts recall the incident of October 2008 when a group of women supporting the red-shirts' rivals, the yellow-shirted Peoples' Alliance for Democracy (PAD), offered up their sanitary napkins around the equestrian statue of King Rama V. The PAD leader Sondhi Limthongkul explained this was to counter attempts to sabotage the power of the statue to protect the nation—harnessing the perceived negative cosmic force of female blood to counteract, or undo, the allegedly evil acts of theirs" ("Symbolism and Beliefs behind Thai Blood Protests" 2010).

4. This essay follows the Royal Thai General System of Transcription (RTGS) for the transliteration of Thai words. Whenever available, the original titles of Thai films are transliterated the way they appear on IMdB.com, recognizing this database as the most likely source for further academic research, regardless of its deficiencies.

5. A secondary category of *nang sayong khwan* (terror films) has been invented to account for newer nonsupernatural horror films, or those that do not feature a ghost, but the term is hardly ever used by Thai filmmakers.

6. Thai horror films can roughly be divided into three subgenres. The most commonplace are horror comedies, featuring specifically Thai spiritual entities, often of animistic origins, such as *phi krasue* (the filth-eating spirit in the shape of a flying female head with entrails) or *phi pop* (the liver-devouring hungry ghost), whose representations do not translate well

outside Thailand (or Southeast Asia). The second group consists of Thai gore movies with stories of magic (usually Khmer black magic, which is seen as particularly potent) used as an excuse for plots featuring graphic bodily destruction. Finally, we have movies that focus on the central figure of a vengeful spirit of the violently dead, known in Thai as *phi tai hong*.

7. This essay uses the current spelling of the director's name as it appears on IMdB.com. However, when the interview with the director was conducted in 2008, the director used another transliteration of his name (Pakhpum Wonjinda).

8. The director of *Gancore Gud*, Apisit Opasaimlikit (better known as hip-hop performer Joey Boy), initially claimed he intended to create a new Thai zombie mythology by blending the concept of a zombie (taken from American movies) with that of the existing local underwater spirits (based on a private conversation with the author in March 2010). The end product, however, did not differ from what we would expect of a regular low-budget zombie comedy.

9. The English title *Formalin Man* derives from a scene in which the singer is injected with formalin in order to enable him to continue to perform.

10. A highly popular traditional form of Thai country music.

11. Any similarity between the character's nickname *Tot* and the German adjective *tot* meaning *dead* is purely coincidental. The Thai nickname transcribed here as *Tot* may or may not be derived from the verb meaning *to block*.

12. Given the fact that one of the film's heroes attempts to fend off the zombies with a fake lightsaber, the English title of the movie can be read as a play on *Star Wars*. At the same time, English titles of Thai films are often coincidental and have been known to change in the process of distribution.

13. This leaves open questions of whether the filmmakers are suggesting a connection between the spread of English as a global language and zombiehood.

14. In his article on the development of science in Thailand, Soraj Hongladarom admits that although Thais have always been keen to benefit from the achievements of Western science and technology, no attempts have ever been made "to integrate the system of thinking underlying Western science into the fabric of Thai culture" (2004, 59). Similarly, contemporary Thais' lifestyles seem open to foreign influences on a superficial, particularly material, level, without giving much thought to, or even rejecting completely, their philosophical foundations.

15. While conceptually zombies can be defined as reanimated corpses driven by instincts rather than intellect, their most iconic representation (derived from Hollywood cinema) portrays them as slow-moving, clumsy, and emotionless creatures capable of ripping their victims to pieces in order to feast on their raw flesh. In newer films, their basic motor skills seem to have improved, but the taste for human flesh and their determination to get it remains the same.

16. On January 17, 2009, the BBC carried the story of the Rohingya refugees who were "sent back to sea in boats without engines, their hands tied, left to their fate," resulting in the loss of at least three hundred lives. Although the military authorities hastened to deny the allegations, many individual police and military officials confirmed the story, explaining that "Rohingyas are seen as a greater security threat . . . because they are Muslim, because they tend to arrive in large numbers at one time, and because they are almost exclusively

men" (Head, "Thailand's Deadly Treatment of Migrants"). On January 27, 2009, Aljazeera reported that claims about the mistreatment of the refugees had been confirmed by a Thai naval officer who explained: "We have to take the engines off the boats or they will come back," adding in lieu of excuses that "[t]he wind will carry them to India or somewhere." An Aljazeera report estimated that "550 of the 992 towed out to sea by Thai soldiers later died" ("Thais Admit Boat People Set Adrift" 2009).

17. "Eighty percent of the migrant workers in Thailand are from Burma. They are particularly at risk, as they face ethnic and political conflict in their home country" ("Thailand: Migrant Workers Face Killings" 2010).

18. Because the article was published online, the page numbers refer to subsequent web pages.

19. On February 23, 2010, *Human Rights Watch* released a 124-page report on the abuse of migrant workers in Thailand based on eighty-two interviews with migrants from Burma, Cambodia, and Laos, culminating in the dramatic statement that "[b]oth documented and undocumented migrants in Thailand are vulnerable to arbitrary acts of violence, intimidation, and extortion from state authorities including police, military, and immigration officers as well as private individuals. These abuses include killings, beatings, sexual harassment and rape, forced labor, abductions and other forms of arbitrary detention, death threats and other forms of intimidation, and various types of extortion and theft" ("From the Tiger to the Crocodile" 2010, 41). Many of the observations in the report mirror the concerns of Amnesty International voiced in the organization's report published on June 7, 2005, which suggests there has been little change. ("Thailand: The Plight of Burmese Migrant Workers" 2005).

20. According to Human Rights Watch ("From the Tiger to the Crocodile"), Thai employees frequently recruit Burmese migrants to deal with the "dirty, difficult, and dangerous jobs" that Thai workers are unwilling to do. As the report states: "Employers find them easier to control because they either do not know of or are too intimidated to assert their rights" (2010, 20). Similarly, Yang (2007) states that "illegal migrants do not have the same bargaining power as Thai nationals, and therefore, are more susceptible to exploitation. Employers use migrants' illegal immigration status and threaten deportation in order to get them to work in unconscionable conditions" (4).

21. In Haitian zombie traditions, with Haiti's history of slavery and labor exploitation, the slaves are often seen as the "living dead," while the process of zombification is used to produce more slaves. Such was, for instance, the case of Clairvius Narcisse, popularized by Wade Davis in his book *The Serpent and the Rainbow* (1985). Narcisse, who was declared dead and buried in 1962, in 1980 returned alive to his home village of L'Estère in Haiti and claimed that he could remember the zombification ritual performed on him, after which he was kept on a farm as a slave for nearly twenty years.

22. Chances are that zombies may finally be making their breakthrough in Thai film. As this essay is going to print, Chalermchatri Yukol's period zombie epic *Phi Ha Ayothaya* is set to open in Thai cinemas on May 14, 2015, and Kulp Kaljareuk's muay Thai zombie action feature, *Fallen Thailand*, is currently in preproduction. If these two films manage to win the hearts of the Thai audience, we will likely see more homegrown Thai zombies in the future.

WORKS CITED

Backpackers. 2009. Directed by Songyos Sugmanakan. Perf. Charlie Trairat, Erika Toda. Segment of *Phobia 2/Ha Phraeng.* 2009. Directed by Banjong Pisanthanakun, Paween Purikitpanya, Songyos Sugmanakan, Parkpoom Wongpoom. Produced for GTH.

Curse of the Sun/Suriyakhaat. 2004. Directed by Kittipong Panyataweesap and Anat Yuangnhern. Perf. Paul Carey, Sitiporn Niyom, Ornjira Lamwilai. Produced for CM Film.

Davis, Wade. 1985. *The Serpent and the Rainbow.* New York: Simon and Schuster.

Formalin Man/Rak Ter Tau Fa. 2004. Directed by Pakphum Wongjinda. Perf. Ekkachai Srivichai, Pimpan Chalaikupp. Produced for Sahamongkol Film International.

"From the Tiger to the Crocodile: Abuse of Migrant Workers in Thailand." 2010. *Human Rights Watch.* February 23, 2010. Accessed July 20, 2010. http://www.hrw.org/en/reports /2010/02/23/tiger-crocodile-0.

Gancore Gud. 2011. Directed by Apisit Opasaimlikit. Perf. Apisit Opasaimlikit, Natee Aekwijit. Produced for Phranakorn Film.

"Government 'Cursed' as UDD Protest Turns Bloody." 2010. *Bangkok Post.* March 17, 2010. Accessed July 20, 2010. http://www.bangkokpost.com/news/local/34533/government -cursed-as-udd-protest-turns-bloody.

Guelden, Marlane. 1995. *Thailand: Into the Spirit World.* Bangkok: Asia Books.

Head, Jonathan. 2009. "Thailand's Deadly Treatment of Migrants." *BBC News.* January 17, 2009. Accessed July 20, 2010. http://news.bbc.co.uk/2/hi/south_asia/7834075.stm.

Hongladarom, Soraj. 2004. "Growing Science in Thai Soil: Culture and Development of Scientific and Technological Capabilities in Thailand." *Science Technology Society* 9 (1): 51–73. doi:10.1177/097172180400900103.

Ladda Land. 2011. Directed by Sopon Sukdapisit. Perf. Saharat Sangkapreecha, Piyathida Woramusik, Sutatta Udomsilp. Produced for GTH.

My Ex 2:Haunted Lover/Fan Mai. 2010. Directed by Piyapan Choopetch. Perf. Ratchawin Wongviriya, Atthama Chiwanitchapan, Thongpoom Siripipat. Produced for Forfilms.

Pee Mak/Pee Mak Phrakanong. 2013. Directed by Banjong Pisanthanakun. Perf. Mario Maurer, Davika Hoorne, Nattapong Chartpong. Produced for GTH.

Resident Evil: Afterlife. 2010. Directed by Paul W. S. Anderson. Perf. Milla Jovovich, Ali Larter, Wentworth Miller. Produced for Constantin Film Produktion, Davis-Films, Impact Pictures.

Resident Evil: Retribution. 2012. Directed by Paul W. S. Anderson. Perf. Milla Jovovich, Sienna Guillory, Michelle Rodriguez. Produced for Constantin Film International, Davis Films/ Impact Pictures (RE5), Capcom Company.

The Return of the Living Dead. 1985. Directed by Dan O'Bannon. Perf. Clu Gulager, James Karen, Don Calfa. Produced for Hemdale Film, Fox Films Ltd., Cinema 84.

Sars Wars/Khun Krabii Hiiroh. 2004. Directed by Taweewat Wantha. Perf. Suthep Po-ngam, Supakorn Kitsuwon. Produced for Charlermthai Studio.

Scared/Rap Nawng Sayawng Khwan. 2005. Dir. Pakphum Wongjinda. Perf. Borvornpoch Jaikunta, Suleeporn Tantragul, Chidjan Rujiphun. Produced for Sahamongkol Film International.

"Symbolism and Beliefs behind Thai Blood Protests." 2010. *BBC News.* March 18, 2010. Accessed July 20, 2010. http://news.bbc.co.uk/2/hi/asia-pacific/8574225.stm.

"Thailand: Migrant Workers Face Killings, Extortion, Labor Rights Abuses." 2010. *Human Rights Watch.* February 23, 2010. Accessed July 20, 2010. http://www.hrw.org/en/news /2010/02/22/thailand-migrant-workers-face-killings-extortion-labor-rights-abuses.

"Thailand: The Plight of Burmese Migrant Workers." 2005. *Amnesty International.* June 7, 2005. Accessed July 20, 2010. http://www.amnesty.org/en/library/info/ASA39/001/2005.

Thailand Yearly Box Office. 2011. *Box Office Mojo International.* Accessed March 10, 2011. http://www.boxofficemojo.com/intl/thailand/yearly.

"Thais Admit Boat People Sent Adrift." 2009. *Aljazeera.* January 27, 2009. Accessed July 20, 2010. http://english.aljazeera.net/news/asia-pacific/2009/01/20091267174292748.html.

28 Days Later. 2002. Directed by Danny Boyle. Perf. Cillian Murphy, Naomie Harris, Noah Huntley. Produced for DNA Films, British Film Council.

Video Clip. 2007. Directed by Pakphum Wongjinda. Perf. Ngamsiri Arsira-Lertsiri, Warot Pitakanonda, Nuttapong Tangkasam. Produced for Sahamongkol Film International.

Who R U?/Krai . . . Nai Hong. 2010. Directed by Pakphum Wongjinda. Perf. Teerapong Liaorakwong, Sinjai Plengpanit, Pongpit Preechaborisutkhun. Produced for Sahamongkol Film International.

Wonjinda, Pakhpum. 2008. "In Conversation with Sronrasilp Ngoenwichit." *Asian Journal of Literature, Culture and Society* 2 (1): 124–35.

World War Z. 2013. Directed by Marc Forster. Perf. Brad Pitt, Mireille Enos, Daniella Kertesz. Produced for Paramount Pictures, Skydance Productions, Hemisphere Media Capital.

Yang, Bryant Yuan Fu. 2007. "Life and Death Away from the Golden Land: The Plight of Burmese Migrant Workers in Thailand." *Asian-Pacific Law and Policy Journal* 8 (2007). Reprinted in *Thailand Law Journal* 1 (12) (2009). Accessed July 20, 2010. http://www .thailawforum.com/articles/Burmese Migrants-in-Thailand-4.html.

"SHE LOVES THE BLOOD OF THE YOUNG"

The Bloodthirsty Female as Cultural Mediator
in Lafcadio Hearn's "The Story of Chūgōrō"

SABINE METZGER

Compared to late nineteenth-century vampire and Gothic fictions, Lafcadio Hearn's "The Story of Chūgōrō" (from the collection *Kottō*, 1902) appears at first glance to be a simple, if not mediocre, tale, devoid of any intricate plot and psychological depth: Chūgōrō, a young man, falls prey to a seductive stranger who, during several nightly rendezvous, deprives him of his blood. However, despite its bloodthirsty female protagonist and despite its evoking what Christopher Frayling in *Vampyres* calls "haemosexuality" (1991, 388), "The Story of Chūgōrō" is not a vampire tale, nor does it blend Western and Eastern supernaturalism. "The Story of Chūgōrō" is a *kwaidan* or "weird tale" from Old Japan, told by his Japanese wife Setsuko Koizumi. Hearn reshaped this tale, as Sukehiro Hirakawa in his "Lafcadio Hearn, a Reappraisal" observes, with "the freedom of a story-teller working from oral sources" (2007a, 13). If Hearn retold the story from Old Japan without recourse to the Gothic and its iconography, he did so for a good reason: Japan has, as Wayne Stein in his article "Enter the Dracula" underlines, "no vampire-tradition" (2009, 241), and Hearn abided by this fact.

Hearn—journalist, novelist, folklorist, and a writer of both travel sketches and ghost stories—was, with his Greek Irish descent, with his upbringing in England and France, and with his years spent in the American Midwest, what Carl Dawson, in his *Lafcadio Hearn and the Vision of Japan*, calls "a man of blurred citizenship" (1992, 5). Although his life and career is otherwise marked by the constant crossing of boundaries—geographical, national, cultural, and generic—he kept literary traditions apart and carefully avoided any intrusions of the West he had left behind. When Hearn in 1889, after having struggled to survive as a journalist in Cincinnati and after intervals in the American South and Martinique, was commissioned by *Harper's Magazine* to travel to Japan and write about his experience of the country, he seized the opportunity. Because he had become disillusioned with Western life, the Orient was, for Hearn and for many of his contemporaries as well, an aestheticist escape promising a spiritual and cultural fulfillment that Western civilization, which he considered "cold and vapid humbug" (quoted in Dawson 1992, 151), could not provide. Hearn never left Japan again and died in 1904 as a Japanese citizen; writings such as *Glimpses of Unfamiliar Japan* (1894), *Gleanings in the Buddha Field* (1897), *Kokoro: Hints and Echoes of Japanese Inner Life* (1896), or his posthumously published *Japan: An Attempt at Interpretation* (1904) and *Kwaidan: Stories and Studies of Strange Things* (1904) earned him the reputation of being Japan's interpreter to the West.

As I argue in this chapter, "The Story of Chūgorō" has to be seen within the context of both Hearn's escape from Western civilization as well as a growing fascination with Japan and its art and culture in America. Hearn's age witnessed not only a flourishing of Gothic and vampire literature, but also, in the wake of the opening of Yokohama, an enthusiasm for Japan. As Nigel Kendall puts it in his introduction to Hearn's *Exotics and Retrospectives*, for a majority of Westerners, Japan was "mysterious and hopelessly exotic" (2001, vii).

What is "startling" and "strange" for Hearn's turn-of-the-century readers is less the fact that the protagonist of his story falls prey to a blood-loving seductress, but rather the fascination with Japan itself, considered to be the exotic per se. With her similarity to the Western vampire, Hearn's bloodthirsty female proves to be a familiar figure in the midst of the unfamiliar—a figure partaking of what could be called a form of the "transcultural supernatural": a neutral territory unfolding between East and West, uniting them but at the same time defying any appropriation.

ESCAPING THE WEST, CIRCUMVENTING TRANSYLVANIA: THE TERMINOLOGICAL VOID

In Lafcadio Hearn's *kwaidan* or "weird tales" from Old Japan, the Western reader encounters figures and themes bearing a striking resemblance to those of nineteenth-century Gothic fiction. "Strip away the Japanese details . . . and one could be in deepest Transylvania," Susan Fisher (2007, 173) observes in "'Weird Beauty': Angela Carter and Lafcadio Hearn in Japan." That Hearn's Japanese ghost stories evoke Transylvanian associations holds true in particular for "The Story of O-Kamē" and "The Story of Chūgorō"—both published in 1902 in Hearn's collection *Kottō: Being Japanese Curios with Sundry Cobwebs*.

In the first story, O-Kamē, two years after having married Hachiyēmon, is attacked by an insidious disease then raging in the province of Toga. The care of the best Chinese physicians proves to be in vain and O-Kamē's strength continually dwindles. On her deathbed, O-Kamē makes her husband promise never to remarry—a wish with which Hachiyēmon, being much in love with his beautiful wife, willingly complies. After his wife's death, Hachiyēmon becomes weaker and weaker. Unable to find a physical cause for his decreasing strength, the physicians suspect "some very unusual trouble of mind" (Hearn 2010b, 50) to be the explanation for Hachiyēmon's poor condition. He finally confesses to his mother "that O-Kamē can find no rest in the other world" (50), that she visits him every night, and that she "looks and acts as when she lived" (51). Alarmed by her son's account, Hachiyēmon's mother consults a Buddhist priest, who advises that O-Kamē be exhumed. When in the presence of the relatives the grave is opened, they find O-Kamē sitting "before them with a smile upon her face, seeming as comely as before the time of her sickness; and there was not any sign of death upon her" (52). After the priest had traced "certain holy talismanic words" (53) in Sanskrit characters upon her body and performed a Sēgaki service for the dead woman's spirit, Hachiyēmon is able to recover his health.

Like so many of Hearn's *kwaidan* from Old Japan, such as "Yuki-Onna" or "The Snow-Woman," which served the painter Bertha Lum as a source of inspiration for her 1916 print "Frost Fairy" (see Meech 1990b, 141), "The Story of O-Kamē" can be read as a tale of love beyond death. Resembling Théophile Gautier's "La morte amoureuse," who, as Erik Butler in his *Metamorphosis of the Vampire* points out, has "too much sensuousness for a mortal" (2010, 63), restless O-Kamē is above all an undead who deprives her husband during their nightly encounters of his physical strength: his vital fluid or his "life-blood." Whereas Hachiyēmon's life can be saved by the intervention of a Buddhist priest, the protagonist of "The Story of Chūgōrō" is less fortunate.

Chūgōrō, an *ashigaru*, a member of "the lowest class of retainers in military service" (Hearn 2010b, 73), suddenly falls into the habit of leaving his master's premises during the night. Although his nightly absences do not go unnoticed by the other *ashigaru*, they decide not to intervene because they suspect a love affair and because Chūgōrō is able to do his work as expected. It is only after the young man begins "to look pale and weak" (74) that they become worried and an elderly servant inquires about the reasons for Chūgōrō's strange behavior. With some hesitation, Chūgōrō tells his comrade his story of the mysterious woman he encountered. She wanted him for her husband and led him to a mysterious building complete with a bridal chamber. Early in the morning, Chūgōrō's new wife begged him to meet her every night at the bridge where they first met, to keep their marriage a secret, and to leave before daybreak—otherwise, both of them would lose their lives. Convinced that his wife is the daughter of a deity, Chūgōrō "promised to obey her in all things" (78). He ends his story by imploring his friend to keep his secret.

The elderly *ashigaru* is surprised by Chūgōrō's story, but does not doubt its truth. Assuming that the young man is "bewitched" (79), he advises him to be careful. In the evening, Chūgōrō waits in vain for his wife and fears he has broken his promise. "Trembling from head to foot" (80) he lies down, and during the night his condition deteriorates. The Chinese physician who is consulted because Chūgōrō is "evidently sick—deathly sick" (80) exclaims, "Why, the man has no blood! . . . There is nothing but water in his veins" (80). Chūgōrō dies at sunset; after having been told his story, the Chinese physician is able to provide an explanation for the young man's mysterious loss of blood. The seductive stranger who lured Chūgōrō to her underwater dwellings "has been haunting this river from ancient time. She loves the blood of the young" (81), he tells the *ashigaru*. During the daytime she took the shape of a "very loathsome creature . . . a great and ugly frog" (82).

Dealing with bloodsucking—be it metaphorical, as in "The Story of O-Kamé"; be it literal, as in "The Story of Chūgōrō"; or with what Butler calls "expropriating and redistributing energies" (2010, 11), both stories could be considered vampire tales. Indeed, "The Story of Chūgōrō" is anthologized in Leonard Wolf's *Blood Thirst: 100 Years of Vampire Fiction* (1997). What characterizes these two stories is not so much the figure of a blood-draining ghostly female or their linkage of the protagonists' loss of blood explicitly with sexual encounters, but the fact that the draining of blood as well as the bloodsuckers themselves are never described in terms familiar to the Western reader, who were acquainted with the dramatization of blood and bite marks, as in, for example, John Polidori's "The Vampyre" from 1819:

> *There was no colour upon her cheek, not even upon her lips; yet there was a stillness about her face that seemed almost as attached as the life that once dwelt there:—upon her neck and breast was blood, and upon her throat where the marks of teeth having opened the vein:—to this the men pointed, crying, simultaneously with horror, "a Vampyre, a Vampyre!" (2008, 12)*

Terms such as *vampirism* or *vampire* are strangely absent from Hearn's stories, along with the whole iconography specific to vampire fiction, such as teeth and bite marks, blood and bloodsucking as a means of reproduction, and gloomy castles and nights of full moons. What the Western reader seems to be able to identify easily is represented by a terminological void. Instead of calling its bloodsucker *vampire*, "The Story of Chūgōrō" offers various suggestions for naming the bloodthirsty stranger by evoking a whole menagerie of figures from Japanese folklore: "Fox-Woman" (Hearn 2010b, 81), "Serpent-Woman" (81), and "Dragon-Woman" (81) are proposed by *ashigaru* as the possible causes for Chūgōrō's loss of blood.

Hearn circumvents and shuns Transylvania terminologically; neither in his fictional nor in his nonfictional writings does he ever refer to his tales as Gothic stories. "While Hearn never used the term Gothic to describe his own work," Fisher writes,

> *he certainly dealt in the imagery and themes that typify Gothic writing. The "Fantastics" that he wrote for the New Orleans Item in the 1880s obsessively repeat such hallmark Gothic motifs as the vampire lover and the graveyard tryst. . . . The tales in Kwaidan are similarly Gothic in mood. (2007, 172)*

Equally absent from Hearn's Japanese ghost stories are the transformations and innovations that Gothic fiction in general and vampire fiction in particular have undergone by the late nineteenth century when he wrote his tales from Old Japan: Andrew Smith, in his *Gothic Literature*, lists a "progressive internalization of 'evil'" as opposed to the earlier Gothic fiction with its "externally manifested sources of danger" (2007, 87) and the use of "doubling as a clear indication" (94) of this internalization. Further, ghosts become the reflection of "social and economic anxieties" (117). Hearn in contrast, although writing at the turn of the century, seems to tell his stories in the most conventional fashion. Wolf, labeling "The Story of Chūgōrō" a "classical adventure tale" (1997, 12), in his *Blood Thirst* anthology observes the tale's lack of "intricate plot development" (12) and its reach "for psychological detail" (12). However, the fact that Hearn does not attempt to diverge from the conventions of the genre with his Japanese tales does not necessarily mean that Hearn is a writer manqué. "Books of ghost stories are my treasure," Hearn once claimed. Being a great admirer of Edgar Allan Poe, Hearn was nicknamed "The Raven" in his youth (Murray 1993, 32), and as a young writer, he shared his Anglo-American contemporaries' appreciation of fictions dealing with the supernatural. As a reviewer of Henry James's stories and translator of Théophile Gautier, Guy de Maupassant, and Pierre Loti, Hearn was well aware of his late nineteenth-century contemporaries' narrative experimentations. James praised him for having acquainted American readers with the works of Loti and for having introduced literary impressionism to the United States (Hirakawa 2007, 5). Therefore, it would be shortsighted to conclude from the simplicity of tales like "The Story of O-Kamé" and "The Story of Chūgōrō" that psychological depth is generally absent from his writing.

Throughout his life, Hearn firmly believed in ghosts and the supernatural—a belief that dates back to his earliest childhood spent with his aunt Sarah Brenane in Ireland. "For the best of possible reasons," he states, "I then believed in ghosts and goblins—because I saw them by day and by night" (quoted in Dawson 1992, 92). Again and again he examined the nature of supernatural experiences. For example in "Vespertina Cognitio," set on a West Indian island, Hearn explores the "ancestral fears of the dark" (2001, 217) and deals with "a dim but voluminous terror" (217) caused by a nightmarish incident—"a Step" (213) in front of the bedroom door, which is perceived as approaching and retreating—that the narrator experiences in a state "half-conscious, dream-conscious" (213). In this autobiographical text, Hearn experiments with the "internalization of 'evil'" characteristics of the fin de siècle Gothic and attempts to find a psychological (and, consequently, rational) explanation for the ghostly apparition. The narrator tries to ascribe his experience to a hallucination caused by the oppressive tropical heat—an explanation he rejects as unsatisfactory, however, since the nightmare is not only experienced by himself but also confirmed by the experience of his West Indian guide. "The Story of O-Kamé" and "The Story of Chūgōrō" are lacking such inquiries into the nature of supernatural experience and into the border area between dream and consciousness. These stories derive their significance from their simplicity, which is anything but a shortcoming. Within the context of Hearn's Japanese writings, his deliberate ignoring of experimentation and generic transformation, as well as his shunning of Transylvania, can be seen simultaneously as an escape from and a criticism of Western civilization.

Hearn had been a great admirer of Japan since the 1884 New Orleans Exhibition, where he saw objects displayed that could easily keep pace with their Western counterparts and thus, as Hitomi Nabae states in "Insect-Music: Hearn's Orphean Song," would "dispel the fixed notion of Japan as the exotic other but allow Japan to claim its presence in the civilized modern world" (2007, 143). Hearn's fascination with Japan was further heightened by his reading of Basil Hall Chamberlain's *Translations of the Kojiki or Records of Ancient Matters.*

As Nigel Kendall observes in his introduction to *Exotics and Retrospectives,* Hearn "never [felt] at home in the West" (2001, x). He had been tossed around in his childhood after his parents' divorce, struggling to survive in the rapidly growing and poverty-stricken Cincinnati of the mid-nineteenth century. Later, he was socially ostracized after his marriage to a former slave at a time when interracial marriage was strongly disapproved of and still illegal in many places (Dawson 1992, 10). Like many of his contemporaries, Hearn was dissatisfied with Western civilization, which he regarded as lacking empathy, rejecting its materialism, its values, and its religion (Hirakawa 2007c, 83). In addition to his underlying fin de siècle antimodernist stance, Hearn's contempt for the West stemmed from his consideration of it as the culture of his much-despised Anglo-Irish father (Hirakawa 2007c, 83). In the East, he hoped to find a spiritual and physical fulfillment that the West could not provide. However, unlike Pierre Loti, for example, he never indulged in mere sensuality. Nor did he adopt the condescending attitude of so many Western writers who visited Japan. Henry Adams, for example, wrote in a letter: "This is a child's country. The whole show is of the nursery. Nothing is serious, nothing is taken seriously. Life is a dream and in Japan one dreams of the nursery" (quoted in Kendall 2001, viii).

In *Japan: An Attempt at Interpretation*, Hearn, in contrast, describes Japan as "a civilization that can be termed imperfect only by those who would also term imperfect the Greek civilization of three thousand years ago" (2008, 5). By comparing Japan to Greece, he evokes his mother's native country and emphasizes Japan's equality with, if not superiority to, Western civilization. He thus concludes, "our Occident has much to learn from this remote civilization not only in matters of art and taste, but in matters likewise of economy and utility" (5). For Hearn, Japan was the country where things were not simply manufactured, but, as he states in *Glimpses of Unfamiliar Japan*, "caressed into existence" (2010a, 58). In both his fictional and his nonfictional writings, he never tires of praising the country's beauty and the refinement of its inhabitants. Hearn's initial enthusiasm, however, finally gave way to a strong disillusionment in the face of Meiji Japan falling increasingly prey to Westernization, and thus, as he writes in "Insect-Musicians," "substituting everywhere for beauty the utilitarian, the conventional, the vulgar, the utterly hideous" (2001, 63).

Hearn's turning to and narrative recreation of Old Japan means, therefore, a second escape from the West, or, as Dawson aptly formulates it, "an exile within the exile" (1992, 30). As Hirakawa observes in his study "Lafcadio's Nightmares," Hearn's interest in ghosts as a writer is to be considered an expression of his antimodernist stance in an age of modernization and Westernization: "If the familiar side of Meiji Japan to Westerners was the Westernization of an East Asian country, Hearn was interested in unfamiliar 'ghostly' aspects of Japan" (2007b, 32). In Old Japan, with its animistic world of Shinto and with its folklore, Hearn found a sphere that was in its temporal remoteness safely out of the reach of Westernization and its devastating influence. And it was Hearn's endeavor to keep Old Japan out of the Western grip, totally disregarding the fact that he himself was a Western writer retelling the tales in English for a chiefly Western audience (see Clubbe 2007, 93–94). Thus the term *Gothic*, frequently employed by Hearn in writings dating from his American years, such as his "Gothic Horror" in *Shadowings* (2007, 213–22), is replaced by "weird beauty," as, for example, in his preface to *Some Chinese Ghosts* (quoted in Fisher 2007, 173). As Fisher observes, this is a notion that is more apt than the term *Gothic* with its Western associations (2007, 173). The "Gothic" tale becomes the *kwaidan* or "weird tale." To speak of his tales from Old Japan in terms of "Gothic stories" would have meant to Westernize them and this holds equally for everything so strangely absent from Hearn's *kwaidan*, like narrative experimentation or the term *vampire* or vampire iconography: Japan has, as Stein in his study "Enter the Dracula" underlines, "no vampire-tradition" (2009, 241). If the nineteenth century's predilection for the irrational and the supernatural has to be understood, as Cody Poulton in her study "Two Springs: Hearn's and Kyōka's Other Worlds" emphasizes, as "a critique of contemporary society" (2007, 162), this critique finds its logical consequence in the simplicity of Hearn's ghostly tales from Old Japan and in their shunning of Transylvania.

The *ashigaru* asks the Chinese physician, "'Who is she?—or what is she?. . .—a Fox-Woman? . . . A Serpent-Woman?—A Dragon-Woman?'" (Hearn 2010b, 81). The end of "The Story of Chūgōrō" cites a whole menagerie of figures from Japanese folklore. Old Japan, Hearn's story seems to imply, has its own names for what the West calls *vampire*. It also has a tradition richer and far more complex than that of the West; the plethora of names is evoked only to be discarded in favor of the frog, and thus associated with the animistic nature of Shinto religion. Hearn leaves it to his readers to fill the terminological void.

FOREGROUNDING THE EXOTIC

What does Chūgōrō tell, if the bloodsucking remains untold? What is "The Story of Chūgōrō" about? Circumventing Transylvania and, consequently, eliding the act of vampirism, Hearn's story elaborates the young man's encounter with the stranger and his being led to her palace in the river: "As we neared the bridge, she pulled my sleeve again and led me down the bank to the very edge of the river," Chūgōrō tells the *ashigaru*:

"Come in with me," she whispered and pulled me toward the water. It is deep there, as you know; and I became all at once afraid of her, and tried to turn back. She smiled, and caught me by the wrist, and said, "Oh, you must never be afraid with me." . . . Into the deep water she stepped, and drew me with her; and I neither saw nor heard nor felt anything more until I found myself walking beside her through what seemed to be a great palace, full of light. . . . The woman led me by the hand: we passed through room after room,—through ever so many rooms, all empty, but very fine,—until we entered into a guest-room of a thousand mats. . . . She led me to the place of honour, by the alcove, and seated herself in front of me, and said: "This is my home: do you think you could be happy with me here?" (76–77)

Before daybreak, Chūgōrō reports, "[S]he conducted me through many rooms, all empty and beautiful, to the entrance. There she again took me by the wrist, and everything suddenly became dark, and I knew nothing more until I found myself standing alone on the river bank, close to the Naka-no-hashi" (78). Although the woman is "very young and handsome" (75), and the youth admits "that her smile was more beautiful than anything else in the world" (77), the story cannot be reduced to the seduction by a sexualized ghostly Other. Chūgōrō's narration elaborates on his being "pulled" by the sleeve (75), his being "led by the hand" (76) to the stranger's palace in the river, and thus to a region radically different from his accustomed surroundings. Inhabited by the stranger and her maids, it is a feminine sphere where Chūgōrō is taken—in stark contrast to the masculine world of Suzuki's *ya-shiki* with the *ashigaru*. Since Chūgōrō is completely unaware of his wife's blood thirst, it is also a world of pleasure and leisure in contrast to the world of the military with its duties and daily routine.

By dwelling on the protagonist's being taken to a region unknown, "The Story of Chūgōrō" becomes paradigmatic for Hearn's writings on the Far East. For leading the turn-of-the-century reader to unfamiliar regions is precisely what both Hearn's fictional and nonfictional writings do. Taking his readers somewhere else, leading them to regions where they have never been before, is a strategy Hearn established as a journalist in Cincinnati, during a time that Dawson refers to as the author's years of "muckraking articles" (1992, 111). As George Hughes points out in his "Lafcadio Hearn and the Fin de Siècle," with his sensationalist articles Hearn "leads his readers to places where, as middle-class respectable citizens, they dared not to go by themselves"(1997a, 87), places such as the slaughterhouses, brothels, and opium dens of the city's Tallow District.

It is almost the same strategy that Hearn pursues in his Japanese travel sketches in which he does not lead the reader to Tokyo or Kyoto, the Western visitors' preferred destinations, but to places like "Matsue—an isolated town on the Japan Sea coast that he calls 'Chief City of the Province of Gods'" (Hughes, 1997b, 107). Hearn rejects the familiar paths of conventional travel writing and seeks the remote that had not been beheld by a Westerner before. His fascination with the remote, the unfamiliar, and the never-before-seen is not only reflected by his choice of destinations, but also by his choice of subjects. In his writing, he explores marginal themes such as frogs in Japanese poetry and Japanese toys; these are isolated concerns, which at the same time constitute, as Nigel Kendall puts it, "the true value of the observant outsider" (2001, xiii).

Hearn also takes the reader to the "foreign and the faraway" (2001,125) in his ghostly tales—however, not only by crossing what Dawson calls the "supernatural threshold" (1992, 101), but also, above all, the cultural threshold. "The local colour is marvellous" (2009, 558) Hearn remarked about the *contes creoles*, and that he foregrounds the "local colour" in his ghostly tales as well becomes evident in the opening paragraph of "The Story of Chūgōrō":

> *A long time ago there lived, in the Koishikawa quarter of Yedo, a hatamoto named Suzuki, whose yashiki was situated on the bank of Yedogana, not far from the bridge called Naka-no-hashi. And among the retainers of this Suzuki there was an ashigaru named Chūgōrō. (2010b, 73)*

In order to convey what he calls "local colour," Hearn renounces the stereotypical cherry blossoms and Orientalist depictions of Eastern cities. Such depictions are omnipresent, for example, in the writings of his contemporary Winnifred Eaton who, under her penname Onoto Wattana, wrote best-selling Japanese romances, such as *A Japanese Nightingale*, without ever having set foot on Japanese soil. Instead, Hearn employs romanized but untranslated Japanese terms, like *hatamoto, yashiki,* and *ashigaru,* terms that he could have easily rendered in English in his retelling of the story. However, replacing the Japanese with English words would have meant, apart from the inadequacy of any translation, to Westernize the tale. Hearn is enamored of the Japanese words as such and uses them lavishly throughout his writings. He often explains and comments on them in footnotes or in appositions: a chest of drawers, for example, is never just a chest of drawers, but a "*tansu,* or chest of drawers" (Hearn 2004, 104). "Language is not just a transparent veil over the culture; it is integral to the otherness of the other culture" (1997b,

106), Hughes observes in his study "Entering Island Cultures." In "The Story of Chūgōrō" (as well as in Hearn's writings on Japan in general), language, therefore, serves to emphasizes otherness. It re-creates and foregrounds Japan as the exotic other. Romanized Japanese terms such as *hatamoto, yashiki,* and *ashigaru* function like poetic forms or metaphors—the *onoma allotrios* or "foreign word" in Aristotle's *Poetics*—due to their "foreignness" or incompatibility with the linguistic surroundings in which they occur. Untranslated and, unless augmented by the author's explanatory comments, also untranslatable for Western readers who do not understand Japanese, they stand out, provoking a clash with the syntagma and interrupting the reading process, thereby directing the reader's attention away from the linearity of the plot to the exotic other per se.

The story's setting and its cast of characters also conveys this "sensation of the foreign and the faraway" (2001, 125)—the "local colour"—based on the story's setting and its cast of characters. "The Story of Chūgōrō" is marked by its minimalistic sceneries: there is the spot in front of the gate of the *yashiki,* the wooden bridge leading across the nearby river, and the stranger's palace in the waters of the river. The Naka-no-hashi Bridge, the riverbanks, and the *yashiki* are devoid of any descriptive details as are the stranger's dwelling with their "bridal chamber" (Hearn 2010b, 77) where the young man spends his nights with the stranger. Apart from the "guest-room of a thousand mats" (76) with its "great alcove at the farther end" (77), its burning lights and "cushions laid out as for a feast" (77), the rooms are "empty." Chūgōrō tells the *ashigaru* that they "passed through room after room,—through ever so many rooms, all empty but very fine" (76), and again, at the end of the night, through "many rooms, all empty and beautiful" (78). The rooms are distinguished by what could be called a "splendour of emptiness," forming a sharp contrast to Poe's interiors and those of Gothic and fin de siècle writers like Huysmans. They evoke the minimalism of Japanese interior design, which was to influence Hearn's contemporaries in the field of architecture and crafts.

The story's cast of characters is equally minimalistic. In his retelling of the tale, Hearn also renounces any descriptive elements or elaboration of the characters' traits—the stranger is merely described as "very young and handsome" (75). The four main characters, reminiscent of the Japanese Noh-play in their small number, are always grouped in pairs: the story's frame focuses on Chūgōrō and the elderly *ashigaru;* on the young man's story of Chūgōrō and the stranger; on the end of the story, after Chūgōrō's death, and on the *ashigaru* and the Chinese physician. Because the tale consists mainly of dialogues, and Chūgōrō's story is embedded in his conversation with the *ashigaru*, the emphasis is on the interlocutors' interaction, which is marked by a strange tranquility. At first, Chūgōrō's nightly absences from the *yashiki* do not cause any conflict; they are even tolerated. When the *ashigaru* takes him "aside" (74), it is not only to admonish him for a violation of rules, but to express his concern for the young man's health. And when Chūgōrō confesses to the *ashigaru* his nightly adventures, it is not only because he is made to do so, but also because of his respect for the latter's concern. After listening to Chūgōrō's bizarre story, the *ashigaru* neither blames nor ridicules the young man, but, convinced that Chūgōrō is "bewitched" (99), concludes that "the lad was rather to be pitied" (79) and that "any forcible interference would be likely to result in mischief" (79). Instead of scolding Chūgōrō, he "kindly" (79) promises to keep his story secret, and even understands the necessity of the young man's keeping his appointment with the stranger on the following evening. In "The Story of Chūgōrō" Hearn depicts human behavior determined by mutual concern, respectfulness, understanding, and politeness; these are qualities for which, in his nonfictional writings, he praises Japanese society, and that extend across the "supernatural threshold" as well. Chūgōrō is by no means forced into the union with the stranger but rather invited: "This is my home: do you think that you could be happy with me here" (77), she asks, and Chūgōrō agrees "out of [his] heart" (77). Apart from her seductiveness, it is the prospect of "happiness" (76) as well as the respect for the gods that makes Chūgōrō accept her as his wife.

"Strip[ping] away the Japanese details" (2007, 173), as Fisher suggests, would deprive "The Story of Chūgōrō" (as any other of Hearn's *kwaidan*) of its impact. The evocation of Japan as the exotic other is not only the essence of Hearn's escape from and criticism of Western civilization—the "sensation of the foreign and the faraway" (Hearn 2001, 125) is also exactly what appealed to Hearn's Western readership at a time when everything Japanese and Japanesque was in vogue. If his writings attempted to take his readers to a region unknown, it was a journey on which they willingly embarked. Hearn's Japanese ghost stories not only coincide with the golden age of the Gothic and the two decades framed by the publications of Joseph Sheridan Le Fanu's "Carmilla" in 1872 and Bram Stoker's *Dracula* in 1897, but as well with the West's increasing fascination with Japan—a fascination that originated, as Julia Meech and Gabriel Weisberg demonstrate in *Japonisme*, in America's becoming acquainted with Japanese art. Weisberg illustrates how the Philadelphia Centennial Exhibition in 1876 as well as the Chicago World's Fair in 1893—with its display of Japanese prints—enabled a vast audience to become acquainted with Japanese arts and crafts, either by visiting the exhibitions or by reading the numerous illustrated articles published in

American periodicals like *Harper's Weekly* (1990a, 17–19). French art dealers, among them notably Siegfried Bing, promoted the spreading of the taste for things Japanese by organizing auctions and sales along the East Coast, familiarizing Americans with the works of Utamaro, Kiyonaga, and Hokusai (see Weisberg 1990, 23–26). In the last two decades of the nineteenth century, Japonisme had experienced what Weisberg calls its "crescendo": by the turn of the century, "so many books and articles had been published on the Far East that few with any interest in culture could have remained oblivious to the seduction of Japanese civilization" (17).

For tales like "The Story of Chūgōrō," Japonisme proves to be a context even more relevant than late nineteenth-century fictions of the supernatural. As Meech concludes, in an age when Japan with its arts and crafts exerted a spell chiefly because it was considered to be "new, which is to say 'exotic'" (1990a, 43), it is precisely the "Japanese details"—Japanese romanized words, settings, and manners—that appealed to the reader, rather than a protagonist seduced and deprived of his blood by a supernatural creature. Although Japan, several decades after the opening of Yokohama, was no longer the terra incognita evoked by an article in *The Friend* in 1851 (anonymous quoted in Weisberg 1990, 15), or Melville's "low-lying, endless, unknown Archipelagos, and impenetrable Japans" (1992, 493), it was still for a majority of Westerners "mysterious and hopelessly exotic" (Kendall 2001, vii). If this applies to Japan in general, it holds true even more for the Old Japan in Hearn's retold tales. By accentuating Japan's exotic otherness, Hearn creates a setting that for his turn-of-the-century readership is far more startling than she who "loves the blood of the young."

BRIDGING THE GAP, APPROACHING EXOTIC JAPAN: THE BLOODTHIRSTY FEMALE AS CULTURAL MEDIATOR

It is significant that the story Chūgōrō tells the *ashigaru* is not a tale of horror. Unaware of her blood thirst, he remembers—without any exception—his nightly excursions to her realm, the "bridal night," and the subsequent nights he spends with his wife as pleasant experiences. Initially startled by the stranger's beauty, her apparent higher social class, and her bold offer, he quickly gains confidence in her. Chūgōrō feels safe and "at home" in the stranger's dwelling, which she offers him to share with her as their "home" (Hearn 2010b, 77).

If, as Poulton claims in regard to Hearn's *kwaidan*, that they are "occulting Japan" (2007, 163), and that they "make the Exotic uncanny" (2007, 164) or "unheimlich" ("uncanny" in the Freudian sense), in "The Story of Chūgōrō," this uncanniness or "unhomeliness" is brought about by the story's setting, by the manners it depicts, and by the romanized Japanese words rather than by the supernatural. It is these elements that evoke, by their effect of defamiliarization, Old Japan and thus constitute the story's uncanniness in the sense that they make the reader feel literally "unheimlich"—"unhomely." Within this exotic and unfamiliar world, Chūgōrō's ghostly bride, the one who "loves the blood of the young," proves to be a familiar figure for the Western reader—particularly in an age when stories of the supernatural flourished. Although she is never referred to as a vampire, and although she does not even leave bite marks, she resembles what the Western tradition calls a vampire—and not just because of her love of blood. The "shape-shift-ing potential" (Butler 2010, 6) and, going hand in hand with the imposture, her portrayal as a "false person" (107) is another feature of Chūgōrō's wife, who takes the shape of a frog during daytime. In his *Metamorphosis of the Vampire*, Butler identifies shape-shifting as one of the vampire's traits.

If not aristocratic like her Western equivalents, such as Lord Ruthven, Sir Francis Varney, Countess Karnstein, or Count Dracula (Butler 2010, 3), she who "loves the blood of the young" appears to Chūgōrō as one of "high rank" (Hearn 2010b, 75) and presumably as the daughter of a deity: "I was neither wet nor cold: everything around me was dry and warm and beautiful" (76). He describes his crossing the threshold to the supernatural in terms that a Freudian reading might interpret as a return to the maternal womb. It is, however, not one of the "intra-uterine settings consist[ing] of dark, narrow, winding passages leading to a central room, cellar or other symbolic place of birth" (1993, 53) that Barbara Creed describes in *The Monstrous-Feminine*, but rather the Freudian "shelter" (1993, 115). With Chūgōrō's entry into the supernatural realm described in terms of a return to the maternal womb (and his way back, through the "dark" [78], reflecting the expulsion from it), "The Story of Chūgōrō" plays with the Oedipal theme that, as Laurence Rickels in his *Vampire Lectures* argues, underlies any vampire tale. Seducing a protagonist who is young, naive, inexperienced, and innocent, she evokes what Creed describes as "the vampire as sexual initiator" (1999, 65). Depriv-ing Chūgōrō of his vital fluids, weakening and thus emasculating him, she reflects the Western female vampire as *vagina dentata* (Creed 1993, 105-6; Nystrom 2009, 66), which, Ernest Jones notes, characterizes vampirism: "the threat of castration; the feminization of the male victim" (quoted in Creed 1993, 70).

These shared attributes, however, do not reveal Chūgōrō's wife as a vampire in disguise, camouflaged by Hearn's omission of Transylvanian iconography. The bloodthirsty female of "The Story of Chūgōrō" differs in a significant respect from those of the West. Chūgōrō's wife, with her seductiveness, her dominance over the protagonist, and her explicit sexual intentions, corresponds to Creed's notion of the "monstrous-feminine" (1993, 62). But simultaneously—since Chūgōrō, being unaware of her doings, has no reason to perceive her as harmful—she lacks the vampire's aspect of the "horrific" (1993, 13) that turns the Western bloodsucker into an expression of nineteenth-century anxieties. Bram Dijkstra, for example, in his *Idols of Perversity*, sees the female vampire with its sexual implications as an expression of male anxieties: "The womb of women was the insatiable soil into whose bottomless crevasse man must pour the essence of his intellect in payment for her lewd enticements. The hunger of the beast was in her loins and the hunger of the beast was the hunger for blood" (1986, 335). Butler, who considers Transylvania as the locus of a "confusion of ethnic categories and political orders" (2010, 112), lists "anxieties about cultural unity" (35) as the motivation for this locus. With its Far Eastern origins, such negative sociocultural connotations are absent from "The Story of Chūgōrō," and Hearn never explores the meaning of the bloodthirsty female in her Eastern context.

The collision between East and West that is so prominent in nineteenth-century vampire fiction, in which the protagonist from Western Europe often travels to an Eastern European region, is in Hearn's story transferred to the act of reading, in which the Western reader is confronted with an Eastern tale. In this context, Chūgōrō's bloodthirsty wife is not revealed as the Eastern equivalent to what the Western tradition calls a vampire, but as something *like* a vampire. Sharing features with the Western bloodsucker, but at the same time differing from it, she is linked to the female vampire by a relation of similarity. Following Paul Ricoeur, this can be seen as a tension between sameness and difference (1979, 146): "To see the like is to see the same in spite of, and through, the different" (146). It is precisely this notion of similarity that Hearn addresses at the end of his autobiographical "Vespertina Cognitio" by commenting upon the nightmarish apparition haunting both the author and his West Indian guide, and identified by the former as a figure from Celtic folklore and by the latter as a "Zombi" (Hearn 2001, 214). It was "a coincidence," Hearn writes, that "had certainly been startling; but the similitude was only partial" (216).

Naming the supernatural, perceiving it as a figure from Celtic folklore or as a zombie, Hearn implies, is culturally defined; however, since the apparition is experienced simultaneously by the author and his guide, the supernatural is able to transcend cultural boundaries. Yoko Makino, discussing the telling of folktales in Hearn's West Indian novel *Youma*, observes that Hearn believes folktales have the power to unite cultures (2007, 110). Hearn was fascinated by ghost stories and folktales not only because of their "weirdness"; he loved them for their capacity to transcend national and cultural delineations as well.

As firmly as he believed in ghosts, he was convinced of the power of ghost stories and folktales to mediate between cultures. He thus assumed the existence of what could be referred to as the transnational or transcultural supernatural. For Hearn, ghosts move on an intermediate, neutral territory, mediating between cultures, a space that is, however, neither a product of hybridization nor a "third space" (see Bhabha, 2004). It is a primary space: a space prior to any differentiation between East and West, or North and South—a space as "primeval" as the "ancestral fears" (Hearn 2001, 207) unfolding between cultures and thus uniting them, but defying any appropriation. It is the space that the one who "loves the blood of the young" inhabits, the space that the Eastern bloodsuckers, like the Fox-Woman, the Serpent-Woman, and the Dragon-Woman of Hearn's *kwaidan*, share with their Western relatives.

Rather than "occulting Japan," Hearn, straddling the nineteenth and twentieth centuries, provides an approach to the exotic other for his Western reader. With its bloodthirsty, shape-shifting, seductive stranger, "The Story of Chūgōrō" lets readers discover the familiar within the exotic. In the midst of otherness, the story points at a similarity that, as a tension between sameness and difference, enables the reader to gain access to the exotic without leveling out its otherness. The bloodthirsty female proves to be a mediator between cultures: like the frog, whose shape she takes during daytime, she is at home both in the East and the West and thus belongs to neither.

WORKS CITED

Bhabha, Homi K. 2004. *The Location of Culture*. Abingdon, UK: Routledge.

Browning, John Edgar, and Caroline Joan (Kay) Picart, eds. 2009. *Draculas, Vampires, and Other Undead Forms: Essays on Gender, Race, and Culture*. Toronto: Scarecrow Press.

Butler, Erik. 2010. *Metamorphosis of the Vampire in Literature and Film: Cultural Transformations in Europe, 1732–1933*. Rochester, NJ: Camden House.

Clubbe, John. 2007. "Lafcadio Hearn as an American Writer." In Hirakawa 2007, 93–102.

Creed, Barbara. 1993. *The Monstrous-Feminine: Film, Feminism, Psychoanalysis*. London: Routledge.

Dawson, Carl. 1992. *Lafcadio Hearn and the Vision of Japan*. Baltimore: Johns Hopkins University Press.

Dijkstra, Bram. 1986. *Idols of Perversity: Fantasies of Feminine Evil in Fin-de-Siècle Culture.* Oxford: Oxford University Press.

Fisher, Susan. 2007. "'Weird Beauty': Angela Carter and Lafcadio Hearn in Japan." In Hirakawa 2007, 169–77.

Frayling, Christopher. 1991. *Vampyres: Lord Byron to Count Dracula.* London: Faber and Faber.

Hearn, Lafcadio. [1898] 2001. *Exotics and Retrospectives.* New York: ICG Muse.

———. [1904] 2004. *Kwaidan: Stories and Studies of Strange Things.* New York: Cosimo Books.

———. [1900] 2007. *Shadowings.* New York: Cosimo Classics.

———. [1904] 2008. *Japan: An Attempt at Interpretation.* Charleston, SC: Forgotten Books.

———. [1894] 2010a. *Glimpses of Unfamiliar Japan.* Vol. 1. Charleston, SC: Forgotten Books.

———. [1902] 2010b. *Kottō: Being Japanese Curios with Sundry Cobwebs.* Charleston, SC: Forgotten Books.

Hirakawa, Sukehiro, ed. 1997. *Rediscovering Lafcadio Hearn: Japanese Legends, Life and Culture.* Folkstone, UK: Global Oriental.

———, ed. 2007. *Lafcadio Hearn in International Perspective.* Folkstone, UK: Global Oriental.

———. 2007a. "Lafcadio Hearn, a Reappraisal." In Hirakawa 2007, 1–15.

———. 2007b. "Lafcadio's Nightmares." In Hirakawa 2007, 30–40.

———. 2007c. "Half a Century after Byron—What Did Greece Mean to the Writer Hearn?" In Hirakawa 2007, 77–92.

Hughes, George. 1997a. "Lafcadio Hearn and the Fin de Siècle." In Hirakawa 1997, 83–103.

———. 1997b. "Entering Island Cultures: Synge, Hearn and the Irish Exotic." In Hirakawa 1997, 104–13.

Kendall, Nigel. 2001. Introduction to *Exotics and Retrospectives* by Lafcadio Hearn, vii–xvi. New York: ICG Muse.

Makino, Yoko. 2007. "Image of 'the Creole Mother' in Hearn's *Youma*." In Hirakawa 2007, 103–10.

Meech, Julia, and Gabriel P. Weisberg. 1990. *Japonisme Comes to America: The Japanese Impact on the Graphic Arts, 1876–1925.* New York: Harry N. Abrams.

Meech, Julia. 1990a. "Collecting Japanese Art in America." In Meech and Weisberg, 41–56.

———. 1990b. "Reinventing the Exotic Orient." In Meech and Weisberg, 95–234.

Melville, Herman. [1851] 1992. *Moby Dick; or, The Whale.* Oxford: Oxford University Press.

Murray, Paul. 1993. *A Fantastic Journey: The Life and Literature of Lafcadio Hearn.* Sandgate: Japan Library.

Nabae, Hitomi. 2007. "Insect-Music: Hearn's Orphean Song." In Hirakawa 2007, 139–51.

Nystrom, Lisa. 2009. "Blood, Lust, and the Fe/Male Narrative in Bram Stoker's *Dracula* (1992) and the Novel (1897)." In Browning and Picart, 63–76.

Polidori, John. [1819] 1998. "The Vampyre." In *The Vamypre and Other Tales of the Macabre,* edited by Robert Morrison and Chris Baldwick, 1–23. Oxford: Oxford University Press.

Poulton, Cody. 2007. "Two Springs: Hearn's and Kyōka's Other Worlds." In Hirakawa 2007, 159–68.

Rickels, Laurence A. 1999. *The Vampire Lectures.* Minneapolis: University of Minnesota Press.

Ricoeur, Paul. 1979. "The Metaphorical Process as Cognition, Imagination, and Feeling." In Sacks, 141–57.

Sacks, Sheldon, ed. 1979. *On Metaphor*. Chicago: University of Chicago Press.

Smith, Andrew. 2007. *Gothic Literature*. Edinburgh: Edinburgh University Press.

Stein, Wayne. 2009. "Enter the Dracula: The Silent Screams and Cultural Crossroads of Japanese and Hong Kong Cinema." In Browning and Picart, 235–60.

Weisberg, Gabriel P. 1990. "Japonisme: The Commercialization of an Opportunity." In Meech and Weisberg, 15–40.

Wolf, Leonard, ed. 1997. *Blood Thirst: 100 Years of Vampire Fiction*. Oxford: Oxford University Press.

OCTAVIA BUTLER'S VAMPIRIC VISION

Fledgling *as a Transnational Neo-Slave Narrative*

TIMOTHY M. ROBINSON

The literary theorist Nina Auerbach proclaims that "every age embraces the vampire it needs" (1995, 145). Her observation that vampires are an ever-changing archetype reflecting societal concerns and anxieties of the particular generation that it derives from is well substantiated. However, the vampire's broad appeal, for the most part, lies with European American writers and audiences, particularly as depicted in literature, film, and television.¹ One might ask why vampires are not represented to a greater degree in African American culture, especially literature—after all, vampires seem an ideal metaphor to describe North American slavery. The slave masters' exploitation of labor was vampiric in that it fed off of the body and minds of black men and women. Nevertheless, the association with vampires and slavery in African American literature did not emerge until the advent of neo-slave narratives. In Toni Morrison's neo-slave narrative, *Beloved* (1987), for instance, the character Beloved is never directly referred to as a vampire; however, she has many traditional vampiric characteristics. Beloved not only returns from the dead, but drains the physical body and spiritual essence of the woman who murdered her when she was an infant— her own mother, Sethe. Denver, Sethe's other daughter, describes Beloved's all-consuming desire and how the "flesh between her mother's forefinger and thumb" is fading while, at the same time, Beloved is "getting bigger" and her stomach "basket-fat" (242). Moreover, the descriptions of Sethe's eyes, which are "bright but dead, alert but vacant" and "paying attention to everything about Beloved" evoke imagery of a someone in the thrall of a vampire's control (242–43). Beloved emerges as the psychological and physical manifestation of America's history of slavery, the horrors of which could drive a mother to murder her own child and call forth the subsequent revenge upon the mother by the child she murdered.

Yet, neither African American writers of antebellum slave narratives nor their contemporary counterparts ever directly utilized the vampire as metaphor until the publication of Jewelle Gomez's neo-slave narrative, *The Gilda Stories* (1991). It recounts the life of a black lesbian vampire and chronicles her adventures as a slave in 1850 and concludes 250 years later in a dystopian future where humans hunt and enslave vampires for the life-giving properties of their blood. In presenting Gilda's story, this novel utilizes a number of long-established black literary tropes associated with slave and neo-slave narratives. Twelve years later, African American writer L. A. Banks's initial vampire series began with *Minion: A Vampire Huntress Legend* (2003). Her novel tells the story of a female musician and a spoken-word poet, Damali Richards, who, with a diverse group of comrades, secretly hunts vampires. Aside from its sharp emphasis on Christian faith, *Minion* seems more a revision of the television series *Buffy the Vampire Slayer* than a novel steeped in the African American literary tradition. Octavia Butler's *Fledgling* (2005), by contrast, which was published two years after Banks's *Minion*, is deeply rooted in the African American literary tradition through her use of the vampire as a trope in what I read as a transnational neo-slave narrative. In a departure from reading *Fledgling* in a purely African American context, I want to situate the novel in the framework of global concerns surrounding transmigration.

Although transnational migration is not a new global phenomenon, the intensity with which individual and group identities are maintained and fashioned as they move between various countries or regions as well as the frequency and the intensity with which this process occurs have reached new levels in the late twentieth and early twenty-first century. Today, however, many migrants who move between borders can be considered transmigrants whose daily lives, according to Nina Glick Schiller, "depend on multiple and constant interconnections across international borders and whose public identities are configured in relationship to more than one nation state" (1995, 48). These migrants are "forging and sustaining multi-stranded relations that link[ed] their societies of origin and settlement" and are establishing "social fields that cross geographical, cultural, and political borders" (Schiller, Basch, and Blanc 1992, ix). Transnationalism, therefore, takes assimilation and conflicting cultural or social norms into consideration as well as the implications for the erosion of boundaries—social, cultural, and economic—between nation-states.

Rather than writing a traditional neo-slave narrative that analyzes the master/slave relationships within the United States, Butler focuses on the relationship between the Ina (who figure as the "vampires" or exploiters) and the human symbionts (who figure as the exploited). Their civilization is portrayed as vascilating between a utopia that physically benefits human symbionts, resolving the Ina's dependency on them for transnational migratory labor, and a dystopia, where the human symbiont's free will is uncertain. *Fledgling* encourages readers to view the nature of the relationship between the Ina and the symbionts as problematic rather than benevolent. Butler focuses not only on economic power relations between these two groups in the broadest sense, but also specifically on gendered relations. Notably, all of these aforementioned African American writers who have utilized vampires or vampirism as a trope are black and female, which establishes a clear convergence between black women's literature in general and the vampire as metaphor in particular.[2] Several specific tropes that often appear in black women's writings can perhaps provide an explanation. According to Bernard Bell, African American women writers employ motifs of racist, sexist, and classist oppression and have predominantly female protagonists. The protagonists of these writers embark on a spiritual journal from victimhood to agency, often based on bonding within a female network, with family and community playing a central role. Bell also notes a strong accentuation on knowledge gained through emotion and the power of black female–centered discourse (see 1987, 242–43).

All of these structural features appear in Butler's *Fledgling*, yoking together vampirism as a trope and African American women's literary tradition, signifying both upon nineteenth-century black women's slave and neo-slave narrative traditions. Unlike early fictionalized and nonfictionalized slave narratives, such as Harriet E. Wilson's *Our Nig; or, Sketches from the Life of a Free Black* (1859) and Harriet Jacobs's *Incidents in the Life of a Slave Girl* (1861), *Fledgling* is a contemporary novel written within the genre of speculative fiction and fantasy. The novel signifies on slave narratives and is heavily couched in vampire lore, underlining Auerbach's thesis that every generation looks to the vampire it needs. I maintain that *Fledgling* is concerned with contemporary rather than traditional "vampiric" issues, including transmigration and its socioeconomic repercussions. By examining relationships between the vampire clan, the Ina, and symbionts, the people upon whom the Ina feed in order to live, Butler interrogates conceptual perspectives of what constitutes one's position as a slave and what constitutes one's position as master. Butler's descriptions of the economic and social interactions between the Ina and their symbionts reveal the complexities of notions such as domination, dependency, manipulation, and free will. The symbionts' interactions within the Ina communities and the human communities are also a commentary upon contemporary debates about transmigration, transnationalism, and transculturalism—the movement of people and their culture from one place to another, especially among developing and industrialized nations.

The vampire, I would argue, is a border-transgressing figure, speaking to issues between migrants and indigenous residents, such as irrational fears of contact, miscegenation, and xenophobia with the other. In Butler's novel, the fear of contact with the other is expressed in the fear of miscegenation between the two groups, the Ina and the symbionts. This aspect of xenophobia frames the narrative and shapes the overall structure of the novel. Similar to the nineteenth-century slave narrative that frequently dealt with miscegenation and laws prohibiting it, Butler also seems especially concerned with those who insist on maintaining blood purity and who will commit to familial devastation or genocide to achieve their goal. A palimpsest narrative that rewrites previously established European American and African American vampire narratives, *Fledgling* examines transgressive race and migratory identities as social constructs through the use of established nineteenth-century African American literary slave narrative tropes that reflect upon oppressive forces in contemporary society.

While such contemporary works incorporating these themes would usually be referred to as neo-slave narratives, I would like to argue that *Fledgling*'s transnationalist discourse requires a more inclusive perspective that moves beyond reductive black/white binaries that one finds in nineteenth-century slave autobiographies and classic neo-slave narratives such as Margaret Walker's *Jubilee* (1966), Sherley Anne Williams's *Dessa Rose* (1986), and Toni Morrison's *Beloved*. In challenging cultural and national identities, *Fledgling* offers up a clear departure from these examples of more traditional neo-slave narratives in terms of the social, racial, and cultural issues that Butler brings to the fore.

"EVERY CULTURE EMBRACES THE VAMPIRE IT NEEDS"

I have already referred to the African American writers' general disinterest in vampire lore and the recent emergence of vampires in black women's literature.[3] However, the dearth of vampires in African American literature and culture does not preclude vampire lore's presence within the black Atlantic. For example, within regions along the west coast of Africa and locations where the transatlantic slave trade originated and held fast for centuries, vampirism often emerged as the prevalent explanation as to why millions of men, women, and children who were taken during the Middle Passage never returned. In recounting her visit to Ghana in 1996, writer Saidiya Hartman describes how she was told stories that seem to rationalize the trauma of this large-scale loss:

> *Everyone told me a different story about how slaves began to forget their past. Words like "zombie," "sorcerer," "witch," "succubus," and "vampire" were whispered to explain it. In these stories, which circulated throughout West Africa, the particulars varied, but all of them ended the same—the slave loses the mother. Never did the captive choose to forget; she was always tricked or bewitched or coerced into forgetting. Amnesia, like an accident or a stroke of bad fortune, was never an act of volition. (2007, 155)*

What seemed incomprehensible required an explanation; those left behind chose a metaphysical account to explain their loss. But there seems to be a certain degree of optimism and subversiveness that is inherent within these stories as well. That not one individual ever returned did not mean that those taken were necessarily killed. It simply meant that those taken must have been made to forget their people, home, and land by some malevolent, supernatural force often thought to be vampires.

Luise White's *Speaking with Vampires: Rumors and History in Colonial Africa* investigates widespread stories of vampires called *mumiani* in eastern and southern Africa. What she finds most pertinent in these stories is the wide geographical and cultural territory these tales cover:

> *Game rangers were said to capture Africans in Colonial Northern Rhodesia; mine managers captured [people] in the Belgian Congo and kept them in pits. Firemen subdued Africans with injections in Kenya but [used] masks in Uganda. Africans captured by mumiani in colonial Tanganyika were hung upside down, their throats were cut, and their blood drained into huge buckets. (2000, 4)*

Thus, the merging of historical facts, myth, superstition, and gossip reconstruct power relationships between the colonists and the colonized through the figure of the vampire. In a revision of the typical representation of the vampire as the invader in European lore, populations in Africa position European imperialists as the outsider, the vampire. As White concludes, these stories about vampires become counternarratives and "the tools with which to write colonial history" (5).

In yet another region of the world influenced by the transatlantic slave trade, the *soucouyant* emerges as a haunting vampire figure among those of African descent in the commonwealth of Dominica, Trinidad, and Guadeloupe. In the traditional folklore of this region, the *soucouyant* is an old woman who strips off her skin at night and transforms into a ball of light. She is then able to enter the homes of unsuspecting victims, sucking their blood while they sleep (see Bane 2010, 127). Most folklorists believe that the *soucouyant* is an amalgamation of French vampire myths and African mythological entities known as *jumbees.* Jumbees are malevolent night spirits or demons that terrorize the living. The *soucouyant* folktale has evolved over time and, in its modern form, is no longer limited to being personified as an old woman (Bane 2010, 81). These accounts, on both the west and east coasts of Africa as well as former colonies in the Caribbean, reveal that the vampire operates as not only a legendary, supernatural, and mythological creature, but that vampire lore is also passed down orally from one generation to the next, resulting in reinterpretations and syncretism. That the vampire is manifest in European, European American, and African diasporic myths and legends underscores the transnational and transcultural nature of the vampire figure.

In fact, if we examine the prevalence of vampire mythology in various European and American cultures across time, discourse about vampires often materializes in historical moments where there is a need to explain the unknown or to rationalize momentous events in human history when collective cultural trauma occurs. In the fifteenth century, Gilles de Rais's search for the "philosophers' stone" led him to torture and kill two to three hundred children. In the sixteenth century, Countess Erzsébet Bathory, also known as the "Blood Countess," kidnapped and killed young girls and then bathed in and drank their blood to maintain her youth and vitality from disease. In the nineteenth century, Vlad Tepes Dracula of Wallachia (or Vlad the Impaler) ordered thousands of people impaled for his own pleasure (see Auerbach 1995, 133). The genesis of vampire tales, which have their origins in Eastern European lore and which later appeared in Western Europe, emerge during cultural crises involving massacres, profound social and economic fears and anxieties, religious persecution, sexual repression, xenophobia, and even en masse killing. It is no small wonder, then, that the European vampire figure eventually made its way to continental Africa and the Caribbean, where slavery and colonialism occurred. According to White (2000), the term *vampire* appears in parts of Africa only after 1918 and the onset of colonial oppression, but the notion of what a vampire does (extracting the blood/life force and killing an individual) was a part of African lore among some groups long before the colonists arrived. Thus, European colonists brought their vampire tales with them and Africans adopted and transformed the tales to explain aspects of European slavery and other traumas such as European biological experimentation on Africans. Although the stories of vampires on East Africa's coast reveal an unknown feature of colonial rule and imply possible experimentations on the natives, on the coast of West Africa the vampire tale is transformed in order to understand personal and communal loss due to the trauma of the transatlantic slave trade. Although vampirism becomes apparent as one explanation of a slave's fragmented cultural and historical memory, according to Hartman, it is the literal and figurative loss of the mother that underpinned the trauma and that was most detrimental (see 2007, 155).

The archetypical mother figure becomes another transcultural metaphor, the antithesis of the vampire, if you will, as the mother in African American literature is known for harboring country, family, and identity, a paradigm that, for the most part, was said to be lost on the slave ships during the Middle Passage to the Americas. Without the Mother/land, slaves had to readjust to a new reality in order to discover their place among a diverse collective of ethnic and cultural groups. Similarly, Butler's protagonist in *Fledgling*, although a powerful vampire-human hybrid, cannot recall anything of substance about her past. Like slaves aboard the transatlantic slave ships, Shori loses all personal and collective memory of her people, critical aspects of her culture, and any historical foundation that might generate a sense of self due to the destruction of her Mothers' clan. The connection between memory and the loss of the mother figure, therefore, merits critical attention. Butler exposes the European American, archetypal vampire tale as white, patriarchal, heterosexist, and authoritarian; she puts forth a vampire tale that is grounded in black culture, is female centered, and is also omnisexual, thereby problematizing the master/slave dialectic.

Fledgling chronicles the story of a fifty-three-year-old vampire, who physically appears to be a ten-year-old black girl. She awakens with amnesia and extreme physical scarring as a result of an attack by unknown assailants. She instinctively returns to the location where she awakened to search for clues to her identity and her vampire origins. Soon after, she finds herself concurrently hunted and befriended by clandestine factions of humans as well as pale, white-skinned vampires called the Ina. The Ina's sensitivity to sunlight causes them—like the vampires—to eschew daytime activities. Shori discovers that she is the product of amalgamated Ina and human blood—in her case, a black human mother, whose genetic predisposition for melanin will permit her offspring the ability to exist in daylight. Thus, by extension, Shori's survival becomes crucial to the survival of the Ina. Indeed, many of the Ina view her as their messiah. Shori later finds out that her Mothers' clan and her Fathers' clan were targeted by Ina factions who disapprove of her family's willful and deliberate miscegenation. The latter half of the novel is concerned with Shori's search for self and the appropriate form of justice to vindicate her family's murder. Shori is, undoubtedly, a revision of the tragic mulatto figure in the vein of nineteenth-century antebellum and postbellum slave narrative fiction.[4] However, although *Fledgling* is firmly rooted in the slave narrative tradition, it goes beyond such expected traditional thematic troping. The novel also explores current global issues such as mass killings and transmigration, as well as contemporary issues involving biological hybridism and recent scientific forays into genetic manipulation and recombinant DNA.

THE NEO-SLAVE NARRATIVE AND ITS DEVELOPMENT

In order to better understand what Butler's intentions are in *Fledgling*, it is important to understand the novel's significant connections to the neo-slave narrative tradition as well as her use of transnational discourse. One of the most significant aspects of the neo-slave narrative form is that this genre advances knowledge of a usable African American past in order to better understand the present. Bell is credited with initially conceptualizing the term *neo-slave narrative* in *The Afro-American Novel and Its Tradition*. In his analysis of contemporary black literature, Bell defines "neo-slave" narratives as "residually oral, modern narratives of escape from bondage to freedom" (1987, 289). Moreover, Bell, borrowing from literary critic Robert Scholes, refers to the inclusion of parody and satire in black literature as *fabulation*; that is, "a return to a more verbal kind of fiction . . . a less realistic and more artistic kind of narrative, more shapely, more evocative" (Scholes quoted in Bell 1987, 284). In *Neo-Slave Narratives: Studies in the Social Logic of a Literary Form*, Ashraf Rushdy defines the neo-slave narrative further as a postmodern exercise that originated in the late 1960s in large part as a response to William Styron's novel *The Confessions of Nat Turner* (1967).[5] Styron's seemingly blatant disregard of historical facts encouraged a new generation of black writers to consciously emphasize a distinctive interplay between blackness, the historical, and a writer's imaginative artistry (see Rushdy 1999, 4–7). For example, both Bell and Rushdy note in their discussion of neo-slave narratives that parody and satire are central to many innovative, contemporary neo-slave narratives—Ishmael Reed's *Flight to Canada* (1972) is perhaps the most celebrated example.[6] However, a majority of neo-slave narratives abstain from parody and satire and instead focus, in large measure, on fictive worlds.[7] Contemporary neo-slave narratives eschew historical accuracy, revise and retell stories of the slave past, and combine African American oral and written traditions.

While such neo-slave narratives have their origins in historical facts, a select number of writers from this generation, most notably Butler and Samuel R. Delany, dared to venture outside the more conventional and popular neo-slave narrative model. Instead, Butler and Delany employ science fiction and fantasy, along with compelling themes such as alternative expressions of sexuality, in ways that not only make use of the black literary tradition, but that also augment the form of the neo-slave narrative tradition. In this way, their work obscures a more direct relationship between the history of slavery in America and historical factualism. Like parody and satire, fantasy and science fiction provide greater divergence from the standard historical neo-slave narrative, and Butler convincingly balances the historical with fantasy and science fiction in *Kindred* (1979).[8] These authors who diverge from conventional forms produce multivalent neo-slave narratives that for some might seem far removed from any apparent direct association with nineteenth-century slave narratives. Nevertheless, whether consciously or unconsciously, they signify upon that tradition. Multivalent narratives—that is, contemporary novels that simultaneously draw attention to and mask their connection to a past tradition—are particularly significant to African American literature because, as Bell points out:

> *[B]lack modernists and postmodernists are definitely influenced by the traditions of Western literature and committed to the freedom of hybrid narrative forms. But because the legacy of institutionalized racism and sexism that shaped and continues to shape their consciousness fosters ambivalence about their culture, and because the struggle for social justice continues, most modern and postmodern African American novelists, like their nineteenth-century predecessors, are not inclined to neglect moral and social issues in their narratives. (1987, 284)*

In other words, novels that employ multivalency are grounded in aspects of both realism and social justice.

Although Butler's *Fledgling* may seem more situated in the genre of fantasy because of its reliance on and reworking of European American vampire mythology and folklore, she also employs science fiction in her delineation of Shori Mathews's world. The Ina are depicted as an alien species separate from humans; they arrived on Earth centuries ago from another world. Nevertheless, Butler connects the world she creates in *Fledgling* both to the past by employing tropes found in slave narratives and to the present by presenting social dilemmas that currently concern our world. By placing the idea of freedom at its center, *Fledgling* is shaped in content and in form by the African American slave narrative tradition. However, Butler's novel links autonomy and freedom as a trope found in slave narratives with a similar trope found in vampire tales: the struggle of human beings for autonomy of body and mind against their vampire "masters."

Even the title of Butler's novel calls forth the slave narrative tradition by evoking ideas of dependence and independence—a *fledgling* denotes a young bird, and *to fledge* means to acquire feathers necessary for flight or independent activity. The motif of flight is prominent in the African American literary tradition, and obtaining the ability to fly is present in folktales such as "All God's Children Got Wings" and "The People Could Fly," where the act of flying symbolizes individual freedom in the literal and figurative sense. These stories, and variations of them, are based on a single historical event, the Ebo slave rebellion off the coast of St. Simons Island, Georgia. The ur-myth is that a group of Africans remembered that they once had the ability to fly and, upon remembering their abilities, flew back to Africa to escape slavery in America. This story of emancipation from the legacy of a traumatic past was also a direct inspiration for an earlier neo-slave narrative, Morrison's *Song of Solomon* (1976). In Morrison's novel, the protagonist, Milkman Dead, must figuratively learn how to fly in order to discover his roots and his true self. In *Fledgling*, Shori too must learn to fly independently and establish her own moral codes of equality in the absence of prior knowledge of the cultural traditions of the Ina. She instinctively establishes a relationship with her symbionts in a way that honors their individuality, despite the possibilities of power, control, and oppression that the Ina could enact against their hosts if they chose to do so.

The narrative perspective of *Fledgling* also mimics the nineteenth-century slave narratives, with the entire novel told from Shori's point of view, demonstrating the power of first-person narrative and "testifyin." Further, both antebellum slave narratives and Butler's fiction utilize similar narrative strategies in describing the precarious position of the slave as witness, participant, and agent. As Lauren Lacey notes: "[*Fledgling*] is constructed so that the reader and the protagonist share the discoveries of her identity; Butler thus creates the conditions necessary for both the unfolding mystery and for the reader to share the discoveries of her identity" (2008, 381). This strategy of narrating one's story to the reader, prevalent in the construction of antebellum slave narratives, made the evolution of the central characters more significant to readers—in other words, the relationship deepens as the reader follows the narrator's progression. This particular narrative form continues in the African American oral tradition, evokes the spoken word in written form, and extends the trope of literacy that is pivotal in slave narratives.

As suggested in Frederick Douglass's *Narrative of the Life of Frederick Douglass* (1845), closely related to development of identity and self-awareness is the association between literacy and knowledge. In slave narratives, a slave's acquirement of literacy almost always ushers in the reward of empowerment and eventual freedom. Shori's initial move from ignorance to knowledge of self begins not with what Henry Louis Gates calls the trope of the "Talking Book," in a scene where a book figuratively "speaks" to the literate but remains silent to the entreaties of the unlettered slave (1988, 131). Shori's knowledge, in contrast, is acquired not through books but through modern, digital technology. By mastering computer technology and learning to navigate the Internet, Shori obtains knowledge about vampirism. Here, Butler utilizes the most current and accessible way of obtaining information—digitally.

This is not to say, however, that books in print form do not play a role in her self-discovery. Butler contrasts digital technology with older methods of information gathering that has, in the past, been achieved by reading books. For example, Shori inquires whether an Ina library exists: "Are there . . . do you have Ina books, histories that I could read to learn more about our people? I hate my ignorance. As things stand now, I don't even know what questions to ask to begin to understand things" (185). Although Shori obtains some understanding through these historical print materials, she is also able to get information from select women in the Ina community, introducing orally transmitted knowledge as well. However, both oral and written knowledge are insufficient in answering her questions about her own past. When she is offered several books to read, Shori rightfully questions their personal usefulness: "I wonder if they'll mean anything to me" (67), she says. Thus, it is the obliteration of her mothers' and father's clan that proves the greatest hindrance to her achieving complete self-awareness. What Shori learns, and what Butler appears to emphasize here, is that only through personal experience and interacting with what Toni Morrison calls "the ancestor" (1984, 343) can an individual truly obtain knowledge of self. Similar to former slaves like Frederick Douglass and Booker T. Washington—who in their autobiographies both emphasized that literacy is paramount to achieving freedom, mastery of the self, and a vital understanding of the world in which they lived—Shori views mastery over the written word as a primary objective.

As indicated earlier, critical to understanding the neo-slave narrative tradition is biracial identity. To further comprehend Shori's biracial heritage, one can look at her name and the manner in which it changes throughout the novel. She is initially named Renee by Wright, her first symbiont, after she requests that he give her a name: "A friend of mine told me it meant 'reborn.' That's sort of what's happened to you. You've been reborn into a new life. You'll probably remember your old life pretty soon, but for now, you're Renee" (13). At this point, her Renee persona has been forged solely through her interaction with human beings. Later, upon encountering her father, she learns that her given name is Shori, which is a Japanese name given to males and which means "triumph"; indeed, Shori is aptly named, for she represents triumph for the Ina and their future. It is through her progeny that they will be able to function in the daylight. Butler's referencing the antebellum slave narrative process of naming and renaming reflects her awareness that despite the rebirth of one's identity, one can still straddle two ontological and psychological planes of existence; it is through the human/vampire hybrid that we see Butler's apparent masking of this important trope in slave and neo-slave narratives. In addition, Shori's dual nature also figures prominently in reading *Fledgling* as a transnational neo-slave narrative. In *The Location of Culture*, Homi Bhabha states that a hybrid figure opens up a space of cultural and racial uncertainty and instability. For Bhabha, this ambivalent space, or "third space," disrupts the unity and homogeneity of racial and cultural identity to create an in-between space that cannot be immediately articulated or predetermined (1990, 211). Ultimately, the hybrid subject disrupts the norm on either side of the binary equation and embodies the impossibility of simplification or essentialization. Shori exists as a hybrid figure, with a biracial but also ultimately transracial identity—both human and vampire. However, these categories remain blurred.

Perhaps even more significant is the way Shori crosses both racial and physical locations. She remains forcibly on the move from both Ina and humans, with no proper or stable home to flee to and hide in in order to escape from those who are hunting her. She is a foreigner—like many contemporary migrants between nations and cultures—with no home, no place to call her own. Ultimately, finding refuge within another Ina community that has little link to her parents, Shori gradually finds full acceptance in a utopian society where racial differences are not paramount; rather, it is the individual's contribution to the collective that matters. In this space, freedom is respected through a process that the Ina refer to as "mutualistic symbiosis" (Butler 2007, 63). This relationship reveals why *Fledgling* is distinctive in its revision of vampire tales because the relationship between vampires and symbionts is in stark contrast to the usual representation of vampires in conflict with humans, with vampires portrayed as monsters that control and manipulate others. The transracial, yet seemingly effortless, moves that Shori makes between and within human and vampire worlds not only mirror the experiences of biracial characters in slave narratives who sometimes passed (both literary and figuratively), but Shori's experience also mimics today's migrants who, by force or by choice, transgress boundaries.

CONCERNS OF THE TRANSNATIONAL NEO-SLAVE NARRATIVE

Concerning Butler's direct and indirect "signifyin'" on nineteenth-century slave narratives, one might ask what constitutes the connection between *Fledgling* as a neo-slave narrative and transnationalism. In what ways do these concepts inform one another? As we shall see, the neo-slave narrative and transnationalism are not antithetical, nor have they ever been. In fact, the discourse of transnationalism and the attendant transformations in culture and identity in black literature has been manifestly present in slave narratives as far back as Phillis Wheatley's poem "On Being Brought from Africa to America" (1773) and Olaudah Equiano's autobiographical narrative (1798). Their recognition of an identity that is distinctly African and their acknowledgment of a European American identity refer to both their roots and to the routes that they have traveled—a foundational hybrid awareness suggestive of W. E. B. DuBois's double consciousness. Butler seems to be encouraging audiences to engage *Fledgling* within this particular context and she enables readers to have access to the past and to literary traditions without totally ignoring the present. As a postmodernist, her fiction draws attention to itself as an artifact that also points to aspects of the real world from both past and contemporary circumstances.

Butler uses the vampire to move beyond simple definitions of American slavery; employing the vampire as a vehicle, she also moves beyond reductive linearity of time and space. Reflective of a simultaneous awareness of historical and contemporary double consciousness as a literary trope, the vampire becomes a cipher that can imply various social, sexual, and religious mores, similar to those found in American slave and neo-slave narratives. Ernest Jones, an early literary critique of vampire literature, recognized that "the two chief metaphorical connotations of the word [*vampire*] are 1) a social or political tyrant who sucks the life from the people . . . [and] 2) an irresistible lover who sucks away energy, ambition, or even life for selfish reasons" (1931, 151). It is the former description that resonates in American slave narratives of the past and also in texts devoted to issues of social justice and crimes against humanity in the globalized present. For instance, Butler's introduction of Shori immediately follows descriptions of the mass murder of her mothers' clan:

> Someone burned your mothers and your sisters as well as all the human members of your family to death here. They shot the ones who tried to get out, shot them and threw most of them back into the fire. How you escaped, I have no idea, but we found the others, burned, broken. (64–65)

Shortly after her reunion with her father and his clan, they too are massacred:

> When I found my father's and brothers' homes, they looked much like the ruin of my mothers' community. The buildings had been completely destroyed, burned to rubble, and then trampled by many feet. My father and my brothers had been there, but they were gone now. I could smell death, but I could not see it. I did not know yet who had died and who had survived. Someone had come for my male family, and whoever it was had been as thorough as they had when they came for my mothers and sisters. (97)

The emphasis on mass killings of one gender to halt further genetic reproduction or perpetuation of ideas from a particular group propels Butler's narrative. Shori concludes that her parents' murders are a direct result of their success in merging black human and Ina DNA. While the Ina have had a symbiotic relationship with humans for centuries, the knowledge that human DNA from a black woman will essentially save the Ina species and allow them to function in the sun causes an irrational fear in certain "pure" Ina. Several Ina are alarmed that her existence and her future progeny will irrevocably and detrimentally transform the relationship between the Ina and their human symbionts, which has consistently relied upon the transmigration of human symbionts between the Ina and human communities. It is here that Butler seemingly draws upon the real-world phenomena of transnational migration.

Transnational migrants often maintain close contact with both their host and their home country and do not cut ties with their countries of origin. Some transnational communities, for example many of those in the Mexican-US border region, maintain, build, and reinforce "multiple linkages" between their homeland and host countries (Schiller 1995, 52). This mirrors the system the Ina maintain with their diverse group of symbionts, while collectively representing a transnational community with multiple linkages. The symbionts are relatively unrestricted and are able to move between borders—in this case, between the Ina communes and their human world. This is primarily because the human symbionts are able to function both during the day and at night, whereas the Ina are forced to be most active during the night.

The symbionts maintain their jobs outside of the Ina communes and return when they are needed or desire to return. A major part of a symbiont's responsibility within the commune is to serve their Ina companions, something that the symbionts appear to do of their own free will. For instance, when a human male expresses a desire to join with Shori, an Ina leader explains that his usefulness goes beyond sustenance: "He has a degree in business administration, and I think you'll eventually need someone like him to help you manage the business affairs of your families" (154). Thus, it becomes clear that when the Ina chooses a symbiont, the symbiont's significance within the Ina commune can be economic, political, or cultural and not just physical or sexual. The Ina hold particular interests that require a simultaneous presence in various social and cultural arenas within the human world as well as within their own.

Certainly, there are both positive and negative associations with transnationalism and migration. The reason for the migration, whether the group moves by force or by choice, is closely tied to the successful or unsuccessful outcome of migration. In addition, there are different types of migration—permanent migration and transmigration, with groups moving back to their point of origin instead of remaining once they have migrated. On the one hand, one of the most horrific consequences of some transnational migrations has been the mass killing of migrating groups because they are portrayed as racially, ethnically, or culturally different. On the other hand, a significant benefit of transnational group migration is the possibility for social mobility and economic prosperity. Within this seemingly positive framework of global capitalism and employment, however, we also find the exploitation of migrating workers in terms of pay, safety, health, and retirement. Butler seems to be most interested in interrogating such intended and unintended repercussions of transnationalism. She explores these consequences by developing the relationship between the Ina and the symbionts even further. The similarities between American slavery as a system of oppression and exploitive transnational globalization processes make the chains that oppress the migrant workforce visible, bringing to mind Karl Marx's vampire metaphor in *Capital: A Critique of Political Economy* (1867).

SUCKING LIVING LABOR VIA TEMPORAL AUGMENTATION

Prior to the publication of *Capital*, Marx associates vampires with the British bourgeoisie, calling their exploitation of the working class "vampire-like." He also asserts that this particular ruling class of England could only subsist "by sucking blood, and children's blood too" ([1867] 1974, 79). In the same vein, Frederick Engels also used the vampire as metaphor in his essay "Labour Movement" (1845). He criticized the ruling class for feeding off labor, referring to capitalists as the "vampire–property holding class" ([1845] 2010). Like Marx, Engels criticized their complicit endorsement of the deplorable conditions in the factories of England, which exploited not only the adult worker, but also children. Thus, both Marx and Engels used a vampire metaphor to express the misuse of various groups of workers across history. Marx was particularly aware of the "the civilised horrors of over-work" and "the barbaric horrors of slavery [and] serfdom" in American slave systems ([1867] 1974, 79). In *Fledgling*, Butler borrows the metaphor of vampires, the Ina, portraying them as the ruling, capitalist class. The workers are, in this case, the symbionts, which essentially function as the Ina's dedicated twenty-four-hour-a-day labor force.

Marx argues that the success of ruling classes rests on the manner in which they extend the duration of labor between daytime and nighttime:

> *The prolongation of the working day beyond the limits of the natural day, into the night, only acts as a palliative. It quenches only in a slight degree the vampire thirst for the living blood of labour. To appropriate labour during all the 24 hours of the day is, therefore, the inherent tendency of capitalist production. But as it is physically impossible to exploit the same individual labour-power constantly during the night as well as the day, to overcome this physical hindrance, an alternation becomes necessary between the workpeople whose powers are exhausted by day, and those who are used up by night. ([1867] 2010, 172)*

In *Fledgling*, the extension of time the labor force must work is particularly significant because it is the prolongation of the workday that primarily motivates the Ina to experiment with human and Ina DNA in order to become mobile during daylight. Until Shori's creation, it was not possible for the Ina to move about freely in the daytime. As a result, the Ina were unable to produce necessities required by their communities during the day; they had to rely on their symbionts to run their economic interests and to protect them during daylight hours. In part, operating as the laborer is the secondary function of the symbionts—to run the daily operations of the commune—while the Ina are forced to remain indoors during the day for protection against the deadly effects of the sun. Their genetic disposition to sunlight forces them to sleep during the day, making the Ina the capitalist class and the symbionts the working class.

The symbionts are more than just laborers for the Ina; through the exchange of saliva and blood, they are bestowed with longer life and enhanced strength and thus they benefit from the Ina. However, the symbionts are also, to some degree, controlled by the Ina, just as Marx describes the worker in *Capital*. After laborers "freely" agree to give their labor to the capitalist, they discover "that in fact the vampire will not lose its hold on him 'so long as there is a muscle, a nerve, a drop of blood to be exploited'" ([1867] 2010, 193).

However, in contrast to the laborers in Marx, the symbionts have greater control over their work and possess a vested interest in the functioning of the commune that they share with the Ina. Undoubtedly, much of America's economic strength during the antebellum period directly resulted from the exploitation of black bodies. Marx's conceptualization of the relation of capital and labor puts forth a clear figurative and literal connection between slavery and vampirism. It is within this context that Butler seems to expand the metaphor of the vampire to include present-day transnational societies and the First World's use of labor from Third-World countries.

The relationship between the Ina and the symbionts is represented in a way that establishes the symbionts' autonomy and ability to make decisions of their own. Butler attempts to present an ideal utopian society where the symbionts are free to question and analyze their condition among themselves and with the Ina—this in spite of the addictive properties of the Ina's saliva and its effect that gives the Ina suggestive influence upon the symbionts' minds. Thus, the relationship between Ina and symbiont becomes even more vexed once a human being is bitten and has been infected with Ina saliva. He or she requires unremitted contact with that Ina; the Ina and his or her symbiont are connected for life. Shori's father later explains the means by which symbionts establish their intimate link to the Ina: "We addict them to a substance in our saliva—in our venom—that floods our mouths when we feed. I've heard it called a powerful hypnotic drug. It makes them highly suggestible and deeply attached to the source of the substance. They come to need it" (73). Not only do they eventually rely on the Ina physically (requiring what appears to be similar to drug withdrawal), but the symbionts frequently move between the Ina community and their human point of origin to maintain the addiction. Also, the humans, once they are bitten, are no longer entirely human; rather, they live longer, are stronger, and have better health. Rather than portraying the usual representation of vampires as the embodiment of evil in their control over their victims, Butler's Ina have a more seemingly sympathetic and mutually beneficial relationship with the humans that they bite, providing them with positive qualities that actually improve human existence. Nevertheless, there is a haunting question concerning the relationship between Ina and humans that persists throughout the novel: are the human symbionts truly free, autonomous individuals or do the symbionts only function to serve the whims of the Ina? Butler leaves the answer to this question open.

As I have argued, however, the relationship between the Ina and the symbionts appears analogous to migrants who sometimes flee or are forced to relocate for a better life, reflecting current labor relationships between industrialized and developing countries. Undeniably, some individual migrants live a better life in the country they have migrated to, but this comes at a cultural and personal price in the loss of their homeland of origin. Moreover, similar to other contemporary neo-slave narratives, Butler questions the very idea of individual freedom and power. Yet Butler expands her interrogation between the Ina and symbionts to include symbiotic relationships in the modern world. If we look at immigrant groups and their precarious position within the confines of countries that they migrate to and the symbolic connections migrant groups maintain with their home countries, the development of the relationship between the symbionts and the Ina becomes apparent. These similarities reveal intricate systems of power that govern these relationships, with one important exception: the Ina seemingly acknowledge and respect their symbionts' points of origin and their accepting attitude is in stark contrast to the way many countries in the West disparage the cultures or places of origin of transmigrants.

As a postmodern, transnational, transracial, and transcultural neo-slave narrative, *Fledgling* critiques depictions of blackness as other. Additionally, it interrogates migration and immigration policies in First-World countries in terms of how these groups are positioned as other, yet as requisite for development and prosperity. Butler, like many other writers of neo-slave narratives, references past iterations of slavery, particularly of the American antebellum period, and shows how slavery, in different formulations, persists in the present. The Ina have developed what they believe is the perfect solution to equality—that is, a *seemingly* mutually beneficial relationship with their symbionts. Here, Butler questions the degree to which relationships among groups can ever be viewed as equal, but rather than underline the negative implications, Butler presents a utopian vision of cultural, racial, and national exchange: the Ina permit their symbionts to work outside of the community and they bring their knowledge-based skills back to the Ina for their benefit. Despite the symbionts' freedom to come and go as they please, they are nonetheless bound to the Ina because of the narcotic effect Ina saliva has on their bodies and minds. They are allowed to move freely between borders (the Ina community and the outside world), but must always return to the Ina in order to obtain the venom that will sustain their body and their sanity. Butler's novel, thereby, provides a profound commentary on the immigration and migration issues currently and immediately affecting the United States and, in particular, its southern neighbor, Mexico. However, Butler's vision entails a broader commentary on modernity and capitalism across the globe, exposing the inequities of globalized capital. It seems that rather than vilifying the body of Mexican immigrants and their supposedly detrimental effect on the US economy and culture, Butler envisions a utopian world where the relationship between Ina and symbiont is mutually salutary.

In rewriting the vampire trope in *Fledgling*, Octavia Butler, like Toni Morrison, Jewelle Gomez, and L. A. Banks, becomes part of a small but vocal group of black women writers who find unique ways to incorporate vampire tropes in their work. In doing so, these black women writers show the strong connections among and intersections between racist, sexist, classist, and ageist oppression. Moreover, Butler demonstrates the influence the familial and the communal exert on an individual's development. However, in contrast to Morrison, Gomez, and Banks, Butler demonstrates the connection between manifestations of slavery in the past as well as oppressive globalizing forces in contemporary society.

She very effectively stretches the possibilities of the vampire genre and places it in conversation with the African American literary tradition in an expansion of its possibilities. Instead of a dystopian world of distrust and hate, Butler imagines a world where the vampire is not at odds with the village, but is a figure that works within a system that is to some extent mutually beneficial. Indeed, in Octavia Butler's *Fledgling*, vampire mythology has traversed the human imagination to become a usable narrative of cultural reproduction freely open to all, making of the vampire a fitting migrant between nations, races, and cultures.

NOTES

1. See Nina Auerbach's *Our Vampires, Ourselves* for a history of "Anglo-American culture through its mutating vampires" (1995, 6). Auerbach argues that vampires "blend into the changing cultures they inhabit. They inhere in our most intimate relationships; they are also hideous invaders of the normal" (6).

2. I am unaware of any African American male writer who has used the vampire or vampirism as a metaphor for the history of slave/master relations. This intersection seems to have been taken up only by African American women writers. Why this is so is a provocative question, but the answer lies beyond the scope of what I explore here.

3. My argument excludes two very popular and successful blaxploitation horror-themed films that were produced in the 70s: *Blacula* (1972) and *Scream, Blacula, Scream* (1973). Although the successful film *Blade* (1998) appeared much later, this black vampire was created by Marvel Comics in the seventies and capitalized on the blaxploitation era of popular film.

4. William Wells Brown's heroine Clotel in *Clotel; or, The President's Daughter* (1853), Harriet Wilson's Frado in *Our Nig; or, Sketches from the Life of a Free Black* (1859), or Frances Harper's postbellum fictional character Iola in *Iola Leroy; or, Shadows Uplifted* (1892) all provide pertinent examples.

5. Neo-slave narratives did not originate in the 1960s. Arna Bontemps's novel *Black Thunder, Gabriel's Revolt: Virginia, 1800* (1936), which concerns a slave rebellion led by Gabriel Prosser in Virginia in the 1800s, is generally considered the first neo-slave narrative. Unfortunately, Bontemps has not received the critical attention that he deserves. I argue, with Rushdy and Bell, that neo-slave narratives began to be written in earnest during the 1960s and 1970s.

6. Other instances include Charles Johnson's novels *The Oxherding Tale* (1982) and *The Middle Passage* (1990).

7. Margaret Walker's *Jubilee* (1966), Alex Haley's *Roots: The Saga of an American Family* (1976), David Bradley's *The Chaneysville Incident* (1981), Sherley Anne Williams's *Dessa Rose* (1986), and Toni Morrison's *Beloved* (1987).

8. *Kindred* simultaneously diverges from and embraces conventional neo-slave narratives: The science-fiction aspect of the novel, Dana's traveling back and forth through time, certainly does not fit the conventional model. However, that a majority of the narrative takes place in the antebellum South and speaks directly to slavery demonstrates that the novel fits the conventional neo-slave narrative model. In short, *Kindred* masks and does not mask its connection to conventional neo-slave narratives.

WORKS CITED

Auerbach, Nina. 1995. *Our Vampires, Ourselves*. Chicago: University of Chicago Press.
Bane, Theresa. 2010. *Encyclopedia of Vampire Mythology*. Jefferson, NC: McFarland.
Banks, L. A. 2003. *Minion: A Vampire Huntress Legend*. New York: St. Martin's.
Bell, Bernard. 1987. *The Afro-American Novel and Its Tradition*. Amherst, MA: Amherst University Press.
Bhabha, Homi K. 1990. "The Third Space: Interview with Homi Bhabha." In *Identity, Community, Culture, Difference*, edited by J. Rutherford, 207–21. New York: Lawrence and Wishart.
Bontemps, Arna. [1936] 1992. *Black Thunder, Gabriel's Revolt: Virginia, 1800*. Boston: Beacon Press.

Bradley, David. 1981. *The Chaneysville Incident: A Novel.* New York: Harper & Row.

Brown, William Wells. [1853] 2000. *Clotel; or, The President's Daughter: A Narrative of Slave Life in the United States,* edited by Robert S. Levine. Boston: Bedford and St. Martin's.

Butler, Octavia E. [1979] 2003. *Kindred.* Boston: Beacon.

———. [2005] 2007. *Fledgling: A Novel.* New York: Seven Stories.

Douglass, Frederick. [1845] 1997. *Narrative of the Life of Frederick Douglass, an American Slave, Written by Himself.* Edited by William Andrews and William S. McFeely. New York: Norton.

Engels, Frederick. [1845] 2010. "Labour Movements." *The Condition of the Working Class in England, 1845.* Transcribed by Tim Delaney. Accessed April 16, 2014. http://www.marx ists.org/archive/marx/works/1845/condition-working-class/index.htm.

Equiano, Olaudah. [1798] 2003. *The Interesting Narrative of the Life of Olaudah Equiano; or, Gustavus Vassa, the African, Written by Himself.* Edited by Vincent Carretta. New York: Penguin.

Gates, Henry Louis. 1988. *The Signifying Monkey: A Theory of Afro-American Literary Criticism.* New York: Oxford University Press.

Gomez, Jewelle. [1991] 2005. *The Gilda Stories.* New York: Firebrand Books.

Haley, Alex. 1976. *Roots: The Saga of an American Family.* Garden City, NY: Doubleday.

Harper, Frances Ellen Watkins. [1892] 1988. *Iola Leroy; or, Shadows Uplifted.* New York: Oxford University Press.

Hartman, Saidiya. 2007. *Lose Your Mother: A Journey along the Atlantic Slave Route.* New York: Farrar, Straus and Giroux.

Jacobs, Harriet. [1861] 2001. *Incidents in the Life of a Slave Girl.* Edited by Nellie Y. McKay and Frances Smith Foster. New York: Norton.

Jones, Ernest. [1931] 2006. *On the Nightmare: The Significant Story of Witchery and Religion.* New York: Kessinger.

Johnson, Charles. [1990] 1998. *The Middle Passage.* New York: Scribner.

———. [1982] 1995. *The Oxherding Tale.* New York: Plume.

Lacey, Lauren J. 2008. "Octavia E. Butler on Coping with Power in *Parable of the Sower, Parable of the Talents,* and *Fledgling.*" *Critique* 49 (4): 379–94.

Marx, Karl. [1867] 2010. *Capital: A Critique of Political Economy.* Vol. 1. *Book One: The Process of Production of Capital.* Translated by Samuel Moore and Edward Aveling and edited by Frederick Engels. Accessed November 12, 2012. http://www.marxists.org/archive/ marx/ works/ download/pdf/Capital-Volume-I.pdf.

Morrison, Toni. [1976] 1987. *Song of Solomon.* New York: Plume.

———. 1984. "Rootedness: The Ancestor as Foundation." In *Black Women Writers (1950– 1980): A Critical Evaluation,* edited by Mari Evans, 339–45. New York: Doubleday.

———. [1987] 2004. *Beloved.* New York: Plume.

Reed, Ishmael. 1972. *Flight to Canada.* New York: Scribner.

Rushdy, Ashraf. 1999. *Neo-Slave Narratives. Studies in the Social Logic of a Literary Form.* New York: Oxford University Press.

Schiller, Nina Glick. 1995. "From Immigrant to Transmigrant: Theorizing Transnational Migration." *Anthropological Quarterly* 68 (1): 48–63.

Schiller, Nina Glick, Linda Green Basch, and Cristina Szanton Blanc. 1992. "Towards a Definition of Transnationalism." In *Towards a Transnational Perspective on Migration: Race, Class, Ethnicity and Nationalism Reconsidered*, edited by Nina Glick Schiller, Linda Green Basch, and Cristina Szanton Blanc, ix-xiv. New York: New York Academy of Science.

Styron, William. 1967. *The Confessions of Nat Turner*. New York: Random House.

Walker, Margaret. 1966. *Jubilee*. Boston: Houghton Mifflin.

Wheatley, Phillis. [1773] 1988. *The Collected Works of Phillis Wheatley*. Edited by John C. Shields. New York: Oxford University Press.

White, Luise. 2000. *Speaking With Vampires: Rumors and History in Colonial Africa*. Los Angeles: University of California Press.

Williams, Sherley Anne. [1986] 2010. *Dessa Rose*. New York: W. Morrow.

Wilson, Harriet E. [1859] 2005. *Our Nig; or, Sketches from the Life of a Free Black*. Edited by P. Gabrielle Foreman and Reginald H. Pitts. New York: Penguin Books.

PART 2

NON/NORMATIVE
SEXUALITIES

APPETITE FOR DISRUPTION

The Cinematic Zombie and Queer Theory

RASMUS R. SIMONSEN

In that compelling, raw, insolent thing in the morgue's full sunlight, in that thing that no longer matches and therefore no longer signifies anything, I behold the breaking down of a world that has erased its borders: fainting away.

— JULIA KRISTEVA, *POWERS OF HORROR*

*W*arm Bodies, Zombieland, World War Z, The Walking Dead, Pride and Prejudice and Zombies: The living dead seem to have infested every corner of popular culture. Zombies have definitely enjoyed a resurgence in recent years—something that appeared unlikely even a decade ago—and the term *renaissance* (rebirth) seems entirely appropriate in this regard (see McGlotten and VanGundy 2013, 101). Be that as it may, I hesitate to call what we are witnessing now a zombie renaissance for the simple fact that, in most cases, what passes for a zombie in contemporary cinema is nothing more than a prop in the Hollywood machine—a stand-in for teenage angst (*Warm Bodies*) or a slapstick dummy (*Zombieland*), for example. None of these millennial "zombies" translate any of the dread or social critique that made George Romero's "ghouls" of the previous century so poignant and, well, scary.

The modern zombie as a flesh-eating ghoul first shambled onto the screen in 1968 with Romero's *Night of the Living Dead.*[1] Earlier in Hollywood history the zombie had appeared in its appropriated Haitian form, as a corpse resurrected by a nefarious voodoo master who puts the dead body to work toward his own wicked enterprise. The zombies we encounter in the beginning of the 1932 film *White Zombie*, for instance, are perfectly docile creatures that pose no immediate threat to their surroundings. Laboring ceaselessly in their master's sugar mill, these undead exhibit no desire to consume human flesh (yet, they can be ordered to kill by their dark master, played by Bela Lugosi). Beginning with his *Night of the Living Dead*, Romero would go on to drastically change the premise of the zombie. While his zombies still stagger slowly and display minimal powers of reasoning, these new undead—in their incessant craving for human flesh—are not made susceptible to the machinations of any evil puppet master. Contrary to the "classical" zombie, then, these "modern" flesh eaters are enslaved only to the infantile drive to consume.

Flesh eating or not, the most appalling characteristic of the zombie is that, neither alive nor dead, it will not conform to a human understanding, or ordering, of things. Human speculation as to what happens postlife comes to a halt in the same moment the dead stumble forth from their graves. No longer can the subject take solace in the romance of a peaceful afterlife. Instead, the romantic consolation has been replaced by the horrific possibility of a postmortem future as a walking, rotting corpse. Indeed, as Marc Leverette points out, the zombie's terrible quality stems namely from the fact that it "offers an unnerving commentary regarding the potential liminality of being human" (2008, 186). And, as he goes on to say, perhaps nothing is more frightening or monstrous as "becoming something that is neither this nor that" (193), which is to say that it is the zombie's inherent uncertain, or undecidable, ontological status that induces dread in the victim.

Given the ontological uncertainty of the zombie, is it possible to attach specific cultural effects to zombie-ness? Is there such a thing as zombie culture? Quoting a number of recent zombie movie titles, the opening paragraph of this essay suggests that the zombie exudes a certain cultural malleability: its in-between-ness, in this regard, is what makes it so adaptable to different contexts. As a vacated human shell, it is at the same time culturally blank, which means that there is seemingly no context too ludicrous or incongruous for it to appear in. I have already noted how the modern-day zombie translates certain characteristics that originated in Haitian culture; in contemporary cinema, the zombie has become an exchangeable object that can be dressed up to fit any genre. Conceptually speaking, as a filmic trope, the zombie transcends boundaries and genres. Some recent films explore the anarchic quality of zombies on a geopolitical scale. As a hyperanxious commentary on globalization, the 2013 film adaptation of Max Brooks's novel, *World War Z*, shows zombies as a massive, undifferentiated predatory unity of violence flowing across the globe. Clearly, zombies do not respect national or geographical barriers. Paying no heed to creed, race, or sexuality, zombies will devour any human form in sight.

As Christiane Brosius and Roland Wenzlhuemer have pointed out, the idea of "flow" is bound up with the idea of transculturalism (2011, 5). Concerning the thematic impetus of this volume, I suggest that it is the transportability of queer theory that propels or gives the zombie its particularly transcultural flow. As Eve Kosofsky Sedgwick stresses in the foreword to her essay collection *Tendencies*, "queer" connotes a certain sense of transversality; it cuts "*across genders, across sexualities, across genres, across 'perversions'*" (1993, viii; emphases in original). Similarly, zombies cut (or gnaw, rather) through definitions of various kinds with each bloody contact. The zombie virus is transported from wound to wound, and the visceral instantiation of the queer zombies in this chapter reaches an apex when the cinematic wound of zombie cinema intersects—flows into—the traumatic reality of the AIDS epidemic, as I will show in my analysis of *Otto; or, Up with Dead People*.

In his essay "The Funk of Forty Thousand Years; or, How the (Un)Dead Get Their Groove On" (2008), Leverette investigates the philosophical problem of the zombie from the point of view of queer theory. He sees the zombie's restless uncertainty as the embodiment of a specifically queer (anti)ontology. While Leverette is not interested in "queer" as a sexual marker—he focuses mainly on the zombie's Derridean or deconstructive potential, which indeed seems to have become the favored point of interest for scholars[2]—I would like to touch upon Harry Benshoff's understanding of the monster as a metaphor for the homosexual in horror films: "To create a broad analogy, monster is to 'normality' as homosexual is to heterosexual" (1997, 2). Rather than constructing a simple this/that binary,[3] however, I insist that the zombie—and by proxy, the queer—can never simply be defined as the opposite of the norm. I refer to *queer* in this chapter not strictly as a sign of identity but as a force, or potential, of disruptive proportions that grows out of what is termed *the abject*. In *Skin Shows*, Judith Halberstam claims that "monstrosity is almost a queer category that defines the subject as at least partly monstrous" (1995, 27)—almost queer, since, like queerness, monstrosity "always represents the disruption of categories, the destruction of boundaries, and the presence of impurities" (27). Within this paradigm, I argue that the zombie represents the queerest of movie monsters, since its existence, as neither living nor dead, is predicated on the destruction of boundaries. Further, drawing on Lee Edelman's queer critique of "reproductive futurity," I argue that the zombie "comes to figure the bar to every realization of futurity, the resistance, internal to the social, to every social structure or form" (2004, 4). The presumably atemporal quality of the zombie, then, disrupts the structure of heterosexual "repro-time" (Halberstam 2005, 5). Indeed, the appearance of this particular brand of the undead halts the signifying practices that inform the reproductive goal of society, which, as Sara Ahmed calls attention to, is always "bound up with the reproduction of culture, through the stabilization of specific arrangements for living ('the family')" (2004, 144). It is perhaps in this regard that we can, at the same time, begin to understand the transcultural impact of the zombie. Zombies are carriers of a virus; as deadly vessels of incurable undeath, they transport the means of destroying culture—understood in this essay as a set of values that are reproduced through heterosexual structures and practices.

Although the zombie does not have a sexual identity per se (since notions such as identity are rendered completely obsolete in dealing with a creature that no longer has an ego), its very presence certainly has an effect on the functioning of sexuality in society. The zombie—as an animated "corpse that is no longer an I" (Leverette 2008, 187)—thus seems to correspond to Phillip A. Bernhardt-House's definition of *queerness* as "anything which actively disrupts normativity, transgresses the boundaries of propriety, and interferes with the status quo in closed social and *sexual systems*" (2008, 159; my emphasis). Similarly, in his review of Eve Kosofksy Sedgwick's *Tendencies*, Eric Clarke emphasizes that "'[q]ueer,' then, would seem to be the lever that pries open the truth of the constitutive (yet constitutively denied) excesses of identity formation of any kind" (1996, 112–13). This seems to be precisely consistent with the queer quality of the zombie; but why, we might ask, has this not been seized upon previous to Leverette's recent account? Perhaps it has to do with the belief that "[q]ueer theory's readings are always about sex relations" (Gelder 2000, 187) and that zombie sex just does not usually happen on screen?[4] At any rate, here I seek to situate the zombie film firmly within a queer reading. Initially, therefore, in my discussion of Romero's *Dead* series I read the emergence of the zombie as an instance of queer interference in the heteronormative institutions of society. This theme is further expanded upon and complicated in rogue filmmaker Bruce LaBruce's take on the zombie genre, *Otto; or, Up with Dead People*, as the zombie is here figured as queer; or, rather, the queer is portrayed as a zombie.

The structure of my argument owes much to Bernhardt-House's reading of werewolves and queerness in the anthology *Queering the Non/Human*, most notably the positioning of "the Werewolf as Queer" and "the Queer as Werewolf." Bernhardt-House borrows two terms from anthropology to guide his reading of the werewolf: the "etic" perspective is used to describe "the viewpoint of an outsider evaluating the werewolf as a symbol and understanding it in terms which are imposed upon it through comparative models rather than on its own merits" (2008, 159); its opposite is the "emic" viewpoint, which engages with the subject's understanding of itself on its own terms. In regard to the emic perspective, the anthropologist will base her/his authority directly on the voice of the subject, or the subject's own ability to categorize her/his immediate world. The Romero zombie, however, is unable to respond to or directly supply the observer with a perspective on human identity distinctions (based on sexuality or otherwise). It is a creature of the in-between that is similarly understood as being radically outside the limits of subjectivity. In my effort to queer the zombie-film genre, I am thus, unabashedly, applying a distinctly etic approach.[5] Invoking Judith Halberstam's paraphrasing of Slavoj Žižek, it is certainly true that "[t]he monster/phantom . . . never stands for a simple or unitary prejudice, it always acts as a 'fantasy screen' upon which viewers and readers inscribe and sexualize meaning" (1995, 10). The very queer undecidability of the zombie nevertheless ensures that the meaning thus enacted can ever only be fleeting.

ZOMBIE AS QUEER

The dead are walking;
I hear the scraping of their shoes upon the floor,
The great rooms echo with their hollow voices;
I hear the creaking of their shoes upon the stairs,
I see them slanting toward their graves.

—WILLIAM ZORACH, "THE DEAD"

Robin Wood suggests that the zombies in Romero's 1978 *Dawn of the Dead*—the second of the *Dead* series—"represent the habits of the past from which the living characters must strive to extricate themselves" (1998, 299). The zombies signify a past that refuses to remain as such; their function is to make us aware of our own shortcomings or failures, which are not simply allowed to fade from consciousness. In all their decrepit ghastliness, the moving corpses in *Dawn of the Dead* indeed make horribly clear how deeply ingrained overconsumption had become in the American psyche in the late 1970s. The majority of the film even takes place in a shopping mall. Refusing the grave, the zombies in this film suggest that consumption is eternal, and if, as the character Peter points out, they are "us," the thinly veiled analogy is that in our race to consume more, we are actually devouring ourselves as we convert the world's limited resources into frivolous luxury items. It is interesting to note that in LaBruce's *Otto; or, Up with Dead People*, one character fittingly refers to the living as having undergone a certain "zombification" process as a result of excessive consumerism.

This relatively straightforward analysis of *Dawn of the Dead* fits with the director's view of his own work. In an interview with Giulia D'Agnolo-Vallan, Romero underscores that "[t]he political dimension of these films is what's important to me" (2005, 23). Similarly, it is tempting to read *Night of the Living Dead* "in terms of the social unrest in the United States in the 1960s," and, correspondingly, "as a critique of the Nixonian 'silent majority'" (Grant 1996a, 6–7; Grant 1996b, 202)—both of which are valid and important readings. Certainly one of the strengths of the zombie, in an analytical context, is that it is a monster that "defies casual explanation, or even simple categorization" (1993, 83), as Steven Shaviro put it in his monumental study, *The Cinematic Body*, and the zombie is therefore particularly open to interpretation. In this way, the zombie evades being read as a monster in the Gothic tradition. The Gothic monster, argues Halberstam, "functions as monster . . . when it is able to condense as many fear-producing traits as possible into one body" (1995, 21). The zombie, however, in its ironic illogical (dis)figuring of the human body, escapes easily fixed meanings and interpretations,[6] and it is exactly this stubbornly oppositional and disruptive value that I exploit when I read the zombie as queer.

In a world where "the failure and inappropriateness of such institutions as family, religion, even traditional humanism, to defeat the legions of the undead" (Grant 1996b, 205) is evident, it becomes pertinent to explore how especially the institution of the family and its correlate, heterosexuality, are rendered illegitimate by the coming of the zombie, which can only properly be responded to (if not defeated) by recognizing its queerness. Shaka Mc-Glotten and Sarah VanGundy also read the zombie in queer terms, and it may be that "the only survivors [in zombie texts] are brave, pioneering heterosexuals who must fight off the threatening (homosexual?) menace" (2013, 113); however, more often than not, these hetero-survivors do not manage to "re-create (an idealized) society through hard work and genital reproduction" (113). Rather, the zombie plague seems to efface the potential of heterosexuality to re-create society *as it used to be*. Not surprisingly, therefore, various critics have read *Night of the Living Dead* as a critique of the nuclear family (see, for example, Wood 2008, 29), with a parallel argument that the zombies are the "logical outgrowth of, or response to, patriarchal norms" (Shaviro 1993, 89). The move away from "patriarchal norms" is discernible in a number of the subsequent zombie films produced by Romero and his fellow filmmakers.[7] As Barry Keith Grant notes throughout his chapter,

"Taking Back the *Night of the Living Dead*: George Romero, Feminism, and the Horror Film" (1996b), zombie films from *Dawn of the Dead* onward have more obviously included progressive, increasingly independent female protagonists capable of survival without their male counterparts. This of course suggests a certain feminist emphasis on the expectation that each successive *Dead* film will be able to offer up an unambiguously gender-equal world, in which women and men fight alongside each other and the sexist impetus of patriarchal society fall by the wayside.[8]

What is missing from these and other similar critical analyses are the zombies themselves. Only by focusing on the living dead can we achieve a more distinctly queer reading capable of foregrounding the collapse of "meaning's eventual realization" (Edelman 2004, 4), which is namely provoked by the zombie plague. The zombie exudes a certain kind of negativity, which convincingly connects with the antifuturity thesis of Lee Edelman's rallying cry against liberal optimism. In *No Future* (2004), Edelman proposes that queer theory should not attempt to liberate the queer from the negative position of abject "other" that conservative politics fervently casts it as: that which is most detrimental to "'the very foundation of Western Civilization'" (16). Rather than fighting for a place in the future of society, we should recognize that this "future" is a heteronormative fantasy, in which queerness—as the abject other—does not fit. To be sure, pure abjection "cannot be assimilated" (Kristeva 1982, 1). However, the social can only "mean" by continually positioning itself in opposition to the "abjectified difference" of the queer, as Edelman suggests (2004, 26). The opening montage of *World War Z*, with its herds of predators and sped-up decomposition of animal bodies, can actually be seen as an apt metaphor for queerness operating as an inhuman force. As a radically unassimilable force, "queer" will unremittingly oppose the insistence of the social order. This is why queer theory is stridently "antisocial" (Caserio 2006, 819). And, in fact, the zombie is driven by the same resistance to the binary logic of normative society.

The zombie is an ideal embodiment of what Edelman sees in queerness as "the force that insists on the void" (2004, 22). Queerness designates the gap between two signifiers, the point at which the pull of signification lessens and identification is suspended. The zombie perversely prolongs this moment, and zombie films on the whole exist as vicious fantasies in which the order of the "normal" is suspended, or cast into crisis. The viewer knows that this gap in meaning—this wound—cannot remain open. For the time being, however, we can revel in the gory intrusion upon the Symbolic reality that would otherwise structure our being according to the logic of repetition and displacement. As Jacques Lacan explains in his "Seminar on 'The Purloined

Letter,'" the vagaries of the signifier on the level of the Symbolic "determine subjects' acts, destiny, refusals, blindness, success, and fate, regardless of their innate gifts and instruction, and irregardless [*sic*] of their character or sex" (2006, 21). In other words, as Edelman explicates Lacan, "we owe our existence as subjects and the social relations within which we live" to the "governing fictions" of the Symbolic order that "we invest ourselves in" (2004, 18). Properly speaking, then, nothing "exists" outside language. In Bruce Fink's phrasing, reality is "that which is named by language and can thus be thought and talked about" (1995, 25). The Lacanian Real, on the other hand, constitutes *"that which has not yet been symbolized*, remains to be symbolized, or even *resists symbolization"* (Fink 1995, 25; latter emphasis mine).

It is this resistance to, or refusal of, the Symbolic that is so pertinent to the event of the zombie. In turn, the regulating, or "performative," practices that we stake our reality on are forcefully challenged, even suspended, by the disruptive arrival of the zombie. The narrative momentum that propels normative living is replaced by "[t]he slow meanders of zombie time" (Shaviro 1993, 98). The disjunctive temporality of the zombie, in Shaviro's words, "emerge[s] out of paralysis of the conventional time of progressive narrative" (98), the same structure that reproductive heterosexuality relies upon.

Instituting gender difference is of course central to the cultural and social structure of heterosexuality. Such concerns, however, are reserved for the living, while zombies, ostensibly, do not abide by the standard parameters of sexuality and gender. Since "zombies seem the least gender-specific creature of all horror film monsters" (Patterson 2008, 108), it thus follows that the gender that had been inscribed upon the living body has been stripped from the rotting flesh of the walking corpse in (un)death. And since, as Judith Butler has shown, the subject does not come into being until a sex has been assumed (1993, 3), the zombie cannot be said to house an "I," or a soul, whether "modern," in Foucauldian parlance (see his introduction to *Discipline and Punish,* [1991], 29), or Christian. The zombie, therefore, is not susceptible to the regulatory practices of society's normalizing impulse. At the moment of zombification, the gender of the newly deceased body is unassumed, for although the undead body still retains clear gender markers (such as clothing and body parts), these will have become devoid of their usual or everyday signification. As a result, the zombie is doomed to (un)live forever in an abject, "uninhabitable" zone (J. Butler 1993, 3). Here we encounter a terrific irony. The zone of the outside is recognized as the land of the dead, but this, in turn, will encroach on the inside, human society, repudiating the living as the excess of the new "norm": nongendered (un)death.

Because the future of society has been suspended, regulatory heterosexuality no longer carries the same authority that it enjoyed prior to the zombie plague. The telos of the heterosexual couple has been subverted, left to linger in limbo indefinitely, or as long as the undead rule the earth. Effectively, heterosexuality is rendered obsolete in the land of the dead. In *Dawn of the Dead*, the three remaining survivors attempt to uphold the pretense of normal life inside the relative safety of the shopping mall. At a poignant moment, Stephen asks Fran to marry him. The setting conforms to all the rules of the proposal ritual: both are costumed in a manner to represent the most exquisite physical qualities of their respective genders, and an intimate candlelight dinner has been prepared for them by Peter. Still, something is missing. As Stephen presents Fran with the ring, she responds by saying, "We can't. It wouldn't be right." Fran recognizes that the social structure that defines and produces heterosexuality is no longer in play, and, thus, the artificiality of not only the specific situation but also the institution of marriage itself is brought to the fore.

More dramatically, in *Night of the Living Dead* the young heterosexual couple of the film—the last hope for humanity to reproduce itself—meets an untimely and gruesome end. The young lovers Tom and Judy are killed in an accidental explosion during a failed attempt to fuel the truck that should have been the vehicle of their escape. The zombies feast on their burned remains in a scene that effectively drives home the point that the time of the "procreative monogamous heterosexual couple as the origin, *telos*, and norm of sexuality" is over (Sedgwick 1993, 74). The narrative movement toward an undivided future is exposed as fantasy in the moment that heterosexual "repro-time" is rendered unviable by the tireless siege of the undead.

In this way, the "Thanatos in drag" (Leverette 2008, 195)—the dead parading around in the uncanny guise of the living—mercilessly intervenes in the performative structure of heterosexuality, the functioning of which is essential to the act of procreation itself. Subsequently, if we substitute "life" for "gender" in the following quote from Judith Butler's *Gender Trouble* (while not exorcising gender from the statement entirely, as it is of course an essential element in the structural formation of "life" itself), we arrive at the following: "*In imitating [life], drag implicitly reveals the imitative structure of [life] itself—as well as its contingency*" (1999, 175). In their stumbling, awkward rendition of life, the very (un)being of Romero's zombies mocks the sacredness of life. In a world populated by the undead, life has become pure pastiche—"parody . . . devoid of laughter" (1991, 17),[9] in Fredric Jameson's memorable turn of phrase. Living has literally become the imitation of a *dead* style (see Jameson 1991, 18). As a survivor in *Land of the Dead* so

accurately says, "They're pretending to be alive, same as us." Indeed, in Butler's exposition of Jameson, "'the original' [life] is revealed to be a copy, and
an inevitably failed one" at that (1999, 176). The only real imitation available
to the genderless zombies is life, but because life itself, culturally and socially
speaking, is comprised of the accumulated disciplinary practices that Butler
and Foucault speak of, the pastiche of the zombies will directly influence the
relations of the living, including gender. Butler's question is pertinent: what
performance can be ultimately effective (see 1999, 177)? The answer to this
question is found in the zombie's nonperformance. Through its apparently
complete lack of motive, the zombie convincingly disrupts the inner/outer
distinction that Butler describes (1999, 176–77). Zombies do not conform to
any gendered acts or gestures, which in Butler's analysis become tantamount
to life. Nor can zombies ever "pass" as truly living humans, since their very
faltering being renders the illusion of life incomplete, with the one exception being their bloody and perpetual attachment to the oral drive (which
nonetheless has no sexual aim).[10]

The zombies' nonperformance effects a crisis in the performances of the
living, who are barred from carrying out their usual routines (see J. Butler
1999, 178). A good example of how the linear progression of heterosexuality
is disrupted can be found in the grisly portrayal of the recently zombified
child, Karen Cooper, killing and eating her parents in *Night of the Living
Dead*.[11] Using *28 Weeks Later* (not technically a zombie film, as the "infected"
are namely that: living infected, not undead ghouls) as their primary example, McGlotten and VanGundy insist that "re-productive futurism, or the
ideology that links images of children to a politics of hopefulness, prolifer-
ates in depictions of children in zombie culture" (2013, 113). However, this is
not the case in *Night of the Living Dead* (nor, as we shall see, in the remake
of *Dawn of the Dead*). I read the scene in *Night* as the refusal of the child
to grow up straight: young Karen refuses to grow into her performance as
a heterosexual female, the bearer of the reproductive futurity that society
demands.

Gender performance requires repetition, the reenactment of already established social meanings. This performance is reliant on the linear time
frame of the heteronormative narrative structure: constituted social temporality. The scene of Karen's parenticide marks the zombie child's (figural)
refusal to travel by the normative map that "chart[s] the emergence of the
adult from the dangerous and unruly period of adolescence as a desired
process of maturation" (Halberstam 2005, 4).

Most literally, in *Night of the Living Dead* the death of the heterosexual
child is what allows for a certain kind of zombie queerness to attach itself

to childhood. All (living) children are assumed by adults to be heterosexual, "while we culturally consider them asexual" (Stockton 2004, 283). According to Kathryn Bond Stockton, it is not until the "(parental) plans for one's straight destination have died [that] the designation 'homosexual child,' or even 'gay kid,' may finally, retrospectively, be applied" (2009, 6–7).

Ironically, the innocence of the straight or normative child—which must vigorously be defended from the corrupting outside world[12]—embodies a certain strangeness, or queerness, which, even as it appears alien to adults, is nevertheless produced by our efforts to keep "the child at once what it is (what adults are not) and leading it toward what it cannot (at least, as itself) ever be (what adults are)" (2009, 30–31). To Stockton, it is this chiastic structure of the child that renders it so markedly queer. It is also this chiasmus that zombification registers so legibly. The queerness of the child is exaggerated the moment it becomes a zombie.

Sexual, as well as ontological, normativity is disavowed by the zombie child, and the scene in *Night of the Living Dead* becomes one of punishment as well: it is as if the newly zombified Karen is saying, "You, my parents, are both implicit in structuring my sexuality as well as my future desires, and for this you must not only die, but be eaten, expelled from sight, abjected!" By reclaiming orality as biologically (rather than psychically) contingent, the zombie child is able to assume clear and unrestrained control of its own "gratification"—the "pleasure of the mouth" (Lacan 1998, 167). While pleasure as a human affect might be denied the zombie, the mouth once again becomes the dominant locus of exploration (whether we can talk about *objet a* as cause of desire in the context of the zombie is debatable). Zombification, therefore, embodies a kind of queer rebirth, and there is indeed something quite infantile about zombies. As a consequence, both adults and children will undergo a regressive movement at the moment of zombification.

Having slain her parents, Karen has no agent of heteronormative law to direct her progression into adulthood. The parents themselves will have become "childlike" in their own transformation into zombies. For young Karen, therefore, the potential and allowed queerness of her childhood can resume unchecked—but only as a zombie. The "not-yet-straight" temporal dimension of childhood (Stockton 2004, 283) is changed into "never-to-be-straight"— never to inhabit any kind of sexuality—as the child becomes infected with the zombie virus. Normal growth is thereby stunted, and the path toward "the official destination of straight couplehood" (283) is forcefully obstructed. Queerness can finally only truly exist apart from life itself, which it refuses as long as living involves conforming to heterocentrist values. The queer child is at once freed and killed in her transformation into (un)death. In the process, the imperative placed on the queer child to either conform or die is subverted (see Sedgwick 1993, 3). She may have escaped the "colonizing narratives of heteronormativity" (Bruhm and Hurley 2004, xxi), but zombification at the same time usurps her own potential for story making.[13]

Night of the Living Dead sufficiently dismantles "the metaphor of the child as a symbol of hope for a better tomorrow" (Halberstam 2008, 275) that Edelman rages against in *No Future*. It is implied that the "Child"—"not to be confused with the lived experiences of any historical children" (Edelman 2004, 11)—carries with it the norms of society, not least of all those pertaining to gender. Hence, the figure of the Child—"as the repository of variously sentimentalized cultural identifications" (11)—belongs to the future, which is always and necessarily deferred. As the bearer of hope for humanity's sustained future, the Child must ruthlessly be defended. Hope, we should remind ourselves, in Halberstam's phrasing, always "goes hand in hand with repro-normativity" (2008, 276), while the family, of course, denotes the central, social locus of such an ideology of reproduction. The queer time of the zombie child, on the other hand, perversely exalts and sustains the undecidability of adolescence that mature, normative society seeks to put under erasure so as to enable the proper emergence of adulthood.

I have already made clear that the family unit is more often than not at the center of attention in zombie films because, to a large degree, the family represents the ordering principle of the individual in the heterosexual social matrix of capitalist Western society. It is likewise fairly certain that "Romero's undead demand the suspension of normal (bourgeois) values" (Grant 1996b, 211), including the family. Such a suspension is recognizable in the birthing scene portrayed in director Zack Snyder's 2004 remake of Romero's *Dawn of the Dead*. The scene in question involves Luda, a minor character who is pregnant at the time of her infection through the bite of a zombie. She dies and is zombified in the middle of labor, as her husband/boyfriend André attempts to bridle his wife's becoming a monster. By so doing, in a futile moment of panic, he tries to reestablish her role as reproductive agent. The child is finally delivered, but it has of course already gone through the zombification process in the womb (figure 4.1). It is born without a gender and future. There is no hope left for the "heteroreproductive couple" (Edelman 2004, 115). To borrow a phrase from Robert Caserio, their "*infantile* belief in the life to come" (2006, 820; my emphasis) has finally been shattered.

The baby was the couple's only means of assuaging the imagined threat to "familial futurity" (Edelman 2004, 116).[14] Insofar as the very potential of birth signals a future, the zombie baby (an homage to the zombified infant in Peter Jackson's *Braindead*) is the most effectively and disturbingly queer of

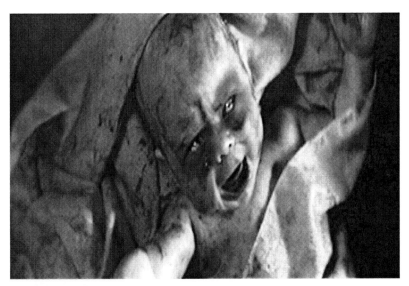

4.1 *DAWN OF THE DEAD*, 2004

all zombies. As the baby-to-be is denied its first breath, in the same instant, the anxiety that frames the repetitive refrain to "the hymn of the meaning of life" (Edelman 2004, 115)—reproduction—is transformed into pure fright. The most horrific and unimaginable outcome of the "what if"—that which might "violate the conditions of its reproduction" (Ahmed 2004, 144)—that the family seeks protection from in the social order has come to (un)life (see Halberstam 2005, 5). This moment in Snyder's reimagining of Romero's classic clearly affirms the disruption of "the coupling of man and woman," the act of which would actually have produced what Sara Ahmed refers to as a metaphorical "'birthing,' a giving birth not only to new life, but to ways of living that are already recognizable as forms of civilization" (2004, 144). The new/un/born has been delivered through the wound that opens up in the Symbolic between two signifiers (life and death), and in this moment it arrests the movement of meaning by breaking up what Lacan in "Position of the Unconscious" calls "[t]he repeating interval" (2006, 715). The very repetitive, jerky movement of the zombified baby itself ironically signifies the obstacle to Symbolic repetition. In his traumatized state, and in a last desperate attempt to keep his family together, André shoots it out with a fellow survivor who seeks to remove the zombie child. The empty cartridge shells—emptied of meaning—hit the floor like pearls from a broken necklace or, in this case, like links of Lacan's signifying "necklace" that have been wrenched from their figural string (2006, 418).

QUEER AS ZOMBIE

Most "survivalist" zombie works present the audience with an external view of the zombies. In other words, we as viewers experience the disruptive impact of the undead from the point of view of the living survivors. Toronto filmmaker Bruce LaBruce turns the tables with his 2008 film *Otto; or, Up with Dead People*, which employs the emic perspective by offering up the viewpoint of the zombie. When the camera shifts to Otto's point of view, colors distort to a monochromatic purple tinge, and the sound track similarly changes to accommodate Otto's disheveled, confused existence. While the zombies in Romero's films impose a queer influence on society, in *Otto* queerness itself is zombified. McGlotten and VanGundy also touch upon this insight in their reading of *Otto*, pointing out that the "liminality of the zombie condition and the tenuous social position of transgressive sexualities link the anxieties induced by zombies and those that arise in response to non-normative gender and sexual alignments" (2013, 112). However, whereas McGlotten and VanGundy focus on the queer pornification of the zombie (which I will consider to some extent), my analysis centers on how LaBruce specifically queers the contagion motif to challenge and disrupt the post-AIDS discourse of contemporary gay culture. In the process, he manages to make zombification the subject of the viewer's sympathetic identification.

Otto tells the story of a recently "turned" zombie's first steps into a world that seems as unfamiliar as ever. As the reanimated corpse of a young gay man, Otto—the main character—tries to come to terms with not only his own new, deceased self but also with the events that led up to his (presumed) death. (Whether Otto is truly undead becomes a matter for speculation as the film progresses.) Heartbreak and familial alienation are on the agenda. Furthermore, at a late point in the film, Otto's former (predeath) boyfriend alludes to a period of hospitalization that Otto underwent for mental illness. Tellingly, during the ex-boyfriend's narrative, several pieces of information are aurally obscured by distorted overdubbing, representative of Otto's unconscious effort to repress the painful memories of his past—his "living" life, so to speak. Zombification, in Otto's case, might then be read as a psychiatric symptom rather than a supernatural occurrence.

It soon becomes clear, however, that Otto's current state of being has not eroded his sexuality, and LaBruce thus presents us with a meditation on this young queer's relation to his (un)living position in society. As a metaphor for queerness, LaBruce's zombie is positioned as the "outside" in the normative discourse of the social, and queer zombiehood that comes to stand in stark contrast to the furthering of life itself. In addition, the ubiquity of "uncouth"

4.2 *OTTO; OR, UP WITH DEAD PEOPLE,* 2008

male-male sex in LaBruce's avant-garde zombie drama challenges notions of propriety with indecorous exuberance in an age devastatingly contaminated by the presence of AIDS.

Early in the film, Otto finds himself engaged in a sexual encounter with a gay man who has met him outside a nightclub in Berlin, where the film takes place. In the midst of sex, Otto is unable to suppress his craving for flesh. As he appears to bite into his sexual partner's mouth and blood drips from the wound, the scene fades to black. A subsequent fade-in sees Otto seated on the edge of the bed, the man lying presumably lifeless beside him. The sheets and walls are covered in blood. Having not been privy to the actual events that led to this, the viewer initially assumes the scene is one of usual gory zombie fare. A moment of surprise ensues, however, when the man suddenly awakens and, in a completely human voice, says: "That was fantastic. Can I see you again?" (figure 4.2). As such, it becomes clear that we are not dealing with a typical zombie kill—the zombie virus is not transferred into the "victim," if he can be called that. Rather, we find ourselves in the midst of what may well be the enactment of a fantasy. It is unclear as to whether Otto is an actual zombie or if his state of being is the symptom of a mental disorder; we as viewers are left wondering what really happened in the bedroom. Did Otto kill the man? Is it an S/M scene involving blood play? Is the "blood" a mere prop that the lovers use to complete the scene? In this way, sex and zombie attack become one, both (im)passionately blood spattered.

This unrepresentable, or undecidable, moment is highly disposed to the workings of fantasy, and we struggle to make sense of the scene. The man's wound initiates the camera's fade-out, which marks the void, or interval, in signification.[15] The diegetic blankness that separates the scene from itself thus allows the viewer to imagine a space where any number of "perverse" gay acts becomes possible; we are invited to "sex" the wound of the Lacanian Real.

In the age of AIDS, the entire scene reads as "unsafe." Blood is liberally exchanged in a gay encounter and, on top of this, if we are to understand Otto to be a full-fledged zombie, he is likely the carrier of a contagion. McGlotten and VanGundy see a link here: "[Z]ombie, like queer, reproduction occurs through contact: including forms of bodily interpenetration—fucking and consuming in Otto—but also the cultural contact that facilitates the world-building that necessarily accompanies the drive to make a more livable life" (2013, 113). The authors only briefly allude to the social fears connecting queers to the origin of the HIV virus, and they neglect to elaborate fully on the kind of "livable life" the contagion trope of zombified queerness might refer to.

The contagion motif itself is necessarily omnipresent in all zombie films, but the almost ritualistic flow of blood that is so central here of course took on an entirely new and problematic dimension after the true impact of AIDS had been discovered in the 1980s. Blood itself was not a "problem" as such in pre-AIDS zombie films; it served as nothing more than an effective and necessarily visible prop that would allow Romero and like-minded directors to bring their visions of apocalyptic zombie dread into full, horrific being. In *Otto*, however, blood takes on the signification of a new, momentous decadence. Embracing the much-too-visceral reality of AIDS means that La-Bruce is able to play with the traditional representation of the homosexual man as a diseased subject—a connoisseur of "unendurable ends" (Edelman 2004, 113)—by letting the infected blood of his queer zombies become the vehicle for on-screen pleasure. However, crucially and ironically, it is not until after having passed from the living that homosexual desires can most clearly be engaged with in *Otto*: zombiehood dedicates a space to the queer subject where the threat of disease and death no longer has any provenance or hold over the possibilities of the flesh.

The original slogan of the film, "Bringing sexy back . . . from the dead" (punning on a song title by Justin Timberlake, "Sexy Back"), underscores LaBruce's desire to comment on or develop a new frame of reference for imagining gay male sexuality post-AIDS, notwithstanding the troubling actuality of the problematic of blood, which still and incessantly threatens to pollute the fantasy. Constant reference is made to the AIDS crisis in *Otto*, even though the word is never actually introduced. This referencing—which takes place in a series of phrases in the film such as "gay plague," "disease-ridden faggots," and "Purple Peril"—makes up for the linguistic absence of *AIDS*. It is, as Lacan says, "the occulted signifier [that] remain[s] present by virtue of its (metonymic) connection to the rest of the [signifying] chain" (2006, 422).[16] "AIDS" itself may have been displaced in *Otto*, but its ghost still lingers.

The queer zombie becomes the mournful image of an "epidemic" that post-AIDS discourse would just as soon forget (P. Butler 2004, 105). In order to move beyond AIDS, one's sexual past must now be repudiated, and the homophobic portrayal of the virile gay male as "the bearer of death" (99) has become appropriated by the gay community itself, in effect. As gay writer Assoto Saint put it during a symposium on gay male literature in America, "We live in an age in which gay sex has a negative connotation: we are seen as disease carriers" (quoted in Duberman 1997, 375). Consequently, the overt sexualization of the gay body has been exchanged for a movement toward desexualization and assimilation "in which members of the gay community [have] started to articulate their political agenda in terms of typically heterosexual aims and practices" (P. Butler 2004, 99).

In "Mourning and Militancy," Douglas Crimp laments that alongside the "dismal toll of death, what many of us have lost [as a result of AIDS] is a culture of sexual possibility" (1989, 11). A whole slew of sexual acts were then placed under prohibition: "golden showers and water sports, cocksucking and rimming, fucking and fist fucking" (11) were, at the very least, barred from the self by a barrier of latex, if not entirely consigned to a place of fantasy. "The attractiveness of fantasy," precisely, "stems from th[e] ability to deliver the goods, to provide the subject with a narrative in which it is possible to access the inaccessible *objet petit a*," as Todd McGowan has noted (2004, 76). The lost object is here "the ideal of perverse sexual pleasure," "the cum never swallowed" (Crimp 1989, 11), as it were. Fantasy grants us access to that which is unsafe or unpleasant—that which cannot conceivably be endured or performed without problem in "real" life—and LaBruce can have his zombies safely engage in otherwise potentially deadly sexual acts. It is Otto who says, during an interview for Medea Yarn's film-within-the-film titled *Up with Dead People*, that "you don't have to worry about dying if you are already dead." Zombification becomes a queer fantasy, therefore, in that it is now possible to imagine sex as far removed from the shadow of AIDS. For the gay zombie, sex can once again be partaken of without any glimpse of the ghostly futurity of suffering and death to spoil the fun.

4.3 *OTTO; OR, UP WITH DEAD PEOPLE*, 2008

The orgy scene that concludes *Up with Dead People* demystifies the threat of death in a sense, as the contagious bodies bathe in blood, engaging with careless abandonment in fucking and sucking (figure 4.3). In LaBruce's fantasy, being undead means endowment with the privilege of having to "die no more." The very artificiality of the scene—we are exposed to its entire staging—overemphasizes how the acting is "perform[ed] in a nonexistent space" (Jackson 1995, 192). The scene is "wonderfully" unhygienic, and Crimp's list of sexual acts has been reclaimed with a vengeance.

But only for a moment, as the fantasy cannot be sustained. The extravagance of the scene highlights the fictionalizing process that memories undergo as they are transformed into nostalgia. The elegiac aura of film in this way impresses upon the nostalgic viewer (see Jackson 1995, 190), who can only connect with the on-screen action by simultaneously acknowledging that his enjoyment is derived from a spectacle of death. No hope in a better, sexier tomorrow is expressed in the process: LaBruce's fantasy does not develop into a discourse about a future in which gay sex can once again escape the harnessing of latex; it is completely self-contained. The scene is a playful monument to gay pleasures, and, for this reason, it begins to seem anachronistic.

But the zombie, as we have seen, refuses and resists temporal restrictions. LaBruce's zombies return as the embodiment of a sexual past that otherwise has been abjected by post-AIDS purists. He constructs something like what

Halberstam refers to as a "queer space" (2005, 6), in which gay sex can be lauded for the achievement to (un)live and fuck "otherwise" in and of itself.[17] LaBruce's orgy scene echoes the sentiment of Ann Cvetkovich as it makes manifest the unwillingness "to accept a desexualized or sanitized version of queer culture as the price of inclusion within the national public sphere" (2003, 5). Otto, indeed, embodies a clear sexual presence as he engages in a relationship with his fellow actor from *Up with Dead People*. In contrast to Romero's zombies, Otto is obviously not desexualized.[18]

Whereas the fantasmatic wound that Romero's zombies inflicted upon mainstream normative postwar American culture became the focal point of a critique of reproductivity as the raison d'être of society, LaBruce's fantasy is localized within the polemical nature of sex debates in a time after AIDS has come to be an inescapable fact of gay life. *Otto* offers LaBruce the appropriate imaginative space to evolve a vision of gay sex that is not only exceedingly queer but sneers at any involvement with assimilatory or normalizing impulses as well. In contrast with the living dead of Romero's films, the zombies in *Otto* are highly sexed creatures. It is even far from certain that they are zombies at all.

The metafictional elements of *Otto* (diegetic worlds colliding) help emphasize the performative aspect of zombification in this film. To be sure, the perverse sexual conduct of the (un)living disrupts the normative performance that gay assimilation necessitates, as the queer zombie stops the passage into "(hetero)normalization" proper (Edelman 2004, 26). In this way, the queer zombie figures as "the inarticulable surplus" (9) that threatens to dismantle gay identity "founded upon assimilation" (P. Butler 2004, 104). We as viewers are not presented with any stable gay identity in *Otto*.

At the close of the film, Otto takes to the highway going north to explore a new way of "death." Clearly, Otto's commitment to queer (un)living does not keep time with the expectations of heteronormative society, and we can be fairly certain that the way leading north does not promise a path to maturity—nor is this desirable. At the close of *Otto*, thus, the transportability of queerness surfaces once more to highlight the boundlessness of undeath— not in a moralizing attempt to warn against the mobility and flexibility of the AIDS virus but in an effort, rather, to emphasize the restlessness of queer negativity: for every gesture toward a stable, reliable tomorrow (as in Otto's near-coupling with his costar from Medea's film), a new impulse to tear at the fabric of the maturation narrative comes pulsing through the screen.

Otto's (un)being exudes a distinctly "queer unbelonging" (Caserio 2006, 819), and the farewell note he leaves on his lover's pillow appropriately reads "Otto: RIP," accompanied by a hand-drawn picture of a tombstone.

4.4 *DIARY OF THE DEAD*, 2007

As Edelman states, "queerness can never define an identity, it can only ever disturb one" (2004, 17), especially one's own.

The zombie is already queer, and the queer is already zombified: they share a metonymic relation, defying cultural normativity equally. As that which "disturbs identity, system, order" (Kristeva 1982, 4), the cinematic zombie presents the viewer with a fantasmatic terrain where heterosexual norms and structures can effectively be disrupted. The zombie is a queer signifier that points nowhere in the signifying chain but to the wound in meaning that it itself established. As a queer cinematic moment, however, the zombie plague is only ever fleetingly present in our exceedingly normative reality. In *Night of the Living Dead*, order is reintroduced toward the film's conclusion as bands of "hillbillies" round up the remaining zombies—a culture-bending encounter if there ever was one. Romero revisits this theme in his recent mock-documentary *Diary of the Dead*, which closes with images even more gruesome and inhumanly cruel than those that bring *Night of the Living Dead* to a conclusion (figure 4.4). Aside from the obvious parallels to the lynching and dismemberment of African American males, these scenes show how heterosexual identity attempts to suture the wound in meaning that queerness signifies. The undead are "sacrificed to a future whose beat goes on, like a pulse or a heart" (Edelman 2004, 154), but as long as the living walk the earth, the queer will return to intrude on their dreams of a wholesome, "straight"-forward tomorrow.

NOTES

1. Note that the word *zombie* is never used to signify the undead in *Night of the Living Dead*; *ghoul* is the preferred moniker. Prior to *Night,* less successful filmmakers had tentatively explored the zombie motif, but it was not until Romero that it reached its modern form (McIntosh 2008, 7–8).

2. See Patricia Molloy's chapter "Zombie Democracy" in *Geopolitics of American Insecurity.* Here she states exactly that "the zombie epitomizes the undecidability of any logical distinction between life and death" (2009, 201).

3. In her book *Skin Shows,* Judith Halberstam certainly warns that "[m]onster-making ...is a suspect activity because it relies upon and shores up conventional humanist binaries" (1995, 143).

4. A notable exception is Peter Jackson's 1992 splatter farce *Braindead,* in which the lead character tries (unsuccessfully) to keep the zombies that he is concealing in his house from having sex with each other.

5. I employ the etic/emic distinction here without simultaneously drawing upon other properly anthropological or ethnographic discursive items that would be likely to follow in its wake, such as "data language." See Marvin Harris's "Emics and Etics Revisited" for an overview of how etic and emic can be applied in the social sciences.

6. Shaviro aptly remarks that the zombie—since Romero—has invoked an exceedingly postmodern sensibility (1993, 84). The cause of zombification is never fully explained, and the zombies become synonymous with that "queerest of rhetorical devices," as Edelman refers to the trope of irony, which, in the de Manian sense, "severs the continuity essential to the very logic of making sense" (2004, 23–24).

7. This is most clearly seen in how Barbara's character is elevated to the position of hero in director (and original *Dead* special-effects master) Tom Savini's 1990 remake of *Night of the Living Dead.* The newly imagined Barbara escapes her original fate and is granted a markedly greater degree of agency than in the original film.

8. Grant complains that Romero's active women always end up as "masculinist" in the end, signaling that we must always in a sense wait for the next installment of Romero's *Dead* films to provide us with an appropriate female hero who can evade the stock archetypes of the horror genre.

9. Romero's films often contain moments or scenes that approach parody and even slapstick. *Dawn of the Dead* arguably contains the most gags out of any *Dead* film. For example, the marauding biker gang is not only brandishing machetes and machine guns in their weaponry against the living dead in the mall, but pies as well. Furthermore, the lumbering, Muzak-style sound track of the theatrical version of *Dawn of the Dead* adds a certain degree of silliness to the otherwise very sinister mood of the film.

10. Since what drives zombies does not correspond to any of the Freudian assumptions regarding the subject's psychical makeup, it would therefore not be accurate to ascribe a cannibalistic impulse—which is sexually motivated in Freud—to the constant and incessant need of the walking dead to devour human flesh either (see Freud's discussion of orality and cannibalism in his case study of the "Wolf-Man").

11. In Savini's remake of the film, Karen's father escapes into the safety of the attic, only to be executed at the film's conclusion by a vengeful Barbara.

12. It is no accident that Harry Cooper insists on keeping his daughter hidden in the basement shelter, as zombies are not the only threat in a setting where Ben's blackness can be assumed as a clear and imminent danger to Cooper's notion of his daughter's pure, white innocence.

13. We might here ask if the zombie child constitutes the leftover excess of all the dead queer children that society has failed.

14. This is the same imagined threat that serves as the backbone for any homophobic argument against gay marriage, adoption, health care, and so on.

15. LaBruce makes skillful use of different cross-fade techniques throughout the film. At the conclusion of the scene in question, the man's now (re)animated body is superimposed on the body of one of the zombies in the film-within-the-film, *Up with Dead People*, thereby metonymically linking the two distinctive diegetic worlds.

16. Indeed, as Lacan remarks in "The Instance of the Letter in the Unconscious," it is not the signifier itself that forms meaning: signification is produced in the spark between two signifiers, according to the process of metaphoric substitution (see 2006, 422).

17. Commenting on the Australian Film Classification Board's recent (and seemingly homophobic) decision not to provide his latest zombie offering, *L.A. Zombie*, with a rating—thereby effectively banning the film from a public screening at the Melbourne International Film Festival—it is interesting to note how LaBruce quite matter-of-factly claims that the queer content of his productions "reaffirms life" ("Bruce Labruce [sic] Zombie Film Banned in Australia").

18. Albeit, the sex between the two actors is of the "vanilla" variant as opposed to the more extreme blood-induced engagement addressed earlier: crisp, white surroundings frame their intimacy and no penetration occurs.

WORKS CITED

Ahmed, Sara. 2004. *The Cultural Politics of Emotion*. Edinburgh: Edinburgh University Press.

Benshoff, Harry M. 1997. *Monsters in the Closet: Homosexuality and the Horror Film*. Manchester, UK: Manchester University Press.

Bernhardt-House, Phillip A. 2008. "The Werewolf as Queer, the Queer as Werewolf, and Queer Werewolves." In *Queering the Non/Human*, edited by Noreen Giffney and Myra J. Hird, 159-83. Hampshire, UK: Ashgate.

Braindead. 1992. Directed by Peter Jackson. Perf. Tomothy Balme, Diana Peñalver, Elizabeth Moody, Ian Watkin. Wingnut Films.

Brosius, Christiane, and Roland Wenzlhuemer. 2011. "Introduction—Transcultural Turbulences: Towards a Multi-Sited Reading of Image Flows." In *Transcultural Turbulences*, edited by Brosius and Wenzlhuemer, 3-24. Berlin: Springer.

Bruhm, Steven, and Natasha Hurley, eds. 2004. *Curiouser: On the Queerness of Children*. Minneapolis: Minnesota University Press.

"Bruce Labruce Zombie Film Banned in Australia." *CBC*. July 21, 2010. Accessed September 20, 2010. http://www.cbc.ca/news/arts/film/story/2010/07/21/zombie-film-bruce-labruce .html.

Butler, Judith. 1993. *Bodies That Matter: On the Discursive Limits of "Sex."* New York: Routledge.

———. 1999. *Gender Trouble: Feminism and the Subversion of Identity.* New York: Routledge.

Butler, Paul. 2004. "Embracing AIDS: History, Identity, and Post-AIDS Discourse." *JAC* 24 (1): 93–111.

Caserio, Robert L. 2006. "The Antisocial Thesis in Queer Theory." *PMLA* 121 (3): 819–21.

Clarke, Eric O. 1996. "All about Eve." *GLQ* 3:106–23.

Crimp, Douglas. 1989. "Mourning and Militancy." *MIT Press* 51:3–18.

Cvetkovich, Ann. 2003. *An Archive of Feelings: Trauma, Sexuality, and Lesbian Public Cultures.* Durham, NC: Duke University Press.

D'Agnolo-Vallan, Giulia. 2005. "Let Them Eat Flesh." *Film Comment* 41 (4): 23–24.

Dawn of the Dead. 1978. Directed by George A. Romero. Perf. David Emge, Ken Foree, Scott H. Reiniger, Gaylen Ross. Laurel Group.

———. 2004. Directed by Zack Snyder. Perf. Sarah Polley, Ving Rhames, Jake Weber, Mekhi Phifer. Strike Entertainment.

Diary of the Dead. 2007. Directed by George A. Romero. Perf. Michelle Morgan, Joshua Close, Shawn Roberts, Amy Ciupak Lalonde. Artfire Films.

Edelman, Lee. 2004. *No Future: Queer Theory and the Death Drive.* Durham, NC: Duke University Press.

Fink, Bruce. 1995. *The Lacanian Subject: Between Language and Jouissance.* Princeton, NJ: Princeton University Press.

Foucault, Michel. 1991. *Discipline and Punish: The Birth of the Prison.* Translated by Alan Sheridan. London: Penguin Books.

Freud, Sigmund. 1971. *The Wolf-Man*, edited by Muriel Gardiner. New York: Basic Books.

Gelder, Ken, ed. 2000. *The Horror Reader.* London: Routledge.

Grant, Barry Keith. 1996a. "Introduction." In Grant, 1–12.

———. 1996b. "Taking Back the *Night of the Living Dead*: George Romero, Feminism, and the Horror Film." In Grant, 200–212.

Grant, Barry Keith, ed. 1996. *The Dread of Difference: Gender and the Horror Film.* Austin: Texas University Press.

Halberstam, Judith. 1995. *Skin Shows: Gothic Horror and the Technology of Monsters.* Durham, NC: Duke University Press.

———. 2005. *In a Queer Time and Place: Transgender Bodies, Subcultural Lives.* New York: New York University Press.

———. 2008. "Animating Revolt/Revolting Animation: Penguin Love, Doll Sex and the Spectacle of the Queer Nonhuman." In *Queering the Non/Human*, edited by Noreen Giffney and Myra J. Hird, 265–81. London: Ashgate.

Harris, Marvin. 1990. "Emics and Etics Revisited." In *Emics and Etics: The Insider/Outsider Debate*, edited by Thomas N. Headland, Kenneth L. Pike, and Marvin Harris, 48–61. Newbury Park, CA: Sage.

Jackson, Earl, Jr. 1995. *Strategies of Deviance: Studies in Gay Male Representation.* Bloomington: Indiana University Press.

Jameson, Fredric. 1991. *Postmodernism; or, The Cultural Logic of Late Capitalism.* Durham, NC: Duke University Press.

Kristeva, Julia. 1982. *Powers of Horror: An Essay on Abjection.* Translated by Leon S. Roudiez. New York: Columbia University Press.

Lacan, Jacques. 1998. *The Four Fundamental Concepts of Psychoanalysis.* Edited by Jaqcues-Alain Miller. Translated by Alan Sheridan. New York: W. W. Norton.

———. 2006. *Écrits.* Translated by Bruce Fink. New York: W. W. Norton.

Land of the Dead. 2005. Directed by George A. Romero. Perf. John Leguizamo, Asia Argento, Simon Baker, Dennis Hopper. Universal Pictures.

Leverette, Marc. 2008. "The Funk of Forty Thousand Years; or, How the (Un)Dead Get Their Groove On." In McIntosh and Leverette, 185–212.

McGlotten, Shaka, and Sarah VanGundy. 2013. "Zombie Porn 1.0: Or, Some Queer Things Zombie Sex Can Teach Us." *Qui Parle* 21:101–25.

McGowan, Todd. 2004. "Lost on Mulholland Drive: Navigating David Lynch's Panegyric to Hollywood." *Cinema Journal* 43 (2): 67–89.

McIntosh, Shawn, and Marc Leverette, eds. 2008. *Zombie Culture: Autopsies of the Dead.* Lanham, MD: Scarecrow Press.

McIntosh, Shawn. 2008. "The Evolution of the Zombie: The Monster That Keeps Coming Back." In McIntosh and Leverette, 1–18.

Molloy, Patricia. 2009. "Zombie Democracy." *The Geopolitics of American Insecurity: Terror, Power and Foreign Policy,* edited by Francois Debrix and Mark J. Lacy, 197–214. Oxon, UK: Routledge.

Night of the Living Dead. 1968. Directed by George A. Romero. Perf. Duane Jones, Judith O'Dea, Karl Hardman, Marilyn Eastman. Image Ten.

———. 1990. Directed by Tom Savini. Perf. Tony Todd, Patricia Tallman, Tom Towles, McKee Anderson. Los Angeles: 21st Century Film Corporation.

Otto; or, Up with Dead People. 2008. Directed by Bruce LaBruce. Perf. Jey Crisfar, Marcel Schlutt, Nicholas Fox Ricciardi, Keith Böhm. Jürgen Brüning Filmproduktion.

Patterson, Natasha. 2008. "Cannibalizing Gender and Genre: A Feminist Re-Vision of George Romero's Zombie Film." In McIntosh and Leverette, 103–18.

Saint, Assotto, et al. 1997. "On Contemporary Gay Male Literature in the United States." In *Queer Representations: Reading Lives, Reading Cultures,* edited by Martin Duberman, 371–77. New York: New York University Press.

Sedgwick, Eve Kosofsky. 1993. *Tendencies.* Durham, NC: Duke University Press.

Shaviro, Steven. 1993. *The Cinematic Body.* Minneapolis: Minnesota University Press.

Stockton, Kathryn Bond. 2004. "Growing Sideways, or Versions of the Queer Child: The Ghost, the Homosexual, the Freudian, the Innocent, and the Interval of Animal." In *Curiouser: On the Queerness of Children,* edited by Steven Bruhm and Natasha Hurley, 277–315. Minneapolis: University of Minnesota Press.

———. 2009. *The Queer Child; or, Growing Sideways in the Twentieth Century.* Durham, NC: Duke University Press.

White Zombie. 1932. Directed by Victor Halperin. Perf. Bela Lugosi, Madge Bellamy, Joseph Cawthorn, Robert Frazer. Edward Halperin Productions.

Wood, Robin. 1998. *Sexual Politics and Narrative Film*. New York: Columbia University Press.

———. 2008. "Freshmeat." *Film Comment* 44 (1): 28–31.

Zorach, William. 1915. "The Dead." *Others: A Magazine of the New Verse* 1 (6): 113.

VAMPIROS MEXICANOS

Nonnormative Sexualities in Contemporary Vampire Novels of Mexico

DANIELLE BORGIA

Since the early nineteenth century, vampire literature has been an accepted way to introduce transgressive representations of sexualities into the cultural imagination of the Western world. The earliest English-language vampire tales expand on the folk legend of the *vardoulacha* from Eastern Europe (specifically Romania, Hungary, and Greece), starting with John Polidori's "The Vampyre" of 1819 featuring the malevolent Lord Ruthven. These sexual transgressions are symbolized by the heightened emotion of fear and disgust with which the human characters regard the vampire protagonists' pleasure in the murders of their victims. As Nina Auerbach, Talia Schaffer, and others have demonstrated, the fictional fear of being preyed on by those whose lives are governed by the carnal pleasure of blood drinking, especially the fear of being irrevocably converted into one of them, represents fear about indulgence in culturally unacceptable sexual behaviors. The sexuality of Count Dracula, the vampire who has most occupied the popular and scholarly imagination since 1897, is "simultaneously different and a parodic mirror" to the sexuality of the human characters, a doubling that "reflects the full complexity of the way one group responds to the sexual customs of another" (1988, 142), as John Allen Stevenson asserts. Whether with Stevenson we read the sexual practices of Count Dracula as representing those of a racially and/or nationally marginalized group, or as figuring the repressed sexual taboos of the dominant culture, vampirism and sexuality are inextricable.

The inseparable fear of and fascination with marginalized sexual behaviors suggested by vampires—including aggressive female sexuality, oral sex, group sex, pedophilia, homosexuality, and necrophilia—communicates the prevailing sexual norms of the author's sociohistorical context and the way that individuals were demonized for transgressing them. Often, the introduction of the vampire and the threats it represents requires its de-struction in order to defend the status quo. In the words of Christopher Craft, "the vampiric abrogation of gender codes inspires a defensive rein-scription of the stabilizing distinctions of gender" (2003, 49). Killing the vampire, then, restores a sharp division between hegemonic masculinities and femininities considered necessary for the smooth functioning of the social order. In other, especially more recent narratives, the vampire is the protagonist that the reader empathizes with and whose sexuality, hegemonic or transgressive, is affirmed.

The narratives of betrayal, conversion, and resistance to conversion that vampire tales contain demonstrate that in the popular cultural imagination, sexual behaviors constitute identities, despite claims by Michel Foucault, Jonathan Katz, and others that sexual practices (specifically homosexual practices) in Europe and the Americas were seen as isolated behaviors, and not associated with permanent identities, until the late nineteenth century. Since then, homoeroticism has often been represented by the literary trope of the vampire, which "fits easily as metaphor for the love that dare not speak its name" (Lord Alfred Douglas quoted in Schaffer 1997, 473), whether in a straightforward manner as in Sheridan Le Fanu's "Carmilla" or through more veiled references as in Bram Stoker's *Dracula*. The text's relative sym-pathy or hostility toward the fictional vampires reflects the cultural context of the author with regard to human sexualities. For example, Anne Rice's *The Vampire Chronicles* introduced the attractive bisexual vampire Lestat to millions of US readers during the 1980s and early 1990s, when the LGBT (lesbian, gay, bisexual, transgender) movement was gaining visibility and popular support.

In contemporary North America, the current craze for literary vampires reflects changes in the dominant sexual narratives of the continent. In the hypersexualized atmosphere of the millennium, the resurgent popularity of vampire novels in the United States, Canada, and Mexico indicates a desire to redefine sexual norms.

Although the majority of twenty-first-century mass-market vampire fic-tions published in English—notably the four best-selling novels by Mormon author Stephenie Meyer, *Twilight* (2005), *New Moon* (2006), *Eclipse* (2007), and *Breaking Dawn* (2008)—ultimately champion a return to conservative sexual mores, other narratives (such as Laurell K. Hamilton's Anita Blake series) reflect more flexible gender roles and more inclusive attitudes to-ward homosexuality, bisexuality, and polyamory. Moreover, the existence of vampire novels that urgently demand monogamous, legally sanctioned heterosexual relationships testifies to the waning of the dominance of traditional configurations of sexuality—as well as the banality of public discourses about sex—in this cultural context. This conservative trend in contemporary US vampire culture has spread to Mexico, with its already more traditional dominant sexual discourse, as a way to reassert the monogamous heterosexual mores sanctioned by the highly influential Catholic Church. For example, the graphic antiabortion messages of *Breaking Dawn/ Amanecer* (2008) were published just one year after abortion was legalized in Mexico City (2007), a change in law that was adopted by only eighteen of the country's thirty-one states and has been overtly rejected by many of its municipal and state legislatures as well as religious organizations (see Lamas 2013, online). The *Twilight/Crepúsculo* series glorifies strictly monogamous, lifelong, heterosexual romantic partnerships begun at a young age that are sanctioned by legal marriage, and the novels firmly proscribe premarital sexual encounters, even between these highly committed partners.

Purity and virginity are the most highly emphasized desirable characteristics for male as well as female characters. The repression and condemnation of female sexuality has a long history in Mexico due to the influence of the Catholic Church, specifically the worship and cultural iconicity of the Virgen de Guadalupe. The condemnation of homosexuality and bisexuality, which continue to be overtly denounced by the Church, has been cemented by influential narratives such as Octavio Paz's *El laberinto de la soledad* (1950). They have also been institutionalized by policing practices that have historically condoned and even perpetrated hate crimes against queer individuals. The most famous of these, *el baile de los 41* held in 1901, consisted of a police raid on a drag ball attended by forty-one gay men from the most elite class of society, who were imprisoned, humiliated, and sent to the Yucatán where they were forced to do hard labor. The public discovery and acknowledgment of the existence of this subculture was a tremendous scandal that has been kept alive in Mexican culture for over a century, popularized by influential literature and illustrations (see Irwin, McCaughan, and Nasser 2003). The number forty-one has been shunned (excluded from addresses, army regiments, police badges, and so on) because it came to symbolize homosexuality as a result of this incident. To date, the Mexican constitution does not specifically prohibit discrimination based on sexual orientation or gender identity, though it does so for other marginalized identities; however, sexuality was included in 2003 in the Federal Law to Prevent and End Discrimination passed by the Mexican Federal Parliament. The law forbids any form of discrimination based on "sexual preferences" but also on "appearance, mannerism, and expression of one's sexual preference or gender" (see "Mexico City Amends Civil Code" 2004, online).

The harassment, violence, and even murder of gays, lesbians, and especially transgender people by law-enforcement authorities chronicled in 1901 continues to this day in Mexico.[1] Yet there is also a growing acceptance of alternative sexual identities in Mexico, reflected to some extent by changes in law and public policy (see "Mexico City Amends Civil Code" 2004, online). This acceptance is reflected by avant-garde vampire narratives that, albeit much less popular with the mass-market readership, are valued by literary critics and academics. This fiction is permeated by empathy and attraction, rather than horror and fascination, for the transgressive vampires. An analysis of three examples of Mexican vampire novels published since 2000, *Vampyr* (2009) by Carolina Andújar, *Amantes de sangre* (2009) by Ramón Obón, and *La sed* (2001) by Adriana Díaz Enciso, traces both the dominant conservative discourses on sexuality in the mass-market novels and the newer acceptance of previously marginalized behaviors and identities in *La sed*.

In contemporary Mexican popular literature, the Gothic narrative of the vampire, which has undeniably been influenced by Meyer's *Twilight* series (translated as *Crepúsculo*), offers a glamorous and romantic return to a social order dominated by conservative gender roles and sexual restraint.[2] The human characters' reactions to their discovery of the vampire nature of the protagonists in these novels, and their resultant fear, censure, and pity of them, reflects current Mexican attitudes toward nonnormative sexualities. For example, some of the best-selling contemporary vampire novels in Mexico, the Colombian Andújar's *Vampyr* (2009) and the Mexican Obón's vampire trilogy *El principe maldito* (2007), *Amantes de sangre* (2009), and *La cofradia secreta* (2010), condemn lesbianism and polyamory.[3] Both *Vampyr* and Obón's trilogy feature a bisexual, promiscuous vampire couple that creates a network of corrupt allies and must be destroyed in order for the heterosexual monogamous love of the protagonists to prevail. Andújar's *Vampyr* (2009), like Meyer's *Twilight* and its sequels, depicts young women who discover that fulfillment consists of relinquishing control of their sexuality (and almost all decision-making responsibility for their lives) to male partners through marriage. In Obón's *Amantes de sangre* (2009), the second of his series, the hegemonic masculinity of the detective protagonist and the malevolent sexuality of the female vampires he encounters express a blatant nostalgia for the uncontested male sexual dominance of women.[4] The popularity of these texts attests not just to Obón's legendary status in Mexican film, but also to the popularity of these narratives of male sexual dominance and female submission, including their demonization of aggressive female heterosexuality.

Some avant-garde fiction introduces more ambiguous portraits of vampires and sexualities through protagonists who are the vampires, not the vampire hunters. One of the most noted in literary circles is Adriana Díaz Enciso's *La sed* (2001), centered on a human-vampire love triangle that brings taboo sexualities to life through haunting encounters of possession and control between two humans and a vampire. The emotional pain that the three protagonists inflict upon each other, unforgettably rendered in Díaz Enciso's vivid narrations of their physical and emotional violence, makes the acceptance and rejection of homosexuality and bisexuality, represented through human sexual, romantic, and platonic relationships with vampires, the central focus of her novel. The differences between mass-market and highbrow literary representations of vampires reflect both the popular resistance toward alternative sexualities in contemporary Mexico and its increasing intellectual and political tolerance of them.

VAMPYR BY CAROLINA ANDÚJAR

Andújar is a young Colombian writer whose website and interviews promoting her first novel, *Vampyr* (2009), position her as an actual vampire in real life outside her fiction.[5] Whether this is the author's fantasy, a marketing ploy, or both, the self-indulgent lust of the male and female vampires that threatens the sexual innocence of the human female protagonists of *Vampyr* depicts a contemporary affirmation of the heteropatriarchal idealization of chastity and monogamy for women. Its demonization of lesbian and bisexual characters supports these hegemonic values, and the plot cements women's submission to male partners even though the female protagonists act independently and show bravery. *Vampyr*'s late nineteenth-century, affluent, Swiss, female boarding-school setting resembles the girl culture of the Irish Sheridan Le Fanu's novella "Carmilla" (1872). As in "Carmilla," the sexual threat to the young virgins appears in the form of lesbian sexuality. Two of the young students, the Hungarian Martina Székely and the Spanish Carmen Miranda, along with their ally Marie, a Swiss maidservant at the school, battle against the forces of evil in the form of a new student, Susana Strossner. The beautiful Susana makes sexual advances toward Marie and manipulates a malleable classmate, Amalia, into having sex with a mysterious man Susana knows. Martina and Carmen, with the help of the local priest, recognize Susana as an ancient Hungarian vampire named Erzsébet Bathory and fight her off with the requisite arsenal of crucifixes, holy water, and incantations. The sinister figure of Susana/Erzsébet casts the aggressive female sexuality, bisexuality, polyamory, and BDSM (bondage, dominance, sadism, masochism) that she represents as evil and corrupt, strongly discouraging the possibilities for readers to consider a broader spectrum of gender and sexuality acceptable.

Both *Vampyr* and *Amantes de sangre* take as their point of departure the legendary historical figure of Erzsébet Bathory (1560–1614), a Hungarian countess who famously kidnapped and murdered more than six hundred young women. Both novels criminalize Bathory as much for her sexuality as for her bloodshed. Rich and related to Slovakian nobility—her cousin was the prince of Transylvania and eventually the king of Poland—Bathory gruesomely tortured her servants and prisoners before killing them. She was popularly, though falsely, rumored to have bathed in the blood of virgins, as recounted in Andújar's novel, to preserve her youth and beauty (McNally 1983, 20). After four noblewomen joined the ranks of the disappeared, Bathory was condemned to live in a tiny cell in her main castle and died four years later. Notably, the "Blood Countess," as she was later called, lured young women to her castle with the promise of an education and the allure of the independence that Bathory herself, as a rich widow, possessed (108). Her cultivation of black magic; her closeness to her aunt, Countess Karla Bathory, who reputedly murdered two of her four husbands and had affairs with women; and her possible links to the family of Vlad Dracula all contribute to the black legend of Erzsébet Bathory. Both Andújar and Obón cast their female vampire protagonists as reincarnations of this historical figure, who was purportedly transformed into a vampire at the time her mortal death was reported. The invocation of this nefarious woman whose sexual practices involved serial killing relates the transgression of hegemonic sexualities that vampirism represents in Gothic fictions to contemporary Mexican crime tabloids. Critics such as Daniel Hallin have observed the ways that contemporary Mexican audiences have become accustomed to *la nota roja*: journalism including reality shows, crime series, and tabloids such as *Alarma!* and *La policiaca* bearing gruesome photos of death scenes (2000, 268). In this context, the novels' linking of the fictional narratives to a historical context through the figure of Bathory lends legitimacy to their censure of nonhegemonic sexualities and both assumes and strengthens its popular support.

The threat of vampirism in Andújar's novel, as the unspoken fear of lesbians, makes its young female protagonists' ability not only to enjoy intimate friendships with each other, but also to live independent lives outside marriage, seem problematically transgressive and dangerous. Upon graduation, Martina's inheritance of the fortune of her aunt, who enjoyed her own single

lifestyle, enables her to live alone. The economic and historical legacy of female freedom that is willed to Martina threatens the dominant social order.
For the young European women of *Vampyr*, money means mobility: "Nos
quedamos hablando horas y fantaseando con ver un mundo que habría
permanecido oculto, sin permisos paternales o de un esposo que dispusiera
de nuestros actos" (We spent hours talking and fantasizing about seeing a
world that would have remained unknown, without parental permission or
a husband that controlled our actions) (Andújar 2009, 143).[6] Martina tells
her lawyer that she never wants to get married, instead preferring to "dedi-
carme a recorrer el mundo sin restricciones de ninguna clase" (dedicate myself to traveling the world without any type of restrictions) (194). For an elite
nineteenth-century woman, this would have been an impossible flouting of
culture and convention; for the millennial upper-middle-class Mexican female reader, such independence is possible, but not generally condoned.

To quell this threat of gender subversion, the neo-Gothic vampire novel
must return Martina and her friend Carmen to the status quo through the
romance plot, by which they voluntarily reject their independence (and the
possibilities for either a lesbian or straight single lifestyle) and reinscribe
themselves in patriarchy for the protection and acceptance that it affords.
The threat of the vampire drives Carmen into the arms of her previously
rejected ex-boyfriend Giovanni and forces Martina to rely on the protection of a mysterious male stranger. Martina, who likes to think of herself as
independent, constantly proves her need to be "rescued" from the clutches
of the vampires, a role that a mysterious male stranger repeatedly fulfills. As
Carmen points out, the threat of vampires has brought Martina romance:
"[t]ienes un protector que te salva cuando estás en peligro" (you have a protector that saves you when you are in danger) (250), she sighs. Martina falls
in love with this shadowy stranger, who later reveals his name to be Adrien
Almos. Adrien, a human who has been bitten by Erzsébet, owes a debt to Edward Cullen of *Twilight*. Like Edward, he is a handsome vampire that refuses
to feed on humans; he stalks her with an uncanny ability to know her every
move; and he expresses intense jealousy. As in the *Twilight* saga, the female
finds these attributes overwhelmingly seductive. Martina suddenly surren-
ders to his magnetic charm, explaining, "[s]abía el riesgo que corría estando
cerca de Adrien. Aun así, no tenía la fuerza de voluntad para separarme de
él" (I knew the risk I was taking in being close to Adrien. Even so, I did
not have the strength of will to separate myself from him) (368). Although
the sexual danger posed by Susana is easily rejected by the protagonist, the
lurking sexuality of Adrien, who might give in to his thirst at any moment,
irresistibly attracts her. His repressed vampirism represents a hegemonic

masculinity in which virility is paired, seemingly necessarily, with a danger that attributes to straight men a possibility of a source of violence and sexual aggression that is innate and biological. Martina's love for Adrien therefore positions the sexual attraction and submission to men as the only culturally acceptable behavior for young women.

The rejection of alternative sexual behaviors is most evident in *Vampyr* when Martina, attending a party at a Parisian castle, finds herself in secluded chambers governed by Erzsébet in which:

> *varias jovenes de escasa edad caminaban desnudas, llevando jarras y volcando su contenido dentro de un enorme baño de sangre. Sus níveas pieles contrastaban con el líquido rojo en que se sumergían, mientras reían y se besaban entre sí . . . dos de las niñas le prodigaban caricias y ella evidenciaba su deleite estremeciéndose y haciendo rechinar su colmillos.*

> *(various women of quite young ages walked about naked, carrying jars and emptying their contents into an enormous bath of blood. Their snow-white skins contrasted with the red liquid in which they submerged themselves while they laughed and kissed each other . . . two of the girls lavished her with caresses and she evidenced her delight by shuddering and baring her fangs.) (239)*

This scene of female group sexuality and sadism immediately makes Martina vomit. The protagonist proves her virginal purity and hegemonic femininity through her body's instinctive recoil from the pansexuality of Erzsébet's vampire women. Clearly, Martina's desire can only be awakened by a man.

Furthermore, *Vampyr* also insists that the sexual attraction to men must be safely controlled by the culturally sanctioned institution of marriage. When Susana's consort, Johannes Ujvary, seduces a susceptible classmate, Martina and Carmen regard the incident as repulsive rather than curious or intriguing. The novel casts this sexual encounter as an issue of female power; the student Amalia submits to Johannes not from sexual temptation or his physical threat, but because of Susana's commanding influence over her. Susana tells Amalia that she cannot share her hard-won secrets of eternal beauty with a virgin: "Quiero mucho ser tu amiga. Quiero poder confiar en ti. Pero sólo podré hacerlo una vez estés con un hombre. Así seremos iguales y . . . podré contarte todos mis secretos" (I want very much to be your friend. I want to be able to confide in you. But I can only do that once you have been with a man. Then we will be equals and . . . I can tell you all of my secrets) (160). Amalia is unpopular and eager to do anything to maintain Susana's confidences: "no quería que Susana pensara que yo era una niña tonta e inexperta. Quería que me considerara digna de su amistad" (I didn't want Susana to think that I was a dumb and inexperienced girl. I wanted her to consider me worthy of her friendship) (169). The shameful emotion surrounding this event, which is discovered and amplified when Martina and Carmen read her diary, and the sinister characterization of Susana, who goes on to convert Amalia into a vampire, suggest a censure of female friends who engage in and advocate sex outside of marriage as well as vilifying women's sexual attractions to each other.

Unlike the weak and contemptible Amalia, the heroine Martina regards the sexual advances of Johannes with horror when he later attempts to force himself upon her. The contrast of her fear of Johannes with her attraction to her rescuer Adrien not only disciplines young, straight, female desire, but also channels it toward men who have the self-control to contain sex within marriage. The hero Adrien is dying because of his refusal to drink blood (read: engage in sex), and Martina helps free him from this torture by discovering the key to unlock a labyrinthine door deep in a castle. This Gothic trope of opening what has been sealed and forbidden to all except these two chosen characters prefigures the legitimate sexuality of Martina, safely contained within her marriage to Adrien by the end of *Vampyr*.

In all of these ways, Andújar's vampire narrative battles to restigmatize multiple sexual possibilities for women, presenting the containment of women's sexuality submissively within straight marriage as the only plausible alternative in an era that actually manifests increasing female sexual independence in Mexico. The novel's condemnation of lesbians reflects a popular Mexican prejudice against *tortilleras*, with their implied rejection of maternal Guadalupana constructions of hegemonic femininity, even as male homosexuality and especially bisexuality is increasingly tolerated and to some extent publicly acknowledged by public figures in recent years.[7] One of the most esteemed vampire novels in the history of Mexican literature, *El vampiro de la colonia Roma* by Luis Zapata Quiroz (1979), features a gay male vampire prostitute as its protagonist. It was not the first work of Mexican literature to contain references to homosexuality, but many consider this novel, quite controversial and even labeled "pornographic" in its day, a historical precedent because of its establishment of homosexuality as an acceptable topic in Mexican literature and of gay men as figures to identify with rather than reject.[8] Despite this gradual acceptance by the literary intelligentsia, the gatekeepers of sexual mores in Mexico have remained highly resistant to queer identities. With regard to high-ranking public figures, extortion and incarceration, as well as the violence that threatens all classes, are still major threats to closeted bisexual and gay males; however, popular demonstrations protesting attacks on queer youth, as well as changes in employment legislation (if not practice), testify as to the influence of the LGBT movement in Mexico.

The reproduction of homophobia in mass-market contemporary Mexican vampire novels such as Andújar's attests to the fact that the tolerance of queer identities in Mexico has been fairly recent and far less widespread than in the United States.[9] The first LGBT organization, the Frente de Liberación Homosexual, was formed at the Universidad Nacional Autónoma de México (UNAM) in 1971, its membership comprised of about 50 percent gay men and 50 percent lesbians (see Mogrovejo 2000, 63–68). The first gay-pride march in Mexico was held on July 26, 1978. Gay marriage was legalized in Mexico, but only in the Distrito Federal, on December 21, 2009, a ruling that reformed article 146 of the civil code and went into effect as of March 2010 (Archundia 2010, online). This context of gay liberation's political gains despite a homophobic hegemony is reflected in elite intellectuals' praise for Zapata and Díaz Enciso in the wake of the popular preference for the authors Andújar and Obón.

AMANTES DE SANGRE BY RAMÓN OBÓN

The representation of the sexual agency of queers and single women as immoral found in Andújar's *Vampyr* also surfaces in male-authored vampire novels popular in contemporary Mexico, such as Ramón Obón's trilogy. Obón is a Mexican lawyer better known as the screenwriter of legendary Mexican horror movies such as Fernando Méndez's *El vampiro* (1957) and *Misterios de ultratumba* (1959), as well as *Con gritos de terror* (1964), inspired by the works of Edgar Allan Poe. Obón's first novel *El príncipe maldito* (2008), centered on the dark crimes of the malevolent male vampire Vládislav, completely sold out its first edition. The second installment of his trilogy, *Amantes de sangre* (2009), which focuses on the female vampire Sophía de Ferenc, has also been very popular.[10] The book jacket advertises the novels with language linked to the horror films Obón is known for: "Prepárese para una pasión maldita que desatará el terror que nadie podrá sobrevivir" (Prepare yourselves for an evil passion that will unleash a terror that no one can survive). Obón's novels, although they employ the main tropes of the Gothic vampire tradition, are part detective, part bloodbath, featuring both long fight scenes in which the male protagonist, RR, asserts his masculinity by defeating mortal men and gory, detailed descriptions of the murderous rampages of the vampires. Both are tied to male sexual dominance over women and in Obón's trilogy, female sexuality is again cast as evil. The book jacket of *Amantes de sangre* makes this explicit: "La muerte tiene forma de mujer, tan sensual como mortífera, tan erótica como sanguinaria, tan apasionada como cruel" (Death has the form of a woman, as sensual as she is deadly, as erotic as she is bloody, as passionate as she is cruel). This narrative, cited repeatedly in the sensual, sinister descriptions of the two female vampires throughout the novel, unites sexuality and death in a way that configures the sexually liberated woman, and sexual desire itself, as a danger to the lives of his readers, who identify with Sophía's sexually restrained enemies, the macho everyman detective RR and the capable policewoman Catherine Bancroft.

In *Amantes de sangre,* the vampires' taking of human victims, mass rampages, and conversion of humans into vampire slaves configure a complicated world of polyamory, bisexuality, and BDSM that bestows them with a power that must be destroyed to preserve the status quo. Like Andújar's *Vampyr,* the plot's criminalization of the vampires condemns nonmonogamous and nonheterosexual behavior. Moreover, the novel prescribes culturally acceptable femininity as characterized by sexual restraint and deference to male authority. The villainous female vampires Sophía de Ferenc and Ditzah Benazir use their sex appeal, described as "los recursos que la Natureleza y sobre todo la experiencia de sórdidos e incontables amantes le habían dotado" (the resources that Nature and above all the experience of sordid and innumerable lovers had given them) (Obón 2009, 113), to manipulate both human and immortal men. In stark contrast, the human heroine Catherine keeps herself aloof, literally shutting the door connecting her hotel room to that of RR despite her desire to be with him. The heroine's appeal is based on the withholding of her body, as opposed to the sexual indulgence of the the vampires. RR's love for the chaste Catherine and his contempt for the female vampires' sexuality champion hegemonic Mexican gender and sexual identities, though adapted to a contemporary, world-traveling, dual-career lifestyle.

The vampire plot of *Amantes de sangre* continually asserts male fears that female sexuality will make women uncontrollable and, worse, able to rule over men. This becomes most clear when RR travels to Veracruz to consult the psychic Esther, a "bruja blanca" (white witch), who induces him to dream, using the native hallucinogenic plant *ololiuhqui.* His resultant vision of Catherine as half-human, half-beast (from the waist down) reveals his deepest fear that Catherine, like Sophía, is capable of a sexual passion that he figures as "animal." The apparition of the ghosts of his wife and child, killed long ago in a car accident, in this dream indicate that he fears loving a woman because it will expose him to vulnerability. This male fear and mistrust of women symbolized by the vampirism and tabooed sexuality of Sophía that RR projects onto Catherine in this dream are shared by Mustafa, one of Sophía's slaves. Mustafa's fear and hatred of Catherine results from their encounter in *El príncipe maldito* when she condemned him to a tiny jail cell. Mustafa wants to rape her for revenge, imagining his ability to take back the masculinity that his arrest had stripped away. Both Mustafa and RR—each in his own way—fear the sexually attractive women's ability to render them impotent.

Sophía is a grave problem for RR not just because of her murderous, rampaging sexual appetite, but also because he cannot control her. Not only has she come back from the dead in this sequel, defying his ability to vanquish the threat of evil she possesses, but she also lures him to unsuccessfully chase after her. She continually evades him, and later takes him captive, holding Catherine hostage. Even when RR knows how dangerous the vampire is, he continues to fear his susceptibility to her charms, musing that "[l]a sensual belleza que mareaba, el hálito de lujuria que desprendía, podían hacerle perder al cabeza y eso sería fatal" (her sensual, dizzying beauty, the air of lechery that she emanated, could make him lose his head, and that would be fatal) (317). This attraction represents the threat of male sexual submission to both women and men, a possibility that men might fear. When Sophía commands him to uncover Vládislav's tomb in twenty-four hours—an impossible task—he is angry to find himself powerless to negotiate with her: "Con aquella mujer maldita no habría demora ni pretextos" (With that damn woman there would be no delays nor excuses) (321). Significantly, Sophía's only interest in taking the blood of RR is related to her plan to use him to release Vládislav. In the figure of this female vampire, the woman who pursues her own sexual gratification weakens the man forced to submit to her for her own ends.

The shame of a woman's rejection or a queer encounter that underlies RR's repugnance for Sophía is deepened by the lesbian encounters of the female vampires in the novel. Sophía selects victims that she converts into vampires to serve as her accomplices in the kidnapping of Catherine and RR. One of her most vicious associates is Ditzah Benazir, an extremely seductive Egyptian belly dancer. Ditzah's worship of Sophía, her desire for Catherine, and the lust that Sophía's male slave Mustafa feels for Ditzah form a complex web of loyalties. Ditzah displays control of her sexuality through fantasy and substitution in order to sustain the vampire hierarchy. The narrative

describes how Ditzah's lust for Catherine "despertaba sus instintos de depre-
dadora. Su mirada se concentraba obsesiva en aquella yugular que palpitaba
imperceptiblemente y en la cual deseaba clavar sus colmillos y succionarle la
existencia" (had awoken her predatory instincts. Her gaze obsessively concentrated on that jugular vein that throbbed imperceptibly and into which
she desired to sink her fangs, sucking out her life) (145). But because Sophía
has forbidden her to kill Catherine, Ditzah "tenía que encontrar con quién
saciar aquel apetito que le daba vida" (had to find someone with whom to sa-
tiate that appetite that gave her life) (145) and sucks the blood of a handsome
young marine instead. Ditzah returns to him for several nights, prolong-
ing her pleasure instead of spending herself at once like the inexperienced
sailor (and by extension, the ignorant average male, who does not have her
sexual expertise). Pain and pleasure are described as occurring in the same
instant when the vampire takes her victim. This mastery of both, within
Sophía's web of immortals, occurs only in the female characters; as a result,
the men form the lowest rank of her servants as henchmen and thugs. Even
though Sophía is ultimately ruled by her love of Vládislav, the women wield
the power; therefore, this world must be destroyed to restore the hegemonic
world order.

Despite this villainization of the vampires in *Amantes de sangre*, ironically, the novel redeems the love of the vampire couple for each other in that
it mirrors the hegemonic romance plot of lovers separated but pledged to
each other for eternity. Their passion for each other is described in heroic
terms. For example, when she returns to where RR and his allies had sealed
Vládislav into a mountain in *El príncipe maldito*, she wails, "Éste es aquel
sitio en donde nuestros enemigos, con sus artilugios abominables, conden-
aron a mi amado a la prisión eternal" (This is the place where our enemies,
with their abominable gadgets, condemned my lover to eternal prison) (320).
Sophía's pain at her separation from her vampire lover Vládislav is portrayed
with pathos, creating both the possibility for sexual "deviants" to return to
the safety of heterosexual monogamy and punishing them for transgressing.

This representation of monogamy depicts Sophía de Ferenc, in a Gothic
fashion, as feeling a deep bond that connects her to her beloved and even
helps her to sense his presence. Sophía has also followed the Romantic pattern of waiting to be reunited with her lover—in this case, for centuries. Yet
she has not refrained from satiating her needs with the bodies of others in
the meantime. She takes victims at will, even a wild pig in the forest, because
"[n]ecesitaba alimentar su cuerpo aunque fuera con la sangre de una bestia
miserable como aquella" (she needed to nurture her body, even if it was with
the blood of a miserable beast like that one) (322). In describing Sophía's

vampirism, the novel characterizes her sexuality as both carnal appetite and an outlet for her emotional frustration (both considered unacceptable sexual motivations for women). The novel similarly casts her lover Vládislav as a dangerous sexual predator when his first action on being released from his tomb is to feed on a large group of victims, a rampage that includes the brutal rape of a female scientist. The discovery of the bloody scene by the police captain reestablishes the hegemonic control of patriarchal social institutions. His authority absolutely dispels any reader sympathy for Vládislav's years of confinement below ground. The criminalization of Vládislav and Sophía, despite the humanity of their passion for each other, carefully directs the reader to condemn promiscuity and to devalue relationships that are not confined to monogamy. The vampires are evil because they do not regulate their sexuality and their emotions like the level-headed RR and Catherine.

Sophía and the reawakened Vládislav are driven by their passion, characterized as savage and uncontrollable; their frenzied sexual encounter when they are reunited starkly contrasts with the interaction of RR and Catherine, who have patiently waited, calculated, and hesitated to enter into a romantic relationship, let alone consummate it. No sexual contact takes place between Catherine and RR in the novel; as is the case in *Vampyr*, the promise of heterosexual monogamy sanctioned by marriage is held out as the protagonists' ultimate goal. Their relieved embrace after they finally kill the two vampires suggests that they will now begin the courtship they had been skirting. This pairing of condemned versus redeeming love follows the Gothic pattern of disciplining the readers' sexuality. Vládislav's violently jealous rage punishes Sophía (and women like her who have used their sexuality to better their social and economic positions) for her independence.

The narrative pays further homage to male dominance and glorifies the submission of even modern, capable women through RR's rescue of Catherine. Despite her career as a brave Interpol agent, she must be delivered from the clutches of Sophía and Ditzah through his intervention; he finds the heroine completely helpless, tied down and even too weak to speak. Ditzah's sensuous feeding on the captive woman also insinuates a lesbian encounter with the policewoman; yet succumbing to RR's possessive claims to her rescues Catherine from this threat. Catherine's submissiveness in her relationship with RR reinscribes her traditional femininity, offsetting her hegemonically masculine qualities of bravery, independence, and lack of emotion.

Amantes de sangre widens its condemnation of women with sexual agency by connecting its vampire story to other legends of evil women. RR is aided by Jeremías, a Jesuit vampirologist who claims that the Civavateo, the spirits of Aztec women who had died in childbirth who haunted crossroads to kidnap children, were actually vampires. Jeremías also surmises that the vampire Sophía has connections to the medieval countess Erzsébet Bathory, and insists that Sophía herself visited Erzsébet in her castle. This connection is confirmed by a New York woman with ties to the case who claims to be the descendant of one of Bathory's daughters. Jeremías's conjectures place Sophía and Ditzah within a global historical framework through which men have blamed women for frightening, unexplained deaths.

LA SED BY ADRIANA DÍAZ ENCISO

Deliberately blurring the binaries of gender and sexuality propagated in the mass-market novels of Andújar and Obón, the vampire love triangle at the heart of Adriana Díaz Enciso's *La sed* (2001) explores bisexuality and polyamory in ways that envision these sexualities as viable. Díaz Enciso transforms the demonized figure of the vampire through the melancholy of her character Samuel, whose haunting desire to be loved (like the US vampire Lestat) defies hegemonic gender categories. In *La sed*, the vampire's immortality and drinking of human blood signals not just sexual and gender transgressions, but also complex emotional states. Its three protagonists, simultaneously human and vampire, are deeply haunted by their inability to connect emotionally with others. Their sexual "thirst" has an almost spiritual component. As Guillermo Samperio's book review states, in *La sed*, "el vampiro se encuentra también trastocado en un ser de infinita tristeza y no en una bestia infernal sedienta de sangre" (one finds the vampire changed into an infinitely sad human being and not a hideous, bloodthirsty beast) (Samperio 2002, 66). Samuel, who committed suicide in the nineteenth century and became a vampire, is obsessed with Izhar, an Egyptian loner who survives by selling drugs in Paris. Desperate to keep Izhar's companionship even after being romantically rejected by him, Samuel offers the younger man a voyage around the world (and home to his native country) on his private yacht in exchange for helping him seduce a vampire companion. The listless detachment of Sandra, a young Mexican woman desperately mourning the death of her father ten years before, makes her Samuel and Izhar's target. The interdependencies that form between the three of them on the ship bind them together in ways that present sexuality as subordinate to emotion for all genders.

Unlike the Gothic vampires of Andújar and Obón, the insatiable thirst that the vampires feel in *La sed* has nothing to do with sexual appetite, of which they retain little. Sandra, when she has been converted to an immortal without her consent or understanding, thinks of herself as having a sexual hunger that supersedes any morality and any other way of relating to human beings, but Samuel corrects her. Sandra, like Samuel, has "la sed," a thirst, for love, so strong that she will try to evoke this emotion from any possible source (strangers, refugees, ex-lovers, and even her best friend's infant). The draining of the source's blood symbolizes the draining of their emotion; the constant thirst reveals the inability of any human to meet the intense emotional need of the vampires. Yet their desperate searching is not portrayed simply as repulsive and criminal, as in *Vampyr* and the *Amantes de sangre* trilogy. Sandra's interiority inspires the reader with compassion for her pansexuality and even pedophilia; it portrays her behavior as motivated by alienation, desperation, and depression.

When Sandra finally realizes that Samuel and Izhar have conspired to make her a vampire, she ironically finds comfort in this terrifying identity. Formerly drifting, unconscious even of her own lack of a will to live, Sandra feels that "[a]hora la percepción de sus sentidos y la gravedad de la revelación de lo que era, poseían una claridad que la vida nunca antes había tenido para ella. Desaparecía la vaguedad que había rodeado sus actos de humana, llevándola sin rumbo por una existencia absurda" (now the perception of her senses and the gravity of the revelation of what she was possessed had a clarity that life had never before had for her. The vagueness that had surrounded her human actions, carrying her aimlessly through an absurd existence, disappeared) (185). Her new vampire focus on feeding, or seizing what she needs from others without the slightest consideration of their own wishes, gives her a purpose. This inhumanely narcissistic drive reflects the suicidal nature that she and Samuel shared in their human forms. Sandra begins to comprehend Samuel's profound love for Izhar and his sexual identity. For example, when she accidentally sees a man whom she realizes that Samuel has seduced for temporary companionship, first when alive and later when dead, she intuitively recognizes that this stranger has only been a stand-in for Izhar, a straight man who cannot return Samuel's love. This emotional intelligence draws her closer to the older vampire. Their deepening connection creates empathy in the reader for homosexuals and a deepened understanding of homosexuality. Izhar cares about Samuel; he simply cannot return the desire Samuel feels for him.

The haunted atmosphere of *La sed* expands traditionally passive Mexican female identities with the internal changes the female protagonist undergoes as a result of her supernatural transformation. In the photos Sandra begs Izhar to take of her, she sees what she had not understood about her new vampire identity. She sees that Samuel's bite has given her what she never had as a human: ambition for self-knowledge and self-determination. Sandra's newfound thirst for her own image is a desire to figuratively create her own life, which she never before wanted to achieve. Yet at the same time, Izhar feels that taking pictures of Sandra allows him to possess her, enabling him to finally feel love for her in addition to the sexual desire he has felt for her from the onset. Correspondingly, Samuel, who has positioned himself as Sandra's creator and master, becomes infuriated when he sees Sandra reveling in these images and destroys them, asserting his authority to control her sexuality and emotions as well as expressing his jealousy of Izhar's fascination with her. Sandra, in having her newfound agency thus challenged, learns to value it. This development explains the emptiness in her human relationships with men: her lack of understanding of the tie between her sexuality and her emotional and spiritual emptiness. This awakening in Sandra symbolizes feminisms extant in Mexico since the Revolution but only now struggling to assert themselves within the hegemonic spheres of social institutions (see Macias 1982).

This supernatural desire for affection that consumes the two vampires also haunts Izhar, though he remains human. He periodically takes a human companion on board the ship with them, but the jealousy of the vampires soon puts an end to these women's lives. He cannot sustain a life in which any human connection he makes is abruptly suspended by Samuel and Sandra's feeding on his companion, attempting to siphon the emotional energy he has casually bestowed on her. He eventually leaves them both. Yet his suicide at the end of the novel reveals that despite his abandonment of them, he cannot bear to live without the vampires' passionate need for him. His inability to go "home" even as he reaches the lands where he once lived demonstrates that he, too, has developed an unnatural thirst, and suggests that the love triangle that has developed is not only destructive, but also sustaining. The multiple relationships and diverse sexualities depicted in the novel do not cease to be tumultuous and unsettling, but by its end, they have become understandable instead of impossible in the cultural imagination. Invoking and inverting the already widely circulated trope of vampirism enables *La sed* to expand the gendered imagination of its contemporary Mexican audience.

Vampyr, Amantes de sangre, and *La sed* demonstrate that vampire fictions can give visibility to sexual identities marginalized by dominant norms even within the parameters of dominant literary discourse. By depicting the desires of the vampires as part of the cultural imagination, these novels acknowledge the growing public visibility of Mexico's queer community and public discourse about nontraditional sexualities such as bisexuality, poly-amory, and BDSM even when they assign negative and criminal connota-tions to them. However, another recent vampire novel, *Vlad* (2010), written by the acclaimed Mexican author Carlos Fuentes, shores up the dominant narratives about sexuality that prevail in the popular Mexican imagination: males as predators, with women and children as easily corruptible prey.[11] The supernatural trope of the vampire sheds light on the real power rela-tions among the gendered identities that the characters represent. The lesbian struggle for visibility within Mexico's academic and political organizations for gender equality, let alone family life, is reflected in their harsh condem-nation in the neo-Gothic vampire novels of Andújar and Obón. In stark contrast, Díaz Enciso's rendering of vampirism asks her readers to question whether it is true that violence arises from the readers' refusals to recognize the humanity of those with nonhegemonic sexual identities or practices. The literary trope of vampirism continues to be used in Mexican literature to explore sexualities that are marginalized in mainstream representation. However, the wide variety of themes expressed in Mexican vampire narra-tives reflects the heterogeneity of the discourses of sexuality in the country itself in the early 2000s.

NOTES

1. See Israel Dávila, "Formal prisión a profesor gay que protestó por discriminación," *La jornada*, 14 mayo 2009; Miroslava Breach Valduncia, "Denuncian despido de una policía por ser homosexual," *La jornada*, 15 mayo 2013; Rodolfo Valadez Luviano, "Condena activista la vejación cometida por policías contra dos gays en Tlapa," *La jornada*, 31 julio 2012; "Maltrato y abuso policial generalizado de lesbianas, gays, bisexuales y personas transgénero," *Amnestia internacional*, doc.es.amnesty.org; "Trabajadoras sexuales transgénero acusan abuso policial en Chihuahua," *La policiaca*, 28 octubre 2014; "México: Hostigamiento de personas trans-género en Aguascalientes," 29 abril 2002, www.omct.org; IGHLRC (International Human Rights Clinic and the Human Rights Program of Harvard Law School), "The Violations of the Rights of Lesbian, Gay, Bisexual and Transgender Persons in Mexico," March 15, 2010, www.globalrights.org.

2. Other English-language vampire novels whose translations have been successful in Mexico include *La Casa de la Noche* series by P. C. Cast and Kristin Cast, *Despertar* by L. J. Smith, and the series *Muerto Hasta el Anochecer* by Charlaine Harris (the basis of the HBO series *True Blood*).

3. The only other mass-market vampire novel written by a Mexican author so far is *Nocturna*, the first installment of director Guillermo de Toro's highly anticipated *La Trilogía de la Oscuridad*, written with Chuck Hogan. For more about the popularity of vampire novels in contemporary Mexico, see interviews with Carmina Rufrancos of Grupo Planeta

and Diego Mejía from Random House Mondadori in Yanet Aguilarsosa's "Seduce la onda vampírica."

4. These themes also appear in Mario Acevedo's Chicano male vampire detective series, which includes *X-Rated Blood Suckers* (2004), *The Nymphos of Rocky Flats* (2006), *The Undead Kama Sutra* (2008), and *Jailbait Zombie* (2009).

5. See, for example, http://vampyrlibro.blogspot.com and http://carolinaandujar.blog spot.com.

6. All translations from the original Spanish texts are mine.

7. For the history of the word *tortillera* to mean *lesbian* in Mexico, see Quiroz Ennis's article "Sobre la etimología de la tortilla."

8. For further information on the history of homosexual themes in Mexican literature from Salvador Novo and Xavier Villarutia to the present, see Luis Martín Ulloa (2007) and León Guillermo Gutiérrez (2012).

9. In Oaxaca, Zapotecan transwomen called *muxe* have been accepted and even revered in society since precolonial times, and since the mid-twentieth century have become *vestidas*, openly cross-dressing (see Stephen 2002, 43).

10. Obón's third novel, *La cofradía secreta*, was released on November 24, 2010.

11. I have not discussed Fuentes's most recent novel because of its lack of popularity and critical acclaim; the only celebrity to have publicly endorsed it is the film director Guillermo del Toro.

WORKS CITED

Aguilarsosa, Yanet. 2009. "Seduce la onda vampírica." *El Universal*. 15 April, 2009. Accessed June 10, 2009. http://www.eluniversal.com.mx/sociedad/2563.html.

Andújar, Carolina. 2009. *Vampyr*. Bogotá: Grupo Editorial Norma.

Archundia, Mónica. 2010. "La primera unión gay, para marzo." *El universal*. January 5, 2010. Accessed January 27, 2010. http://www.eluniversal.com.mx/ciudad/99607.html.

Auerbach, Nina. 1995. *Our Vampires, Ourselves*, Chicago: University of Chicago Press.

Craft, Christopher. 2003. "'Kiss Me with Those Red Lips': Gender and Inversion in Bram Stoker's *Dracula*." In *Bloom's Modern Critical Interpretations: Bram Stoker's "Dracula,"* edited by Harold Bloom, 39–69. Philadelphia: Chelsea House.

Díaz Enciso, Adriana. 2001. *La sed*. México: Secretaria de Cultura Puebla: Colibrí.

Foucault, Michel. 1978. *The History of Sexuality*. Vol. 1. New York: Pantheon.

Ennis, Quiroz. 1998. "Sobre la etimología de la tortilla." *Debate Feminista* 9:269–77.

Gutiérrez, León Guillermo. 2012. "Sesenta años del cuento mexicano de temática gay." *Anales de literature hispanoamericana* 41:277–98.

Hallin, Daniel C. 2000. "*La Nota Roja*: Popular Journalism and the Transition to Democracy in Mexico." In *Tabloid Tales: Global Debates over Media Standards*, edited by Colin Sparks and John Tulloch, 267–84. London: Rowman and Littlefield.

Irwin, Robert McKee, Edward J. McCaughan, and Michelle Rocio Nasser. 2003. *The Famous 41: Sexuality and Social Control in Mexico, 1901*. New York: Palgrave Macmillan.

Katz, Jonathan. 1996. *The Invention of Heterosexuality*. New York: Plume.

Lamas, Marta. 2013. "La despenalizacion del aborto en el Distrito Federal." *La jornada.* 29 noviembre 2013.

Macias, Anna. 1982. *Against All Odds: The Feminist Movement in Mexico to 1940.* Westport, CT: Greenwood Press.

McNally, Raymond T. 1983. *Dracula Was a Woman: In Search of the Blood Countess of Transylvania.* New York: McGraw-Hill.

"Mexico City Amends Civil Code to Include Transgender Rights." June 15, 2004. Accessed July 20, 2010. www.iglhrc.org

Mogrovejo, Norma. 2000. *Un amor que se atrevió a decir su nombre: La lucha de las lesbianas y su relación con los movimientos homosexual y feminista en América Latina.* México: Plaza y Valdés.

Obón, Ramón. 2009. *Amantes de sangre.* México: Ediciones B.

Samperio, Guillermo. 2002. "El gótico de Adriana Díaz Enciso: *La sed.*" *La cultura en México/Siempre!* May 29, suppl. 48 (2554): 66–67.

Schaffer, Talia. 1997. "'A Wilde Desire Took Me': The Homoerotic History of Dracula." In Bram Stoker, *Dracula,* edited by Nina Auerbach and David J. Skaal, 470–82. New York: W. W. Norton.

Stephen, Lynn. 2002. "Sexualities and Genders in Zapotec Oaxaca." *Latin American Perspectives* 29:41–59.

Stevenson, John Allen. 1988. "A Vampire in the Mirror: The Sexuality of Dracula." *PMLA* 103:139–49.

Ulloa, Luis Martín. 2007. "El tema homosexual en la literatura mexicana." Presented at the Universidad de Guadalajara, Mexico, 2007. http://www.naua.se/Mexico07/Pub/Documentos/Luis_Ulloa_P.pdf. Accessed September 11, 2008.

HYBRIDITY SUCKS

European Vampirism Encounters Haitian Voodoo in
The White Witch of Rosehall

MONIKA MUELLER

Annie Palmer, "the white witch of Rose Hall," was a Jamaican plantation owner of British descent, who, according to the widespread
lore about her, not only killed her three husbands in the 1820s but
also practiced voodoo[1] and acquired a reputation for excessively whipping
her slaves. Her legend has inspired two novels, a folk song, and several performances. While Johnny Cash's 1973 song "The Legend of Annie Palmer"
focuses on Annie as a sadistic slave owner and husband killer, Herbert G. de
Lisser's 1929 novel *The White Witch of Rosehall*—the thematic focus of this
essay—presents the legendary Annie as a "white witch" who instrumentalized both Haitian voodoo and European vampirism in order to dominate,
and in some cases also to kill, the people who happened to cross her path.
In doing so, she also became a symbol of the brutality of colonial presence
in the Caribbean.

The legend of Annie Palmer is part of Jamaican oral history and varies
depending on the source one consults. Annie Palmer was born around 1800
in England (Pifer 2001, 177); according to one version of the story, her parents came to Haiti in 1812 and died soon thereafter, leaving the task of raising Annie to a nanny who was a voodoo practitioner (see Pifer 2001, 177).
Another version, however, has it that her parents did not die right away and
deliberately introduced her to a highly renowned voodoo priestess, who was
socially respected and far from only being a nanny (see de Lisser [1929] 1958,
135–36). Around 1818, Annie moved to Jamaica and soon married Robert
Palmer, the first of her three husbands. Drury Pifer gives a vivid account of
Annie and her relationship with the three men who fell victim to her initial
attractions:

When the English man, John Palmer, first saw her, he was bowled over.
She resembled the clever heroine in a Jane Austen novel. It would never
have occurred to the gentleman that this lovely creature had been up
to her elbows in blood rituals. . . . [S]he was dainty enough to convince
any lover that what she needed most was male protection. (2001, 177)

John Palmer purportedly died of arsenic poisoning, but Annie claimed that
a fever had carried him off. Her second husband went the same way. Number
three, however, was stabbed and then finished off by having hot oil poured
into his ear (see Pifer 2001, 177–78). In addition to killing her husbands, Annie also transgressed social norms by allegedly having sexual relations with
slaves, whom she often subsequently murdered (see "The White Witch of
Jamaica" 2011, online). Mike Henry writes in his 2005 romance novel *Rose
Hall's White Witch: The Legend of Annie Palmer* (a somewhat sanitized up-
date of de Lisser's story of Annie): "[I]t was rumoured that Annie could only
find satisfaction from the choicest of her slaves, who were favoured by late
night calls and visits" (viii). Pifer, who tells Annie's story in his account of
the life of American tycoon John Rollins, the man who bought Rose Hall
Plantation and turned it into a resort, succinctly characterizes Annie Palmer as "the colonial Caribbean at its worst" (2001, 177). "Raised with all the
privileges granted the European," he writes, "the oversexed Annie reveled in
superstitious rites and steamy voodoo rituals conjoining blood and sperm,
death and sex" (177).

Annie Palmer acquired her spiritual skills from a Haitian native high
priestess "who had marched with the armies of Dessalines and Christophe
when these set out to free Haiti from the French domination" (de Lisser
[1929] 1958, 135). In the two novels about her, which are based on the diary
of the bookkeeper Robert Rutherford—who became Annie Palmer's lover
soon after he began to work on her plantation—she not only employs her
much talked about "evil magic" to dispose of her unwanted husbands, but
also brings it into play when she decides to kill the native Jamaican housekeeper[2] Millie, her rival for the love of Robert Rutherford. Her Euro-Haitian
"vampire's voodoo" actually turns out to be more powerful than *obeah*, the
Jamaican folk magic and religion. Millie's grandfather, Takoo, a well-versed
obeah practitioner, miserably fails in protecting his granddaughter and saving Millie from Annie's fatal curse. In order to take his revenge, he finally has
to resort to strangling Annie.

Herbert G. de Lisser was an eminent Jamaican literary figure by the
time of the publication of *The White Witch of Rosehall*, which is one of the

better-known works among his prolific output of twenty-five novels and
novellas. As the editor of Jamaica's most important newspaper, the *Daily
Gleaner*, he was able to garner attention for his novels by publishing them
in his newspaper (Rosenberg 2007, 63). De Lisser's book has met with criticism of literary scholars like Rhonda Cobham, who argues that with Annie,
de Lisser created a deliberately "superior" European character, which shows
his privileging of whiteness and white characters (see Cobham 1986, 174).
I, however, argue that de Lisser did not create Annie in order to privilege
unadulterated whiteness, but rather relied on the European vampire tradition combined with the Haitian voodoo tradition in order to present his
character—who draws on both traditions—as an emblem of the abuse of
colonialist social privilege and power.

De Lisser was a "brown Jamaican" (Rosenberg 2007, 63) of "very old Jamaica ancestry, Portuguese-Jewish . . . with a modicum of African blood"
(Roberts quoted in Rosenberg 2007, 64). As a writer who "became the
spokesperson for the white elite," even though he "allied himself with the
Afro-Jamaican middle classes at the beginning of his career" (64), he literally
"incorporated" a conflicted Euro-Jamaican hybridity, which is reflected in
his creation of Annie Palmer as a literary character.

In *The White Witch of Rosehall*, de Lisser presents Annie's superior spiritual power as the result of European and Caribbean cultural fusion. As a
creole hybrid herself, by culture rather than by "blood," in Jamaica she cleverly uses this power over people who believe in voodoo. Annie's spiritual
powers derive from an evil hybridity that cleverly instrumentalizes what is
presented by de Lisser's nineteenth-century English narrators as the worst
of two worlds: a stereotypically "African" susceptibility to a belief in sorcery
and a stereotypically "European" ability to use rationality as a key ingredient in its manipulation of the appropriated African belief system. By means
of her vampiric nature, Annie Palmer, in her apparent quest to become the
epitome of the cruel colonizer, transcends gender boundaries and assumes
a power over everything and everybody that a woman would not ordinarily
have.

Although the fact that Annie Palmer's white witchery was influenced by
the tradition of Haitian voodoo is evident after even a cursory reading of
the novel, it is less obvious that her black arts are equally informed by the
European vampire tradition that de Lisser also considered as his cultural
heritage. The connection with the European tradition is revealed in a comment by the character Rider, a "defrocked" minister, who remarks that Annie
as a Jamaican "Old Hige" is "only the Vampire of other countries" ([1929]
1958, 159). So far the vampire trope has not received much critical attention,

yet readers familiar with Sheridan Le Fanu's novella "Carmilla" (1872) will soon realize that Carmilla—and other mostly female vampire characters from European lore—also served as a major source of de Lisser's inspiration for Annie. Like some of her European forebears, Annie likes to drink the blood of young females and she also likes to flog and torture servants. In this, she seems to follow the sixteenth-century Hungarian "Blood Countess," Erzsébet Bathory, who allegedly killed more than 650 female servants after tormenting them by sticking needles into the "girls' flesh and pins under their fingernails" or using "an iron to scald the faces of lazy servant girls" (McNally and Florescu 1994, 127). Mike Henry additionally associates Annie Palmer with the fifteenth-century Transylvanian impaler, Vlad Tepes, a.k.a. Count Dracula, when he reports that Annie displayed the decapitated head of an unruly female servant in a basket and also had the head of another "servant placed on a bamboo stake at Rose Hall and left to decay in the sun for all to see" (2005, v).

Like Le Fanu's Carmilla, who has Hungarian roots and sometimes takes the shape of a black beast, Annie, the "Old Hige," who has European as well as Haitian roots, is also in the tradition of the European *strigoaica*, "an evil creature who sleeps during the daylight hours, flies at night, can change into an animal form such as a wolf, a dog, or bird, and sucks the blood from sleeping children" (McNally and Florescu 1994, 120). Actually, not only Annie (who was instructed by a Haitian voodoo specialist), but also Carmilla is associated with voodoo—which might seem strange at first, but certainly illustrates that tales about various types of folk magic have circulated throughout the world for a long time. When she first makes her appearance at the Styrian *schloss* owned by Laura's English father, Carmilla is in the company of a "hideous black woman, with a sort of coloured turban on her head, who was gazing all of the time from the carriage window, nodding and grinning derisively towards the ladies, with gleaming eyes and large white eye-balls and her teeth set as in fury" (Le Fanu [1872] 2003, 98–99). Nevertheless, the identity of this scary black woman is not disclosed at any point in Le Fanu's story. One might speculate that the "hideous woman" is a figure of demonic empowerment for hitherto powerless and silenced women and that Le Fanu, in a move parallel to that of postcolonial women writers who feature vampires (see Khair and Höglund 2013, 6), uses her to allot dangerous occult power to Carmilla: "[T]he vampire figure is seized . . . and becomes the recuperated Other, recreated as equal and different," "inflect[ed] . . . with a different social and political meaning" (Wisker 2013, 51).

Both Le Fanu's Carmilla and de Lisser's Annie indulge in their vampirism by drinking the blood of female servants and lower-class people, whom they exploit and have no respect for. Unlike Annie, who sucks her rival Millicent's blood to kill her, Carmilla, in addition to killing servants through her vampire's habit, sucks the young noblewoman Laura's blood out of love: "Carmilla" is first and foremost the story of a young female vampire's erotic love for another girl and thus considered the first lesbian vampire (see Auerbach 1995, 41; Signorotti 1996, online). However, in spite of their possible qualification as love bites, Carmilla's violations of Laura, and of her previous victim Bertha, very much resemble Annie's act of sucking blood from Millicent.

Before being attacked, Laura either dreams about a beautiful woman (later identified as Carmilla) or perceives a black cat that jumps on her bed and then turns into a female figure; in one instance she even sees a blood-drenched Carmilla in her dream. The result of a vampire's visit is an unmistakable mark, as an attending physician explains in "Carmilla":

> *The punctures which she described as having occurred near the throat were . . . the insertion of those two long, thin, and sharp teeth which, it is well known, are peculiar to vampires; and there could be no doubt, he added, as to the well-defined livid mark which all concurred in describing as that induced by the demon's lips, and every symptom described by the sufferer was in exact conformity with those recorded in every case of a similar visitation. (141)*

Like Carmilla's victims, Annie's victim Millicent also has the vampire's mark upon her and thus is also doomed to die because her life force has been sucked out:

> *[Millie] opened her bodice. Two firm rounded breasts were displayed. In the little hollow flanked by the soft promontories was a blistered space, about the size of a shilling. Purple against the golden brown of the glossy skin it stood out; and the skin was almost broken. It looked as though it had been caused by a blow which, a trifle harder would have drawn blood. (148)*

Millicent's encounter with her vampire is less romantic than Carmilla's; she is bitten by Annie, but the vampire's possessive love is for another. Millie becomes a victim of a colonial power struggle that the white woman Annie is determined to win. She has understood the power dynamics involved and tells her lover Robert about Annie's vampiric nature: "[Annie Palmer] was here, sucking all me blood; she is an Old Hige, a witch, a devil. She want to kill me because she want you for her own self" (de Lisser [1929] 1958, 150).

The Caribbean vampire figure, the "Old Hige," is known by various names. Giselle Anatol explains:

The soucouyant . . . Old Hige/Old Hag, volant . . . are all women who shed their skin at night and stealthily attack their neighbors, sucking their blood before returning home to re-don their slippery outer coverings. Because the soucouyant is typically characterized as the epitome of evil, I argue that stories about her effectively socialize women to obey patriarchal mandates, and condition men to expect women to do so. (2009, online)

The female vampire of the European tradition is likewise "the epitome of evil," but in its historical context, evil works toward female empowerment, as I argue in the following. I am convinced that de Lisser deliberately placed Annie Palmer in the European tradition alongside the Caribbean tradition in order to show how her vampirism fed into her status as a brutal colonialist and slave master. Gina Wisker draws attention to the connection—here embodied by Annie Palmer—between colonialism (rather than exclusively class) and vampirism when she writes:

The trajectory of construction, allure and repulsion which the vampire represents in fiction mirrors the behavior of imperialist colonizers who were fascinated with foreign lands, and so traded, invaded, enslaved, dominated. . . . From such an imperial and colonial turn the vampire is one small step. (2013, 50)

As critics have pointed out, both Le Fanu's "Carmilla" and de Lisser's *The White Witch of Rosehall* feature female protagonists who defy the assigned gender roles of their times by conducting the homosocial exchange of a "love object" strictly between women. Both protagonists engage in bloody cruelties and transgressions that are coded as typically male; in Annie's case, such cruelty is absolutely needed as part of her scheme for self-empowerment.

"Carmilla" features a story of vampiric love that is obviously lesbian whereas *The White Witch of Rosehall* focuses on the homosocial—against a colonial background—rather than the homosexual. As Elizabeth Signorotti emphasizes, "Le Fanu refrains from heavy-handed moralizing, leaving open the possibility that Laura's and Carmilla's vampiric relationship is sexually liberating and for them highly desirable" (1996, online).

Signorotti identifies Le Fanu's intentions as clearly protofeminist, arguing that he "chronicles the development of a vampiric relationship between two women, in which it becomes increasingly clear that Laura's and Carmilla's lesbian relationship defies the traditional structures of kinship by which men regulate the exchange of women to promote male bonding" (1996, online).[3] Luce Irigaray, basing her argument on insights by the anthropologist Claude Lévi-Strauss, and using the more common example of male-male relationships to comment on the homosocial exchange of the "objects" of love and/or marriage, has shown that in societies censuring homosexuality, homosocial exchange relationhips express homosexual relations:

> [H]omosexual relations . . . are just as subversive, so they . . . are forbid-den. Because they openly interpret the law according to which soci-ety operates, they threaten in fact to shift the horizon of the law. . . . Exchanges and relationships, always among men, would thus be both required and forbidden by law. . . . Thus all economic organization is ho-mosexual. That of desire as well, even the desire for women. Woman ex-ists only as an occasion for meditation, transaction, transference between man and his fellow man, indeed between man and himself. (1985, 193)

Signorotti points out that Le Fanu shows that this law is disregarded by transgressive women: "Le Fanu allows Laura and Carmilla to usurp male au-thority and to bestow themselves on whom they please, completely exclud-ing male participation in the exchange of women, normative as discussed by Claude Lévi-Strauss" (Signorotti 1996, online). While Le Fanu thus rather openly presents female homosexual desire, de Lisser focuses on homosocial desire expressed by a female slaveholder who needs to reverse the patriar-chal gender structures in order to achieve her goal of becoming a particu-larly cruel female colonizer.

In *The White Witch of Rosehall* it is the young, naive Englishman Rob-ert Rutherford rather than a woman who is exchanged between two strong women in a patriarchal, colonial setting. To explain the mechanism of ho-mosocial exchange in de Lisser's novel, one only needs to adapt the passage quoted from Irigaray by replacing the word *woman* with *man*. The agents of exchange are the white plantation owner Annie Palmer and the independent housekeeper Millie, who proudly insists that she is an independent entrepre-neur rather than a servant. Annie customarily commands and kills men; she thus is a perfect agent in the exchange of Robert, who is an ideal exchange object because he is made weak by the fact that he is several years younger than Annie and does not know how life in the Caribbean works. In addition to not wanting to lose Rutherford, Annie cannot stand the idea of being outdone by "a colored servant."[4] Thus, it does not come as a surprise that

Annie Palmer strives to be part of the patriarchal structure of the colonial Caribbean, which is characterized by "hegemonic masculinity associated with conquest, control and the consolidation of power by privileged men" (Thame 2011, 77). Millie, the free Jamaican housekeeper, stands no chance against Annie in this contest—by turning her into a zombie in the course of the power struggle between the two women, Annie, in the context of Caribbean lore, also turns her into a slave.

In the end, both transgressive women, Carmilla and Annie, can only be stopped through the use of brute force exercised by males as representatives of "real patriarchy." Carmilla is killed by Laura's uncle and an especially skilled vampire slayer in the only reliable way that will kill a vampire for good: a stake is driven through her heart. Annie, however, is only throttled to death by Millie's grandfather, Takoo. But this need not mean that their evil female reign is over; vampires, as Le Fanu reminds us, are revenants: "The spectre visits living people in their slumbers; *they* die, and almost invariably, in the grave develop into vampires. This [also] happened in the case of the beautiful Mircalla, who was haunted by one of the demons" (Le Fanu [1872] 2003, 147). According to the logic of the perpetuation of vampires, Carmilla has turned Laura into a vampire and Annie has made Millicent her heiress.

In her quest to usurp the white male role of a slaveholding plantation owner, Annie Palmer exhibits a great deal of apparent perversity and unusual cruelty. It is no wonder that those who write about the figure of Annie Palmer have felt the need to explain the psychological motivations behind both her cruelty and her gender-bending dress choices. If one sees Annie as an exemplification of the vampire's lust for blood, or "hæmosexuality" (1991, 388) as Christopher Frayling has aptly named it, one can categorize her as a case of "sadism in woman," which, according to Krafft-Ebing, sometimes manifests itself in vampirism.[5] Indeed, de Lisser has his narrator explain Annie Palmer's sadistic penchant for whipping slaves as an outbreak of lust for blood:

The first flogging she had seen had made her ill, yet she had found a terrible fascination in it. She had gone to see another, and yet another; that first tasting of blood as it were, had awakened a certain lust in her which had grown and strengthened until it had become a powerful and abiding obsession. Had she lived fifty years before, when slaves could still be procured from the coasts of Africa, and when the law gave the slave-owner more power over the life of a slave than it did in these days, she would sometimes have had an erring bondsman or woman whipped to death in her presence. ([1929] 1958, 80)

In addition to showing such decidedly unladylike behavior, Annie—like the female helper who accompanied the Hungarian "Blood Countess" (see Mc-Nally and Florescu 1994, 128)—goes about her plantation in men's clothing, as Robert is told by Millicent. At first Robert is reluctant to believe this, but when Annie, who is only four feet eleven, stands in front of him "in a black suit which had evidently been made for her," holding "a heavy riding whip in her hand" and sporting an "imperative and stormy" manner, he can no longer dismiss this as "the invention of the slaves" (104). In the scene following Annie's appearance in male attire, she attacks Millicent with the whip. Later, she also wears the same masculine outfit when she ventures out to put her fatal spell on Millicent. By going on this spectacular gender bender, Annie masculinizes herself in the service of an empire that, according to Elleke Boehmer, "fears always the pollution, disorder and unmanning that come from without" (2013, vii). Thus, her transgression of gender boundaries ironically also undermines her purpose because it serves to uphold empirical power structures that are purely masculine by hierarchical definition.

Mike Henry glibly remarks in the context of Annie's unfeminine posturing and voracious sexual appetite in his "Brief Historical Foreword" to his 2005 book *Rose Hall's White Witch* that "[h]er sexual desires knew no boundaries and moved from one sexual need to another, be it flagellation or cross-dressing—Annie did it all" (viii). De Lisser's and Henry's descriptions seem to indicate that Annie was highly dissatisfied with her role as a female, a role that did not foresee for her to be an "innately" cruel colonialist and slaveholder. In light of Annie's penchants for flogging her slave lovers and her desire for Millie's blood, she also appears to be a sadist, according to Freud's definition in *Three Essays on the Theory of Sexuality*:

> *The most common and most significant of all the perversions—the desire to inflict pain upon the sexual object, and its reverse—received from Krafft-Ebing the names of "sadism" and "masochism" for its active and passive forms respectively. . . . As regards active . . . sadism, the roots are easy to detect in the normal. The sexuality of most male human beings contains an element of aggressiveness—a desire to subjugate; the biological significance of it seems to lie in the need for overcoming the resistance of the sexual object by means other than the process of wooing. ([1905] 1962, 23–24)[6]*

While Annie is not male, her sexuality seems to be "actively male" in keeping with this definition and she might therefore be one of the women who—according to Freudian psychologist Joan Rivière—assume womanliness and wear it as a mask "to hide the possession of masculinity" ([1929] 2000, 73). As a sadist, Annie assumes traits that are not only (allegedly) masculine, but also colonialist, as is supported by Aimé Césaire's description of colonial relations: "I look around and wherever there are colonizers and colonized face to face, I see force, brutality, cruelty, sadism, conflict, and in a parody of education, the hasty manufacture of a few thousand subordinate functionaries" ([1950] 1995, 205).

In addition to outright sadistic, physical violence, Annie Palmer has even more awful spiritual torments in store for her servants and slaves. The reaction of the local population to her "sorcery" shows just how skillfully she used her Euro-Haitian powers to subdue those who believed in them. Tutored by a Haitian voodoo priestess, Annie allegedly acquired skills of commanding "the spirits who inhabited and animated everything" (de Lisser [1929] 1958, 136). Because of her special powers, she is able to terrorize Jamaican believers in obeah by making portents of ill omen, such as the horrible "Threefooted Horse," appear in the sky. The narrator explains the appearance of the creature in terms of the effect it has on the local audience: "It was not only by bodily fear that she held them, by dread of the whip and the iron chain, but by far more potent spiritual terrors, by . . . the conviction that she could summon fiends from the pit to work her will if she were minded to do so. And tonight she had done so" (119). Later, Millie is transformed into a will-less zombie by Annie's spiritual terrors: "[I]t was clear she believed that she could move only with great difficulty. Her fixed belief that her blood had been sucked and she was doomed had sapped her will, and her body reacted sympathetically to her extraordinary obsession" (152). In reference to Millie, Annie Palmer thus acts as both a Euro-Caribbean vampire and the zombie-making *bokor* of Haitian lore. Moreover, she is a perfect representative of (masculine) colonial power as defined by Boehmer in "Empire's Vampires": "From the day the colonizer takes possession until the day he reluctantly departs . . . his activities connote the extraction of the very stuff of life, the life-blood, from those—the colonial other—who have absolutely nothing other than abject life in abundance" (2013, vii).

The writer and anthropologist Zora Neale Hurston was one of the first Western anthropologists to draw attention to the fact that it takes a mix of psychological and scientific knowledge to create a zombie. In her 1938 book *Tell My Horse*, Hurston presented the central findings of her 1937 field trip to Haiti—where zombies were seen doing slave labor—as follows:

It was concluded that it is . . . a matter of the semblance of death induced by some drug known to a few. Some secret probably brought from Africa

and handed down from generation to generation. These men know the
effect of the drug and the antidote. It is evident that it destroys that part
of the brain which governs speech and will power. ([1938] 1983, 206)

Although Hurston was right about the "secret drug" theory that here locates murderous rationality in Africans (rather than in the Westerners that de Lisser's narrators attribute it to), she could not prove it to be true. Scientific evidence of the poison theory was finally presented in the 1980s by Canadian ethnobiologist Wade Davis, who identified tetrodotoxin (which is found in numerous types of fish) as the poison used by Haitian *bokors* (see Davis 1988, 160).

Not having the advantage of relativizing twentieth-century explanations at hand, de Lisser's narrator and characters present the inexplicable "supernatural" events in the novel in terms of stereotypically binary African/Caribbean and Western/European modes of behavior. The Jamaicans in de Lisser's novel actually believe that Annie is an Old Hige, and thus can suck out a person's life force, but the Englishman Rider provides a state-of-the-art nineteenth-century psychological explanation for Annie's strange powers. Based on his knowledge of the effects of mesmerism, he tells the stupefied Robert Rutherford that "Annie Palmer may have a power which is of the mind, not of hell" (de Lisser [1929] 1958, 161).

In this dramatic situation, Annie's Jamaican antagonist and former ally, Takoo, is shown to be relatively powerless in comparison to Annie. He is unable to use his own obeah skills to stop Annie's spell because he does not know that Annie is on the prowl and also because Annie, on top of practicing her powerful obeah, uses a type of European (stereotypically "rational") mind control that can be very sure of its results. Her superiority as a voodoo practitioner is clearly the result of her cultural hybridity. As Rider explains to Rutherford, the voodoo priests who taught Annie were excellent amateur psychologists as they were "versed in all the old African sorcery" (128–29), but Annie is later also identified by Rider (with a clearly racialist European bias) as a reincarnation of Lucrezia Borgia (see 239). This Old-World connection, according to Rider, added some "stereotypically European" rationality and calculation to her "native skills" and thus perfected them. In his conversation with Rutherford, Rider also locates Annie's spiritual skills in a nineteenth-century European discourse by comparing her to the German Franz Anton Mesmer, who successfully "mesmerized" French citizens: "[W]hat I mean is that perhaps she causes people to see things she herself thinks of; it is a vision of her mind that she projects into space, now in the form of a spectral horse, now in the form of a shadowy vampire" (de Lisser [1929] 1958, 160–61).

Robert Rutherford ultimately sees only one solution to Millie's zombifica-tion in light of all of these contradictory explanations: Annie is to undo the spell she has cast on Millicent because "only Mrs. Palmer . . . can induce her to believe that she is no longer bewitched" (162). But Annie refuses, knowing that the spell has passed out of her control, for "[s]he could set agencies of harm in motion; [but] she could not control their effect" (222–23). So Mil-licent eventually dies, even though Robert and Rider try to convince her by means of rational arguments of the fact that she is not physically sick, and even though they also invoke Christian religion. Subsequently Takoo, in a final showdown, kills Annie without the use of obeah by strangling her with his bare hands.

Literary critics have wondered what exactly de Lisser's objective might have been in creating the literary character of Annie Palmer and how it might have fit the agenda of privileging light-skinnedness that they have perceived in his work. Rhonda Cobham argues in her "bio-bibliographical" article on de Lisser that the fact that in *The White Witch of Rosehall* "the White witch's voodoo is shown to be more potent than that of the Black obeahman" (1986, 174) is part of his general strategy of privileging white-ness, observing that de Lisser "goes out of his way to ascribe any notable acts of bravery, leadership or even ruthlessness . . . to White, or almost-White characters" (174). She attributes this to the fact that the light-skinned and "socially white" Afro-Jewish writer, influenced by the British author James Anthony Froude, who viewed the West Indies as a place of corruption,[7] held a generally unfavorably view of dark-skinned blacks.[8]

Unlike Cobham, who attributes Annie's cruelty to her "superior white-ness," Leah Rosenberg (who argues that racial hybridity, culminating in the type of a "clear sambo," was de Lisser's racial ideal)[9] imputes Annie's outra-geous behavior to the stereotypical cruelty of the "foreign white creole" in the West Indies:

[D]e Lisser transforms Annie from a white Jamaican woman into the daughter of an Irishman and an Englishwoman raised in Haiti and tu-tored in voodoo. Her crimes were born of the inferior cultures of Haiti and Ireland, not of Jamaica. Morever, Annie embodies the negative characteristics that English discourse historically attributed to white creole (Jamaican) women. . . . [W]hite creole women were depicted as flogging their slaves to satisfy petty jealousies. Fluent in the creole lan-guage and other practices of slaves, they were no longer fully European. (2007, 84)

Rosenberg devotes a few pages of her chapter on de Lisser's career as a Jamaican journalist and writer to the question of why de Lisser chose to publish *The White Witch of Rosehall* in his journal *Planter's Punch*. He usually instrumentalized the journal as an outlet to praise Jamaica's high-class white ladies, as, for example, the Duchess Atholl in the issue that also features Annie Palmer. Rosenberg thus writes:

> *The intentional juxtaposition of Palmer's story with de Lisser's carefully constructed image of white women foregrounds the contradiction between the two and begs the question, How did de Lisser mean his contemporary readers to understand his outrageously decadent and degenerate heroine? What was her role in de Lisser's project of remaking the image of Jamaica, past and present? (2007, 82)*

With his portrayal of Annie, Rosenberg concludes, a bit anticlimactically, de Lisser must have wanted to rehabilitate "the image of Jamaica's contemporary ladies by making Mrs. Palmer appear even more flawed than she had been in the earlier versions of the legend" (82).

In light of the fact that in the figure of Annie Palmer de Lisser pits European and Caribbean traditions of "magic" mind manipulation and their "rational" explanations against each other in a tour de force of supernatural conflict, I think that it is does not make much sense to interpret Annie and her spiritual feats in terms of de Lisser's presentation of "white superiority" or his interest in the "social engineering" of Jamaica. De Lisser's Annie is a vampire from Jamaican folklore rather than a real figure of Jamaican social life and therefore it is difficult to picture her as useful to de Lisser's project of "remaking the image of Jamaica, past and present," as referred to in Rosenberg's quote. Annie's status as a vampire and voodoo practitioner adds a great deal of ambiguity to her character and makes her a very slippery figure. Historically, a vampire can hardly be thought of as a model citizen who might be used to illustrate any kind of social or even "racial" superiority. As Laurence Rickels points out in his *Vampire Lectures*, in Europe "the wicked or excommunicated person, the perjurer, apostate, the person who died under a curse, and the person . . . who was buried without proper rites" (1999, 4) usually made for a suitable vampire. Even more interesting in this context is the fact that the vampire—exemplified by the legends of the Blood Countess or Count Dracula, who tormented local peasants—has often stood for economic exploitation, such as the "parasitic relationship between the aristocracy and the oppressed middle and lower classes" (Signorotti 1996, online). The planter aristocrat Annie Palmer fits very well into this line of cruel and perverted oppressors because in her case economic exploitation is exacerbated by race oppression.[10] Bolstered by the social status bestowed upon her from her white heritage as well as her acquired knowledge of Caribbean cultural currency, Annie effortlessly transgresses the boundaries imposed by her gender and dominates everybody from her slaves to her lovers. Therefore, I suggest that in light of both the creolization of her evil magic and her vampiric nature, de Lisser's Annie Palmer can be better understood as a study in the abuse of power and an emblem of the vampiric nature of colonialism than an illustration of de Lisser's notion of actual "superior whiteness."

The many versions of the life and fall of Annie Palmer show that her life story continues to fascinate those who hear about it. Therefore, it should not come as a surprise that as late as 2010, Jane Crichton's "revisionist" play, which provides a "softer" Annie with a rationale for her deeds, won numerous awards;[11] that British playwright Sol B. River published a postcolonial version of the play in 2003; and that in 2005 Mike Henry published yet another novel version of the legend, aimed at catering to tastes more enlightened and "modern" than those of de Lisser's presumed audience. Unlike de Lisser, who mentions Annie's apparent "oversexedness" but does not dwell on it, Henry frankly describes Annie's perverse appetites for both white and black men. However, he sanitizes his version by totally forgoing de Lisser's racialized psychological speculations, even announcing in his prologue that he aims at "sav[ing] the reader from feelings of bitterness let alone race-hatred" (M. Henry 2005, iv). Yet by eliminating the fascinating tension of the plot-elements dealing with race he also runs the risk of turning Annie's story into a run-of-the-mill historical novel featuring very predictable stock Gothic elements. Thus, despite its obvious shortcomings, de Lisser's less politically correct version still remains much more intriguing—and debatable.

NOTES

1. I use the given spelling instead of a Creole spelling such as *vaudun;* de Lisser's novel clearly is situated in the traditions of popular culture rather than Haitian religion.

2. As the male protagonist of the novel finds out, a Jamaican "housekeeper" is defined as a young woman who is self-employed and who is also willing to offer her services as a live-in lover.

3. It should, however, be noted that Laura, the narrator, cannot help but think of Carmilla's "uncanny" desire for her in terms of heterosexual desire and male cross-dressing in the style of a Shakespeare comedy. She reports, for example, that she could boast of "no little attentions such as masculine gallantry delights to offer" (Le Fanu [1872] 2003, 105), and

wonders about the possible "insanity" of Carmilla's behavior: "Was she notwithstanding her mother's volunteered denial, subject to brief visitations of insanity; or was there here a disguise and romance? . . . What if a boyish lover had found his way into the house and sought to prosecute his suit in masquerade? . . . But there were many things against this hypothesis, highly interesting as it was to my vanity" (105).

4. Rutherford, whose personal characteristics apparently also include loyalty and gallantry, at one point even assumes an active role in the exchange triangle when he considers prostituting himself to Annie in order to save Millie's life. However, Millie dies before he can do so. Interestingly, Annie, likewise, later offers to prostitute herself to her former lover, the overseer Ashman, in exchange for Ashman's promise to kill Robert.

5. Richard von Krafft-Ebing reports a case of sadistic female vampirism in his section on "Sadism" in his *Psychopathia Sexualis*: "A married man presented himself with numerous scars of cuts on his arms. He told of their origin as follows: When he wished to approach his wife, who was young and somewhat 'nervous,' he first had to make a cut in his arm. The she would suck the wound and during the act become violently excited sexually. This case recalls the widespread legend of the vampires, the origin of which may perhaps be referred to such sadistic facts" ([1886] 1991, 396).

6. In *Three Essays on the Theory of Sexuality*, Freud, following Krafft-Ebing, acknowledges that female sexuality can be sadistic too (see Freud [1905] 1962, 23–24). Krafft-Ebing writes on the subject: "[S]adism in which the need of subjugation of the opposite sex forms a constituent element, in accordance with its nature represents a pathological intensification of the masculine sexual character; in the second place, the obstacles which oppose the expression of this monstrous impulse are, of course, much greater for woman than for man. Yet sadism occurs in women, and it can be explained by the primary constituent element— the general hyper-excitation of the motor-sphere" ([1886] 1991, 396).

7. In *The English in the West Indies or the Bow of Ulysses*, Froude, according to Cobham, "argued that the Whites in the West Indies had become so debased as a result of isolation from the benign intellectual traditions of the mother country that they were incapable of drawing the bow of Ulysses—that is, of self-rule" (1986, 168). De Lisser apparently adopted this view.

8. In an article in the *Jamaica Times*, de Lisser characterized "the black Jamaican" with stereotypical excess as follows: "Good humoured and impulsive, an admirable imitator when well taught but with no inventive faculty whatever. . . . He has no literature, and no art. His music is of the rudest. He is sometimes brave to recklessness and sometimes a deplorable coward" (quoted in Cobham 1986, 168).

9. Rosenberg writes that "[d]e Lisser built on race theories that celebrated hybridity, most directly [Sydney] Olivier's theory presented in *White Capital and Coloured Labour* (1906) that interracial people were superior to monoracial people" (2007, 72). She goes on to explain that he predicted that Jamaica would over time develop such a racial type of its own and that if hybridity was maximized, Jamaica "would produce a national racial type equivalent to a 'clear sambo,' a classification de Lisser defined in *Twentieth-Century Jamaica* as a person 'with about one-fourth or one-fifth of white blood'" (Rosenberg 2007, 72).

10. Annie Palmer is also a perfect representative of a "rapacious modernity," described by Paul Gilroy in *The Black Atlantic* as "complicity of rationalism with the practice of white supremacist terror" (1993, 118).

11. Krista Henry writes that Crichton decided to present an apologetic version of Annie Palmer's life in her play because "she found it disturbing that a young female was evil without just cause": "Crichton imagines Palmer as a frustrated and abused woman who took out her grievances on the people around her. Sticking mainly to the story that has been passed down through generations, Crichton adds a few quirks to show that Palmer was just a woman who was upset at the way her life was going" (2009, online). Leah Rosenberg mentions several other earlier Annie Palmer performances, without going into detail about them: "The story of Annie Palmer has been reinscribed into Jamaican national arts in two of Jamaica's national pantomimes, *The Witch* (1975/76) and *Miss Annie* (2002/3) as well as in the work of the National Dance Theatre Company" (2007, 90).

WORKS CITED

Anatol, Giselle. 2009. "Vampires from the Caribbean: The Soucouyant." December 4. Accessed September 24, 2012. http://www.gothic.stir.ac.uk/guestblog/vampires-from -the-caribbean-the-soucouyant/.

Auerbach, Nina. 1995. *Our Vampires, Ourselves.* Chicago: University of Chicago Press.

Boehmer, Elleke. 2013. "Foreword: Empire's Vampires." In Khair and Höglund, vii–ix.

Césaire, Aimé. [1950] 1995. "Discourse on Colonialism." In *Slavery and Beyond: The African Impact on Latin America and the Caribbean,* edited by Darién J. Davis, 199–208. Lanham, MD: Rowman and Littlefield.

Cobham, Rhonda. 1986. "Herbert George de Lisser (1878–1944)." In *Fifty Caribbean Writers: A Bio-Bibliographical Sourcebook,* edited by Daryl Cumber Dance, 166–77. New York: Greenwood Press.

Davis, Wade. 1988. *Passage of Darkness: The Ethnobiology of the Haitian Zombie.* Chapel Hill: University of North Carolina Press.

de Lisser, Herbert G. [1929] 1958. *The White Witch of Rosehall.* Kingston, Jamaica: Macmillan Caribbean.

Frayling, Christopher. 1991. *Vampyres: Lord Byron to Count Dracula.* London: Faber and Faber.

Freud, Sigmund. [1905] 1962. *Three Essays on the Theory of Sexuality.* New York: Basic Books.

Gilroy, Paul. 1993. *The Black Atlantic: Modernity and Double Consciousness.* London: Verso.

Henry, Krista. 2009. "Childhood Memories Bring Annie Palmer to Life." *The Gleaner.* August 16. Accessed September 24, 2011. http://jamaica-gleaner.com/gleaner/20090816/ ent/ent8.html.

Henry, Mike. 2005. *Rose Hall's White Witch: The Legend of Annie Palmer.* Kingston, Jamaica: LMH Press.

Hurston, Zora Neale. [1938] 1983. *Tell My Horse.* Buena Vista, CA: Turtle Island.

Irigaray, Luce. 1985. *This Sex Which Is Not One.* Ithaca, NY: Cornell University Press.

Khair, Tabish, and Jonathan Höglund, eds. 2013. *Transnational and Postcolonial Vampires: Dark Blood.* London: Palgrave.

Krafft-Ebing, Richard von. [1886] 1991. "Psychopathia Sexualis: Sadism." In Frayling, 390–97.

Le Fanu, Sheridan. [1872] 2003. "Carmilla." In *Three Vampire Tales*, edited by Anne Williams, 86–148. Boston: Wadsworth.

McNally, Raymond T., and Radu Florescu. 1994. *In Search of Dracula: The History of Dracula and Vampires*. Boston: Houghton Mifflin.

Pifer, Drury. 2001. *Hanging the Moon: The Rollins Rise to Riches*. Newark: University of Delaware Press.

Rickels, Laurence A. 1999. *The Vampire Lectures*. Minneapolis: University of Minnesota Press.

Rivière, Joan. [1929] 2000. "Womanliness as a Masquerade." In *Psychoanalysis and Woman: A Reader*, edited by Shelley Saguaro, 70–78. Houndmills, UK: Macmillan.

Rosenberg, Leah Reade. 2007. *Nationalism and the Formation of Caribbean Literature*. New York: Palgrave.

Signorotti, Elizabeth. 1996. "Repossessing the Body: Transgressive Desire in 'Carmilla' and Dracula–Vampire Story Retold with Masculine Themes Added." *Criticism* 38. Accessed November 2, 2011. http://findarticles.com /p/articles/mi_m2220/is_n4_v38/ ai_18981386/.

Thame, Maziki. 2011. "Reading Violence and Postcolonial Decolonization through Fanon: The Case of Jamaica." *Journal of Pan African Studies* 4 (7): 75–94.

"The White Witch of Jamaica." 2011. Accessed March 25, 2011. http://scaryplace.com ./Jamaica.html.

Wisker, Gina. 2013. "Celebrating Difference and Community: The Vampire in African-American and Caribbean Women's Writing." In Khair and Höglund, 46–66.

PART 3

CULTURAL
ANXIETIES

REVAMPING DRACULA ON THE
MEXICAN SILVER SCREEN

Fernando Méndez's El vampiro

CARMEN SERRANO

Cinematic representations of the monstrous and the supernatural are an inextricable part of film history, and the vampire is among its international stars. *The Devil's Manor* (1896), by French film pioneer Georges Méliès, is considered one of the first films to play with the vampire theme. In it, a bat-like creature flies into a Gothic castle and then is transformed into a sinister cloaked figure (see Abbott 2004, 12). In 1922 director F. W. Murnau made the critically acclaimed German expressionist film *Nosferatu,* which presents one of the most frightening versions of the aristocratic vampire as described in Bram Stoker's novel *Dracula* (1897). Since then, the vampire figure has found numerous embodiments throughout the world and in various media.

Like the vampire, the filmic image is reborn, parodied, abused, and killed, only to resurrect again. Typically, the fear-instilling vampire films appear to satisfy popular taste for a while, but interest quickly subsides, resulting in parodies such as *Abbott and Costello Meet Frankenstein* (Charles Barton, 1948) and *The Fearless Vampire Killers; or, Pardon Me, but Your Teeth Are in My Neck* (Roman Polanski, 1967). Nevertheless, there is always a new group of spectators ready to consume the latest articulation of the vampire. This is exemplified in the recent *Twilight* saga film series (2008–2012) based on Stephenie Meyer's series of novels with the same titles, which were extraordinarily successful, especially among teenage girls. The popularity of these films along with the revenues generated inevitably led to the production of more vampire films, which include, to name just a few, *Daybreakers* (Michael Spierig and Peter Spierig, 2009), *Dark Shadows* (Tim Burton, 2012), *Abraham Lincoln: Vampire Hunter* (Timur Bekmambetov, 2012), and *Let Me In*

(Matt Reeves, 2010), which is the American remake of the Swedish film *Let the Right One In* (Tomas Alfredson, 2008).

Prior to the latest renaissance of bloodsucking creatures on the big screen, the appeal of the supernatural and the monstrous had been thoroughly exploited by US film studios, which produced the first American horror film series between 1931 and 1939. Among the most famous terror-inducing film series of this era are *Dracula* (Tod Browning, 1931), *Frankenstein* (James Whale, 1931), *Dr. Jekyll and Mr. Hyde* (Rouben Mamoulian, 1931), and *White Zombie* (Victor Halperin, 1932). *Dracula*, starring Bela Lugosi, was a sensational success, selling over 50,000 tickets in just two days (see Phillips 2005, 13). In the end, the film grossed more than twenty-five million dollars, which is all the more remarkable given that the country was in the midst of the Great Depression (see Flynn 1992, 39).

These films were not only popular among US audiences; they were also successful internationally, especially in Latin America. With the advent of sound in 1927 and because the Hollywood studios wanted to maintain their stronghold in Spanish-speaking countries, more than one hundred Spanish-language films were made by Hollywood studios from 1930 through 1935 (see Pinto 1973, 474). The most famous of these Spanish-language film versions was *Drácula* (1931), by the US film director George Melford. The film used Spanish-speaking actors and was shot at night using the same sets, script, and shot list as Tod Browning's English *Dracula*.

Even though both films were produced simultaneously, the Spanish film version of *Dracula* was finished several weeks before its English counterpart and was screened in Los Angeles in January 1931. In April of that same year, the Spanish-language version of the film premiered in Mexico City, where it played throughout the month (see Skal 1990, 41). According to John Flynn (1992), the Spanish *Dracula* continued to play for many years in various Spanish-speaking countries, an indication of the popularity of these films in Latin America. Following the success of the Spanish version of *Dracula* and other Hollywood horror films in the 1930s and 1940s, Mexico experienced its own national vampire film boom, which began in the 1950s and lasted well over a decade. Some of the Mexican films include *El vampiro* (Fernando Méndez, 1957) (The Vampire); *El ataúd del vampiro* (Fernando Méndez, 1958) (The Vampire's Coffin); *El mundo de los vampiros* (Alfonso Corona Blake, 1960) (The World of the Vampires); *El Santo contra las mujeres vampiro* (Alfonso Corona Blake, 1962) (El Santo against the Female Vampires); and *Las vampiras* (Federico Curiel, 1969) (The Female Vampires). As in the United States, the initial films were first-class productions that were aesthetically complicated and fear-provoking, whereas the later films could only be described as low-quality parodies. For example, in *El Santo contra las mujeres vampiro*—a real camp classic—"El Santo" (a professional wrestler who appeared frequently on television) overtakes and defeats the demonic, albeit gorgeous, vampire vixens who plot to bring about the apocalypse by unleashing vampire monsters on earth.

The vampire figure in the Mexican context might at first seem like an unlikely appropriation of a foreign cultural symbol, yet there is a complicated and meaningful relationship between the vampire monster and the vampire bat that draws on Mexican culture being negotiated in these films. The Mexican vampire films illustrate how the vampire monster travels from place to place and is seemingly transformed in each context, thereby revealing the circumstances in which it is produced. Because the vampire figure has appeared in literature and film in various countries, it is worth exploring how the vampire is recast in different national contexts. This underscores the ways in which the vampire monsters destabilize specific constructions of belonging and, most important, how these vampire films express anxieties concerning national boundaries and citizenship at specific social and political crossroads. Here, I analyze the ways in which the articulation of the vampire in Mexico differs from the typical form of the vampire produced in films in Europe and the United States. At the same time, I discuss how the vampire embodies Mexican fears having to do with foreign outsiders; specifically, the immigrant and the colonizer.

The vampire is a mythical being that was already part of the pre-Columbian Mexican imaginary, which influenced European vampire folklore and subsequent vampire literature and film. The chronicles relating to the conquest of America in the fifteenth century introduced the first vampire bats—a species capable of killing cattle and even humans—to the European imaginary. This bloodsucking bat of the Americas was very different from the innocuous European fructivore, which had no metaphoric association with the figure of the vampire monster. Before the identification of the Latin American bloodsucking bat species by explorers and travelers, the vampire monster was usually described as a zombie-like dunce and was associated with other animals. The vampire monster was thought to be able to transform itself into a cat, dog, wolf, rat, or other creature, but the vampire was not necessarily associated with the bat. However, upon European sighting and reporting, the vampire bat species was subsequently incorporated to the vampire folklore in Europe (see McNally and Florescu 1994, 125–26). In his Gothic novel *Dracula* (1897), Bram Stoker amalgamates the American bat species and the vampire monster. In effect, he creates the quintessential vampire that not only spawns the filmic model, but also establishes the modern image of the vampire still current in popular culture. The French biologist Comte de Buffon used the term *vampire* in the mid-eighteenth century to describe the bloodsucking bat species of South America; however, it was Charles Darwin who further disseminated the existence of the bloodsucking bat species when he described it after his famous *Voyage of the Beagle* (1839). In his discussion of the vampire bat he notes the following:

> *The Vampire bat is often the cause of much trouble, by biting the horses on their withers. The injury is generally not so much owing to the loss of blood as to the inflammation, which the pressure of the saddle afterwards produces. The whole circumstance has lately been doubted in England; I was therefore fortunate in being present when one (Desmodus d'orbignyi, Bat.) was actually caught on a horse's back. We were bivouacking late one evening near Coquimbo, in Chile, when my servant, noticing that one of the horses was very restive, went to see what was the matter, and fancying he could distinguish something, suddenly put his hand on the beast's withers, and secured the vampire. In the morning the spot where the bite had been inflicted was easily distinguished from being slightly swollen and bloody. The third day afterward we rode the horse, without any ill effect. ([1839] 1909, 32–33)*

Travelers who ventured throughout the Americas from the fifteenth century through the twentieth century often wrote about their experiences with these bats, fueling the imagination of those who received their letters. The consequential incorporation of the bat into European vampire folklore is not so difficult to imagine. Even as late as 1922, travelers were still amazed by this creature. William Beebe describes his experiences with the vampire bat in *Edge of the Jungle*:

> *For three nights they swept about us with hardly a whisper of wings, and accepted either toe, or elbow, or finger, or all three, and the cots and floor in the morning looked like an emergency hospital behind an active front. In spite of every attempt at keeping awake, we dropped off to sleep before the bats had begun, and did not waken until they left. We ascertained, however, that there was no truth in the belief that they hovered or kept fanning with their wings. Instead they settled on the person with an appreciable flop and then crawled to the desired spot. (18)*

The chronicles of the conquest and the subsequent travel letters only helped fuse the association of the bat with the vampire monster that began to appear in literature. One of the first literary works to have associated the bat with the vampire monster is the serially published English Gothic novel *Varney the Vampire* (1845) by Thomas Peckett Press and James Malcolm Rymer. However, it is Stoker who crystallizes the image of the vampire as we generally know it today: the vampire is an aristocratic, refined man, with the supernatural ability to hypnotize his victims, read minds, and transform himself into an animal. At the same time, he is almost always an ambitious being seeking to infect and conquer new lands. In *Dracula*, Stoker makes various allusions to the beasts from South America:

> *I have not seen anything pulled down so quick since I was on the Pampas and had a mare that I was fond of go to grass all in a night. One of those big bats that they call vampires had got at her in the night, and what with his gorge and the vein left open, there wasn't enough blood in her to let her stand up, and I had to put a bullet through her as she lay. ([1897] 1996, 150–51)*

This description of the vampire bat in the Americas clearly altered European vampire folklore; however, when the monster was reappropriated and used in Latin American texts and films in the twentieth century, it seemed to lose its original autochthonous pre-Columbian association.

Bats in Latin American autochthonous cultures were not usually associated with evil; instead, they were perceived as powerful creatures, mediums, and sometimes gods. For example, in the Tajin pre-Columbian stone sculptures of Veracruz, vampire bats are depicted as gods that are important in postsacrificial ceremonies (see Kampen 1978, 117). At the same time, the powerful bats also appear in the *Popul Vuh*—the book of creation and epic myths of the Quiche Maya, which was transcribed from oral tradition to written text by the Dominican monk Francisco Ximenez in the seventeenth century. In it a "death bat," or *camoazotz*, takes the head of one of the twin heroes, which is then carried to the ritual ball game. According to J. Eric S. Thompson, in several of the codices (for example, those of Borgia, Porfirio Díaz, or Codex Fejérváry-Mayer), anthropomorphized bats are depicted as involved in human sacrifice (see Thompson 1966, 180–81). The Zotzil Maya, who live on the plateau of Chiapas, used to call themselves *Zotzil uinic* or bat men, claiming that their ancestors had found a stone bat that they took as their god (see Thompson 1966, 176). In other words, the first bat men could be found in the Americas.

The pre-Columbian bat's association with the sacred is erased when the American bat species reaches the opposite shore of the Atlantic. There, the bat becomes a fear-instilling and malignant being, these being among the usual qualities associated with the contemporary vampire. In an ironic twist of fate, the vampire bat, the autochthonous bloodsucking creature from the Americas that informed Stoker's own creation of the vampire monster in *Dracula*, returns home in the twentieth century transformed and repackaged in print and celluloid form in which the vestiges of his previous incarnation have seemingly been buried.

Before the conquest, the vampire bat belonged to the sacred or the mythic underworld; however, after the conquest the vampire bat became almost solely associated with the profane. More specifically, the vampire bat returned to the Americas as its evil double, recalling many doubles from literature and film. For example, Dr. Jekyll and Mr. Hyde are one and the same individual, but divided between the man of reason and the uncontrollable monster. Dr. Frankenstein is in incessant conflict with his other, the very monster he has created. Once he has given life to the aberrant being, his singular mission is to destroy it, but never realizes this goal. Yet another example can be found in Dorian Gray: he is the eternally young, refined gentleman, while the painting, his other, is his aging and decrepit evil half. These men, who perhaps had good intentions, are haunted and persecuted by their other, and one of them will usually perish. In the case of Mexico, it is the monstrous other, the European vampire, that annihilates the memory of the autochthonous bat deity that once was.

RELOCATION OF ANXIETIES: DISEASE, XENOPHOBIA, AND THE FOREIGN

Critics often interpret the vampire monster as a subversive intruder that infects and reproduces itself, threatening national borders. According to David Punter, the invasion of the other expresses fear having to do with perceived racial degeneration, which corrupts notions of identity (see Punter and Byron 2004, 232). The vampire is usually understood as the other that threatens to transgress borders or boundaries from the outside. In her book *Skin Shows*, Judith Halberstam argues that the vampire condenses many different kinds of threats into one body:

> For Dracula is the deviant or the criminal, the other against whom the normal and the lawful, the marriageable and the heterosexual can be known and quantified. . . . [H]e is the boundary, he is the one who crosses. . . . [H]e threatens stability. . . . He is a composite of otherness

that manifests as the horror essential to dark, foreign, and perverse bodies. (1995, 89–90)

In other words, part of what constitutes this body's peculiarity is its ethnicity (see Halberstam 1995, 91). Halberstam argues that Dracula resembles the Jew portrayed in British anti-Semitic discourse in the late nineteenth century:

In Dracula vampires are precisely a race and a family that weakens the stock of Englishness by passing on degeneracy and the disease of blood lust. Dracula, as a monster/master parasite, feeds upon the English wealth and health. He sucks blood and drains resources, he always eats out. (1995, 95)

The othering that Halberstam here identifies in the novel has been observed in vampire films as well. In Murnau's *Nosferatu*, the repulsive rodent-like Count Orlock (associated with the bubonic plague) invades a small German town. Critics, including Ken Gelder in *Reading the Vampire* (1994), have argued that it is difficult not to interpret this film as anti-Semitic because the image of Count Orlock so closely resembles the images of Jews depicted in pre-Nazi propaganda. The vampire embodies a coded expression of cultural fears that requires unpacking. William Hughes suggests the following:

For criticism, though, the vampire frequently remains a "menace" even when its threat is not regarded as implicated sexuality. Indeed, there appears to be a critical imperative that dissociates the vampire from conventional humanity, polarising the un-dead in a cultural Other whose practices constitute an intervention into the integrity of race and nation or an invasion to the sanctity of home and family. (2012, 201)

This visual projection of the deviant, aberrant other reemerges in the 1931 US film production of *Dracula* starring Bela Lugosi. If the vampire encodes anxieties about a foreign other, who can we read as this other? In his discussion of *Dracula*, Kendall Phillips suggests that the film's monster was the perfect embodiment of chaos brought on by extreme economic turmoil. With xenophobia becoming more pronounced due to increased immigration, those arriving from war-devastated Europe were especially vulnerable to aggression directed at immigrants (see Phillips 2005, 16). At the same time, within the social-political context in which these films were produced, there were also very specific foreign, dark bodies threatening notions of national identity. Like the immigrants arriving from Europe, Mexicans arriving in the

United States were vulnerable to hostility. According to the historian Manuel Gonzales, after the financial collapse that led to the Great Depression there was an increase in racial tensions in which ethnically marked Americans—especially those from Mexico—were suspect. Mexicans in the United States were often depicted in the media as diseased, as sexually deviant, and as nocturnal criminals. Mexicans, like other ethnic Americans—and like vampires—were perceived as a seeming threat to the integrity of race and nation. These damning descriptions of an entire culture and its people that were not uncommon at the time, coupled with the desire to be rid of the "Mexican Problem," led to the repatriation of approximately 400,000 Mexicans between 1929 and 1937 (see Gonzales 1999, 148). This was an exclusionary process in which certain citizens could never really assert their rights in spite of having US passports; this was further reinforced by the fact that some of those deported were US citizens of Mexican heritage. Thus, it seems likely that the cultural anxieties embodied in the vampire figure as described by Phillips were focused not only on immigrants arriving from Southern and Eastern Europe, but also those coming from Mexico.

The first major Hollywood horror films were produced between 1931 and 1939, which coincides with the repatriations of Mexicans between 1929–1937; therefore, it is worth exploring the many ways in which horror films articulated fears having to do with Mexican immigration specifically. Juan Bruce-Novoa has read American science-fiction films from mid-century as reflecting fears of alien encroachment. He says the following:

> Of course, alien visitation films share a fear of the unearthly, nonhuman origins of the migrant. Both alien considered here begin as undesirables: more than merely the unknown, they present a potential threat materialized in the violation of earthly boundaries presumed inviolable. (2011, 17)

EL VAMPIRO—WHAT DOES SPEAKING SPANISH MEAN?

If the vampire can be interpreted as resulting from a gesture of othering, what happens when Mexico has its own vampire film boom? Is there an other? If so, who is this other? In the case of the film *El vampiro,* it is a white, foreign, aristocratic, and perverse body that threatens Mexican identity. Given the violent past of conquest and colonization, Spain would seem like the most likely candidate for representation by an invading body. Or, if not Spain, perhaps this film articulates fears of a US invasion through the vampire figure. Mexico has had a contentious relationship with the United States that is akin to the vampire relationship: one of seduction and consumption. However, as I describe later in more detail, it is vis-à-vis France and French culture that the film *El vampiro* seems—perhaps somewhat surprisingly—to reaffirm Mexican identity.

The Mexican critic Carlos Monsiváis describes how emerging Mexican film companies "nationalized" the Hollywood model to create a successful homegrown industry. He also argues that the Mexican film studios not only created films that would please popular taste by following a formula that had proven to be financially lucrative, but they also promoted cultural nationalism through the exaltation of edifying symbols: historical events, local humor, national celebrations, local traditions, and religion (see Monsiváis 2003, 265). These signifiers of Mexican identity, or *mexicanidad*, are played out in very specific ways in *El vampiro* in which the villainous other and the heroes can best be understood within national conceptions of belonging.

El vampiro, the 1957 Mexican horror classic, is one of the most esteemed films in its genre and was considered one of Mexico's most successful films in that year. The film was not only a box-office hit in Mexico, but also became a cult classic internationally. These films were eventually dubbed in English and were shown on television in the United States in the 1960s (see Shaw and Dennison 2005, 227–28). The tremendous success of *El vampiro* resulted in the immediate production of its sequel, *El ataúd del vampiro* (The Vampire's Coffin).

The plot of *El vampiro* follows a predictable vampire-film model. Here, two innocent victims, Marta and Enrique, arrive on the dangerous terrain of the Count in Sicomoros, Mexico. Instead of Count Dracula, we find the equally ominous and sinister Count Lavud, also known as Mr. Duval. Mr. Duval has a plan to illicitly acquire Marta's family hacienda by slowly turning the family members into vampires. Marta's aunt Eloisa has already been turned into a vampire, while her other aunt, María Teresa, has been buried alive in the family crypt. Ultimately, Enrique and María Teresa will have to cast out the vampire in order to save the family estate and restore order.

The film has all the usual characteristics of the classic vampire film as first established by Murnau's *Nosferatu*, but transferred to rural Mexico in the mid-twentieth century. Rather than in a Gothic castle, the story takes place in a once-magnificent hacienda, whose surrounding land is haunted by vampires. This hacienda has the customary architecture associated with the Gothic castle, including trapdoors, secret passageways, a crypt, libraries, and subterranean labyrinths. Furthermore, instead of the superstitious

Transylvanians often found in various vampire films, Mexican Catholic mestizo peasants adorn the screen. The opening scene shows a vampire attacking a young aristocratic woman in a grand Mexican hacienda sometime in the mid-1800s, but then cuts to a scene in rural Mexico in the 1940s, where all of the subsequent action unfolds.

Typically, the heroine first arrives at the site where she will inevitably be seduced and bitten by the aristocratic vampire. As in the opening scenes in the films *Nosferatu* and the Browning *Dracula*, a mysterious carriage arrives with an equally mysterious shifty-eyed henchman in order to transport the unwitting victim and hero, Marta and Enrique, to the vampire's terrain. The carriage driver in this film is not only transporting Marta and Enrique, but he is also transporting soil brought from Bakonia, Hungary, in a crate addressed to Mr. Duval, the villain.

As I have described earlier, the vampire in the film *El vampiro* has lost its associations with the pre-Columbian deity, the death bat, or the sacred medium. This Mexican filmic vampire inherits many of the characteristics of the vampire conceived by Bram Stoker and represented in the films *Nosferatu* and *Dracula* (both the English and Spanish versions): an aristocratic, refined, and erotic evil soul seeking to devour victims and conquer lands.

The villain is the elegant and distinguished Mr. Duval, who is dressed in foreign-looking noble garb with a large pendant, all of which is reminiscent of Bela Lugosi's Dracula costume. At the same time, there is one additional feature present in this vampire that was not part of the visual representation in vampire films up to this point (see Cotter 2006, audio commentary): he has canine-like fangs. Stoker's vampire does have this feature; however, in films up to 1957, the sharp teeth were not usually visually represented. Stoker describes the Count in the following way:

> *His face was a strong—a very strong—aquiline, with high bridge of the thin nose and peculiarly arched nostrils; with lofty domed forehead, and hair growing scantily round the temples, but profusely elsewhere. His eyebrows were very massive, almost meeting over the nose, and with bushy hair that seemed to curl in its own profusion. The mouth, so far as I could see it under the heavy moustache, was fixed and rather cruel-looking, with peculiarly sharp white teeth; these protruded over the lips, whose remarkable ruddiness showed astonishing vitality in a man of his years. For the rest, his ears were pale and at the tops extremely pointed; the chin was broad and strong, and the cheeks firm though thin. The general effect was one of extraordinary pallor. ([1897] 1996, 22)*

Perhaps such large canine teeth would have offended spectator sensibilities at the time; yet, after *El vampiro,* these fangs would be incorporated into almost every subsequent film. At the same time, on his journey to visit the Gonzales family, Mr. Duval steps out of his carriage momentarily to feed on a peasant child and he does so in the presence of the child's mother. Such a scene would have been unusual for vampire films before 1957. In this way, the Mexican vampire is gifted with more animalistic or aggressive behavior than previously seen in films. He is, in effect, a more intimidating vampire than his filmic predecessors.

Mr. Duval is trying to purchase the hacienda, Sicomoros, from the esteemed Gonzales family that owns the estate on which Count Karol de Lavud, the villain's brother, is seemingly buried. Mr. Duval has two sinister aims: to resurrect his dead brother, who was murdered one hundred years ago by the town peasants, and then, along with him, to conquer the rest of the country. His plan will only work if he is able to purchase the hacienda from the Gonzales siblings: Emilio, Eloisa, and María Teresa.

The rest of the family does not realize that Eloisa has already been turned into a vampire and that she is scheming along with Mr. Duval to take the land they refuse to sell from Emilio and María Teresa. They first try to eliminate María Teresa by giving her a secret powder that places her in a living-dead state. Because she is presumed dead, she is buried alive in the family crypt. With María Teresa's supposed death, Marta, her niece, is now in a vulnerable position as heir, therefore becoming yet another obstacle and object of Mr. Duval's evil desire. He, of course, plans to convert her into a vampire as he did with Eloisa.

It is significant to point out that the name Count Lavud is a palindrome for Duval, which clearly appropriates a play on words not uncommon in vampire literature. Examples of wordplay are present in the novel *Carmilla* (1872) by Joseph Sheridan Le Fanu, in which the female vampire is known by the anagrammatic names Carmilla, Mircalla, and Millarca. Similarly, the hero, Enrique, will later discover Mr. Duval's sinister lineage when he holds a mirror up to Count Lavud's epitaph and deciphers the name. What is significant about the surname *Duval* is the origin, which is clearly French, suggesting the role of France in the Mexican imaginary and national identity after the French invasion of 1862 and the reign of Maximilian. At the same time, the title *Count* is a clear reference to European nobility, which further marks him as a foreigner in Mexican land.

REAFFIRMING THE MEXICAN NATIONAL IMAGINARY

The reaffirmation of national identity is not only played out in the image of the vampire, but also realized through other characters. Most important, María Teresa, who is buried alive but later saved by her faithful and very Catholic servants, is visually different than her vampire sister, Eloisa. The fair-skinned and ageless Eloisa is more akin to the typical vampire vixen: young, seductive, erotic, and evil. At the same time, she is elegantly dressed in a black fitted gown with a plunging neckline. One of the first supernatural appearances begins with the introduction of Eloisa's character. As Marta and Enrique are walking at night toward the hacienda, Eloisa magically appears at the crossroads and secretly follows them. When she arrives at the hacienda, she is transformed into a bat and then mysteriously reappears at the top of the staircase to greet Marta. This appearance and transformation reveal that evil has already violated the sanctity of the Gonzales home.

Eloisa's placement at the crossroads is also very significant. The crossroads is a metaphorically charged space that is most commonly used to describe one's figurative position in life, but it is also frequently used as a metaphor for the transition to the afterlife. In Eastern European folklore, it is often the place where those suspected of vampirism are interred because the crossroads bears the form of a cross. A wide range of deviant behavior can mark one as a potential vampire. For example, those who have died by suicide or while drunk can become vampires. Criminals, bastards, witches, magicians, and even the excommunicated are among those who can become vampires and are therefore buried at the crossroads (see McNally and Florescu 1994, 121–23). It is believed that when they return as the undead, they will be confused at the intersections of roads and hence be unable to find their way home. This place where the roads meet is also important in Mexican folklore, because the mythical monster *Cihuatateo* is sometimes considered to be a vampire who stalks travelers at the crossroads. *Cihuatateo* is the "Celestial Princess" and demonic female who roamed paths and haunted crossroads to maim and kill (see Clendinnen 1991, 82). The placement of Eloisa at a crossroads clearly situates her in a place that denotes evil.

Seemingly, Eloisa has invited the vampire to cross the threshold and she has given herself to Mr. Duval, thereby becoming a traitor to the family. The female duplicity played out in this film recalls representations of La Malinche, Hernán Cortés's interpreter, guide, and mistress, as well as later a quintessential symbol of national betrayal. She played an important role in the conquest of the Aztec empire in the sixteenth century and has since been made into the archetypal traitor and thus without honor. In this way, the film plays with the Mexican imaginary in which female betrayal could be understood in very specific historical terms.

María Teresa, on the other hand, is very different from her traitorous sister, Eloisa. Unlike her sister, she has darker and more mestizo features. She also has long, black, disheveled hair with long, gray streaks that make her look haggard. Instead of wearing a fitted gown, she wears a cloak-like black dress. More important, she appears in almost every scene carrying a large crucifix, which underscores both her faith and her yearning to exorcise the vampires. She is neither an object of desire nor the source of malevolence, but rather the quintessential devout Catholic and mestizo woman who will ultimately bring about the demise of the monsters. Even though she is presumed dead, she wanders through the secret passageways and trapdoors of the hacienda like a spirit seeking to protect the family from the menacing vampires.

While Eloisa might remind spectators of the ultimate betrayal embodied in the image of La Malinche, María Teresa's character evokes yet another culturally important female, but in this case she is the epitome of virtue, the Virgin Mary. María Teresa's name may refer not only to the Virgin Mary, but her name could also be alluding to the *Virgen de Santa Teresa del Niño Jesus* or *Santa Teresa de Avila*, both important Catholic saints of the Carmelite order who are said to be under the protection of the Blessed Virgin Mary. Although the romantic hero, Enrique, accompanies and saves the heroine from the clutches of the vampire, it is the saintly female figure who will cast out the evil from the hacienda. With seemingly supernatural strength, María Teresa is ultimately responsible for annihilating the vampires. In the final climactic scene, she strangles her sister, the vampire and traitor, and she also drives a stake through the heart of Mr. Duval, therefore singlehandedly ending the vampire invasion. It is unusual to have a female figure as vampire killer portrayed in such aggressive terms. In the novel *Dracula*, it is Van Helsing and other male figures who drive the stake through the hearts of many of the vampires, but here there is an inversion of gender roles. In *Nosferatu*, for example, Count Orlock dies as a result of seduction on the part of a woman who is his object of desire. In the final scene of that film, he is so engrossed with sucking her blood that he does not notice the threatening sun rays that cause him to disintegrate. Thus, the female provokes the vampire's annihilation through seduction and not through direct physical violence.

In *El vampiro*, the female figure is the one who has the power to vanquish evil and prevent an apocalypse. When cast within the Mexican context—with a prevailing Catholic culture in which *La Virgen de Guadalupe* receives the most fervent veneration—it is not surprising that the virgin-like mestizo

woman is the one to banish the demonic monsters. Since Mexican independence, *La Virgen de Guadalupe* has been a symbol of *mexicanidad*: she
is the synthesis of the Indian goddess and the Virgin Mary. In his study of
the Mexican madonna, William B. Taylor describes the phenomena in terms
that are pertinent to this discussion:

> *The story of the apparition in 1531, just ten years after the Aztec capi-*
> *tal at Tenochtitlan fell to Cortés, is rich in providential possibilities—a*
> *dark-complected Virgin appears to a lowly Indian in Tepeyac, the sa-*
> *cred place of pre-Columbian goddess, leaving her beautiful image on the*
> *Indian's cloak. Then, in a spontaneous surge of Indian devotion, natives*
> *flock to the site of the miracle, embracing her image in their spiritual*
> *orphanhood as if she were the new mother restoring order in the super-*
> *natural world as well as in the here and now. She combines the Indian*
> *past with the Spanish present to make something new, a proto–Mexican*
> *Indian Madonna who will gradually be accepted as well by American*
> *Spaniards and* mestizos *as their own thus forming the spiritual basis of*
> *a national independence movement in the early 19th century. (quoted*
> *in Poole 1995, 5)*

The vampire killer, María Teresa, could be seen as the incarnation of *La Virgen de Guadalupe*; like her, she restores order in the supernatural world by
casting out the vampires from the hacienda and, by analogy, from Mexico.
María Teresa's role in the film recalls images of the various representations
of the Virgin Mary holding a spear over a dragon to prevent the apocalypse.
This is a very significant detail because the same image is replayed in the
final scene when she is standing over the vampire with a stake. As Raymond
McNally has already noted, Dracula's name was associated not only with
the devil but also with a dragon. The historical Dracula's (Vlad the Impaler)
family crest included the image of a dragon—the name *Dracul* signifying
dragon in Romanian (see McNally and Florescu 1994, 8–9). In the end, María
Teresa is the national heroine who vanquishes the foreign other who was
threatening the sanctity of home and nation.

The film seemingly recalls national myths through its representation of
female characters, and it also reaffirms Mexican identity vis-à-vis France
and French culture. In terms of national identity, Mexico has had a complex
relationship with France: on the one hand, France is a cultural and intellectual model for Mexico, especially among the elite, but on the other hand,
France is also a country that invaded Mexico twice during the nineteenth
century. These incursions are emblematic moments in the construction of

Mexican nationalism. Furthermore, the film was released in 1957, which also happens to be the centennial celebration of the 1857 constitution. In Mexico, as in other Western cultures, centennial celebrations have always been important moments used to reaffirm national identity, which suggests that the constant and unrestrained mention of the centennial by several of the characters in the film is purposeful. By recalling the centennial of the first vampire assault that was said to have happened sometime around 1840, the film seems to point to the first French invasion of Mexico, known as the Pastry War (1838). In this odd historical episode, a French pastry chef complained to French King Louis-Philippe that his shop had been looted by Mexican officials. France used this affront along with defaulting loans to invade Mexico and recover some of those debts (see MacLachlan and Beezley 2010, 61–62). The Battle of Puebla, which took place on May 5, 1862, is a military triumph that is important in the Mexican imaginary: the well-armed invading French soldiers sent by Napolean III were defeated by their poorly armed Mexican counterparts, some of whom only had machetes. The Battle of Puebla is often cited to underscore Mexican valor and courage in the most dire of circumstances.

Due to years of civil unrest, Mexico was in a weakened position, rendering it susceptible to invasion. Napoleon III of France—often described in vampiric terms by Victor Hugo—was ready to feed on the wealth of a weaker nation. The historian Kristine Ibsen's description of Mexico echoes this vampire metaphor: "Defenseless, and weak, the homeland had been left vulnerable to the parasitical European powers" (quoted in MacLachlan and Beezley 2010, 25). Under the guise of a "civilizing mission" and uniting the "Latin race," Napoleon III of France chose to invade Mexico (see Ibsen 2010, 2). Given that the occupation of Mexico was both politically and financially advantageous, he sent troops to Mexico under the pretext of collecting outstanding loans. In 1864, Napoleon III also named Archduke Fernando Maximilian, along with his wife Carlota of Belgium, emperor and empress of Mexico. The temporary occupation that ended in 1867 was short-lived and resulted in the execution of Maximilian and the expulsion of the French troops. The film subtly alludes to the Napoleonic invasion and to the empress when the tomb of Count Lavud first appears on the screen. The date printed on the epitaph reads "Enero 19, 1840," which corresponds to the birth year of Carlota of Belgium (June 7, 1840) and the month and day of her death (January 19, 1927). As Ibsen underscores, the emperor and empress were significant figures in the imagining of national identity and therefore the inclusion of these dates cannot be accidental: "Extravagantly theatrical yet resistant to preconceived divisions and easy categorizations, the story of the ill-fated emperors has alternately been regarded as the last vestige of a dying order, and as the catalyst for the formation of Mexican national identity" (2010, viii).

More important, in terms of historical context, this 1957 film was released as the government was seeking dramatic ways to commemorate the 1857 constitution, the reforms, and the death of Benito Juárez (see Weeks 1987, 114). These centennial celebrations lasted from the late 1950s through the late 1960s. Benito Juárez, a mythic hero for many, was called the "Moses of equality" and became one of Mexico's most deified symbols (see Ibsen 2010, 8). He is one of the most popular historical figures who embody *mexicanidad*: a man of Zapotec Indian ancestry and humble beginnings who eventually became president of the country. In an act designed to reaffirm the republic and to repudiate the assault, he was also responsible for the execution of Maximilian, despite international pleas. As a way to remember his contribution to the restoration of the republic, the government erected a large monument of Juárez on the site of Maximilian's execution during the centennial celebrations (see Weeks 1987, 114). A coin bearing the bust of Juárez was also minted in 1957. These official commemorative celebrations and gestures underscore that the resistances to the multiple French interventions are important moments in the national imaginary that help to define Mexican identity: Mestizo, Indian, Criollo, Spanish, but never French.

Similarly, José Vasconcelos, a philosopher and an influential figure in the forging of a national identity in postrevolutionary Mexico, wrote on this subject in his book, *La raza cósmica* (1925). In it, he celebrates *mexicanidad* by recalling the various cultures that constitute the nation: Indians, colonizing Europeans (from Spain), and African slaves. In other words, in official discourse, the indigenous cultures, the Spanish conquerors, and the African slaves are recognized as belonging to the Mexican national identity. This confirms the observation of critic Carlos Monsiváis (2003) that the Mexican film industry promoted cultural nationalism through the incorporation of edifying moments such as national celebrations and historical events. It is thus not surprising that many of the characters in the film recall the centennial of the vampire invasion, reminding the spectator of the important moments in the national past. In other words, this film could be understood as another form of reaffirming notions of identity by emphasizing the threat embodied in the vampire, which, as I have argued, is negotiated through Mexico's complicated involvement with France in the nineteenth century.

In my discussion, I have followed the journey of the vampire from the Americas to Europe and back in order to analyze the ways in which the monster is articulated in each cultural context. In the films, the vampire is a menacing figure that arrives seeking to infect, invade, and conquer. At the same time, he is potentially a subversive other that transgresses borders and threatens stability. The vampire figure can be understood as an agent that expresses certain cultural fears at very specific social and political crossroads. As many critics have suggested, in US and European films, the vampire figure embodies anxieties and fears about immigration, in particular because the films were produced during a time when certain ethnic groups were treated aggressively and even expelled from their adopted homelands.

When the anthropomorphized bat was reappropriated by Mexican filmmakers in the 1950s, the vampire men and the bat deities—such as those found in pre-Columbian culture and codices—seem to have been permanently buried under the Europeanized vampire monster. In its place, the monster that appears on the Mexican silver screen is yet another version of the literary vampire as first created by Bram Stoker in the nineteenth century, a projection that we can find in almost every film ever since. In *El vampiro*, as in other vampire films, the menacing monster that invades, crosses borders, and threatens identity must be cast out or killed so that order may be restored. In the case of Mexico, the foreign threat embodied in the vampire calls to mind historical events having to do with French invasion and expulsion, which were founding moments in the nation's history, as seen in the many centennial celebrations of the late 1950s.

WORKS CITED

Abbott and Costello Meet Frankenstein. 1948. Directed by Charles Barton. Perf. Bud Abbott, Lou Costello, Lon Chaney Jr., Bela Lugosi, Glenn Strange. Produced by Robert Arthur.

Abbott, Stacey. 2004. "Spectral Vampires: *Nosferatu* in the Light of New Technology." In *Horror Film: Creating and Marketing Fear*, edited by Steffen Hantke, 3–20. Jackson: University Press of Mississippi.

Abraham Lincoln: Vampire Hunter. 2012. Directed by Timur Bekmambetov. Perf. Benjamin Walker, Rufus Sewell, Dominic Cooper. Produced by Timur Bekmambetov, Tim Burton, and Jim Lemley.

El ataúd del vampiro. 1958. Directed by Fernando Méndez. Perf. Abel Salazar, Ariadna Welter, Germán Robles. Produced by Abel Salazar.

Beebe, William. 1922. *Edge of the Jungle.* New York: Henry Holt.

Bruce-Novoa, Juan. 2011. "Border Crossings and (Trans)nationalism in Film: Paradigms of Attitudes towards Immigration: Science Fiction Films as Allegories in the Mid-Century." In *Aesthetic Practices and Politics in Media, Music, and Art Performing Migration*, edited by Rocío G. Davis, Dorothea Fischer-Hornung, and Johanna C. Kardux, 15–29. New York: Routledge.

Clendinnen, Inga. 1991. *Aztecs: An Interpretation.* Cambridge: Cambridge University Press.

Cotter, Robert. 2006. Audio commentary on *El vampiro*. DVD. San Francisco, CA: CasaNegra Entertainment.

Dark Shadows. 2012. Directed by Tim Burton. Perf. Johnny Depp, Michelle Pfeiffer, Eva Green. Produced by Graham King, Christi Dembrowski, Johnny Depp, David Kennedy, Richard D. Zanuck, et al.

Darwin, Charles. [1839] 1909. *The Voyage of the Beagle*. New York: P. F. Collier.

Daybreakers. 2009. Directed by Michael Spierig and Peter Spierig. Perf. Ethan Hawke, Willem Dafoe, Claudia Karvan, Michael Dorman, Sam Neill, Vince Colosimo, Isabel Lucas. Produced by Chris Brown, Sean Furst, and Bryan Furst.

The Devil's Manor. 1896. Directed by Georges Méliès. Perf. Georges Méliès, Jeanne d'Alcy. Produced by Georges Méliès.

Dr. Jekyll and Mr. Hyde. 1931. Directed by Rouben Mamoulian. Perf. Fredric March, Miriam Hopkins, Rose Hobart. Produced by Rouben Mamoulian.

Dracula. 1931. Directed by Tod Browning. Perf. Bela Lugosi, Helen Chandler, David Manners. Produced by Tod Browning and Carl Laemmle Jr.

Drácula. 1931. Directed by George Melford. Perf. Carlos Villarías, Lupita Tovar, Barry Norton. Produced by Paul Kohner and Carl Laemmle Jr.

The Fearless Vampire Killers; or, Pardon Me, but Your Teeth Are in My Neck. 1967. Directed by Roman Polanski. Perf. Jack MacGowran, Roman Polanski, Sharon Tate, Alfie Bass, Ferdy Mayne. Produced by Gene Gutowski.

Flynn, John L. 1992. *Cinematic Vampires: The Living Dead on Film and Television, from "The Devil's Castle" (1896) to "Bram Stoker's Dracula" (1992)*. Jefferson, NC: McFarland.

Frankenstein. 1931. Directed by James Whale. Perf. Colin Clive, Mae Clarke, Boris Karloff. Produced by Carl Laemmle Jr.

Gelder, Ken. 1994. *Reading the Vampire*. London: Routledge.

Gonzales, Manuel G. 1999. *Mexicanos: A History of Mexicans in the United States*. Bloomington: Indiana University Press.

Halberstam, Judith. 1995. *Skin Shows: Gothic Horror and the Technology of Monsters*. Durham, NC: Duke University Press.

Hughes, William. 2012. "Fictional Vampires in the Nineteenth and Twentieth Centuries." In *A New Companion to the Gothic*, edited by David Punter, 197–210. Oxford: Blackwell.

Ibsen, Kristine. 2010. *Maximilian, Mexico, and the Invention of Empire*. Nashville: Vanderbilt University Press.

Kampen, M. E. 1978. "Classic Veracruz Grotesques and Sacrificial Iconography." *Man*, n.s., 13 (1): 116–26.

Le Fanu, Sheridan. [1872] 2003. "Carmilla." In *Three Vampire Tales*, edited by Anne Williams, 86–148. Boston: Wadsworth.

Let Me In. 2010. Directed by Matt Reeves. Perf. Kodi Smit-McPhee, Chloë Grace Moretz, Richard Jenkins. Produced by Donna Gigliotti, Alex Brunner, Simon Oakes, Tobin Armbrust, et al.

Let the Right One In. 2008. Directed by Tomas Alfredson. Perf. Kåre Hedebrant, Lina Leandersson, Per Ragnar. Produced by Carl Molinder, John Nordling, and Warren Riviere.

MacLachlan, Colin M., and William H. Beezley. 2010. *Mexico's Crucial Century, 1810–1920: An Introduction*. Lincoln: University of Nebraska Press.

McNally, Raymond T., and Radu Florescu. 1994. *In Search of Dracula: The History of Dracula and Vampires*. Boston: Houghton Mifflin.

Meyer, Stephenie. 2005. *Twilight*. New York: Little, Brown.

Monsiváis, Carlos. 2003. "Función corrida (El cine mexicano y la cultura popular urbana)." In *Los estudios culturales en México*, edited by José Manuel Valenzuela Arce, 261–95. México, DF: Fondo de Cultura Económica.

El mundo de los vampiros. 1960. Directed by Alfonso Corona Blake. Perf. Mauricio Garcés, Erna Martha Bauman, Silvia Fournier. Produced by Abel Salazar.

Nosferatu. 1922. Directed by Friedrich W. Murnau. Perf. Max Schreck, Gustav von Wangenheim, Gerda Schröder, Alexander Granach. Produced by Enrico Dieckmann and Albin Grau.

Phillips, Kendall R. 2005. *Projected Fears: Horror Films and American Culture*. Westport, CT: Praeger.

Pinto, Alfonso. 1973. "Hollywood's Spanish-Language Films: A Neglected Chapter of the American Cinema, 1930–1935." *Films in Review* 24:474–87.

Poole, Stafford. 1995. *Our Lady of Guadalupe: The Origins and Sources of a Mexican National Symbol, 1531–1797*. Tucson: University of Arizona Press.

Prest, Thomas Peckett, and James Malcolm Rymer. [1845] 1970. *Varney the Vampire; or, The Feast of Blood*. New York: Arno Press.

Punter, David, and Glennis Byron. 2004. *The Gothic*. Oxford: Blackwell.

Recinos, Adrián. 1969. *Popul vuh, libro común de los quiches*. La Habana: Casa de las Américas.

El Santo contra las mujeres vampiro. 1962. Directed by Alfonso Corona Blake. Perf. El Santo (Rodolfo Guzman Huerto), Lorena Velázquez, María Duval, Jaime Fernández, Augusto Benedico, Ofelia Montesco, Javier Loya. Produced by Alberto Lopez.

Shaw, Lisa, and Stephanie Dennison. 2005. *Pop culture Latin America! Media, Arts, and Lifestyle*. Santa Barbara, CA: ABC-CLIO.

Shelley, Mary Wollstonecraft. [1818] 2012. *Frankenstein*. London: Penguin.

Skal, David J. 1990. "The Spanish Dracula." *American Film* 15 (12): 38–41.

Stevenson, Robert Louis. [1886] 1961. *The Strange Case of Dr. Jekyll and Mr. Hyde, and Other Famous Tales*. New York: Dodd, Mead.

Stoker, Bram. [1897] 1996. *Dracula*. New York: Barnes and Noble.

Thompson, J. Eric S. 1966. "Maya Hieroglyphs of the Bat as Metaphorgrams." *Man*, n.s., 1 (2): 176–84.

El vampiro. [1957] 2006. Directed by Fernando Méndez. Perf. Abel Salazar, Germán Robles, Ariadne Welter. Produced by Abel Salazar. DVD. San Francisco, CA: CasaNegra Entertainment.

Las vampiras. 1969. Directed by Federico Curiel. Perf. John Carradine, María Duval, Pedro Armendáriz Jr. Produced by Jesús Fragoso Montoya and Luis Enrique Vergara.

Vasconcelos, José. [1925] 1966. *La raza cósmica: Misión de la raza Iberoamericana, Argentina y Brasil*. Mexico DF: Espasa-Calpe.

Weeks, Charles A. 1987. *The Juárez Myth in Mexico*. Tuscaloosa: University of Alabama Press.

White Zombie. 1932. Directed by Victor Halperin. Perf. Bela Lugosi, Madge Bellamy, Joseph Cawthorn. Produced by Victor Halperin.

Wilde, Oscar. [1890] 2012. *The Picture of Dorian Gray*. London: Penguin.

THE REANIMATION OF YELLOW-PERIL ANXIETIES IN MAX BROOKS'S *WORLD WAR Z*

TIMOTHY R. FOX

With the 2006 publication of *World War Z: An Oral History of the Zombie War*, novelist Max Brooks made history, both literally and figuratively. Literally, according to *Publishers Weekly* (2011, online), Brooks broke barriers and made publishing history with sales of all formats (hardcover, paperback, audio) reaching 600,000 within just five years of the book's release. The 2013 release of the feature-length film produced by and starring Brad Pitt only served to help further boost sales of the novel ("Best Sellers" 2006, online), making sure it remained on top-sellers lists long after its initial publication.[1] Not only is *World War Z* the first zombie-themed book to achieve such strong sales figures in such a short period of time, but it may well be the first contemporary zombie-themed novel in the history of horror fiction to have found its way onto the *New York Times* Top 10 Bestsellers list (Deutsch 2013, online).

Figuratively, of course, Brooks "made" history insofar as *World War Z* is fashioned not in the traditional novelistic format, but as a "historical document," a compilation of reportage on the fictional postapocalyptic scenario of viral zombies overrunning the world and the human effort required to repulse this global plague. The text mimics the style of interview transcription made popular by the published oral-history works of Pulitzer Prize–winning Studs Terkel.[2] *World War Z* features the fictional first-person accounts of dozens of individuals who lived through and in many instances played important roles in fighting what has come to be known as "the zombie war." The underlying plot of the novel is of a viral plague that begins in China and spreads worldwide through the black market for organ transplants and illegal immigration. The virus kills its victims and reanimates them as cannibalistic zombies capable of spreading the disease. Nations throughout the world are overrun, the sole exception being Israel, which was prepared for the pandemic, and geographically isolated Cuba. The novel generally criticizes the lack of insight on the part of government ministers and military planners who allowed the plague to spread. The "war" is won through the slow advance of a sniper-based military strategy, an approach that takes many years.

Although *World War Z* is entertaining and well researched, and Brooks generally is successful in giving voices and identities to his multiple "narrators," the novel also betrays a number of negative traits easily identified as contemporary variants of traditional Yellow-Peril thinking or anti-Asian anxiety. This popular novel may not be identical to the "massive ethnic slur" (Button 2006, 427) that was Yellow-Peril fiction of an earlier time in American cultural history, but it does contain elements of what might be construed generally as reflecting contemporary American anti-Asian anxieties (see O'Sullivan 2000, 28). As I demonstrate here, the best-selling novel *World War Z* builds on an undercurrent of racially motivated antagonism toward Asians that goes beyond a mere nationalistic response to the rising geopolitical and economic power of China. If that is the case, then it can be assumed that the ongoing popular appeal for *World War Z* is based not only on the novel's varied, entertaining, and creative plot structure, but on its subtle expression of both the nationalistic and the racial anxieties that serve as emotional touchstones for those within the United States who fear that the demise of the nation's liberal democratic society is at hand.

WHAT IS YELLOW PERIL?

Most simply defined, the belief in the Yellow Peril entails the irrational fear of conquest or domination by an Asian power, specifically a Chinese or Japanese invader. But to understand this irrational fear, it is necessary to understand the historical depths of its roots. The general anxiety of the Yellow Peril arises not from historical circumstances, but from the metaphysical foundation upon which modern Euro-American sociopolitical worldviews are drawn. Yellow-Peril anxiety has its roots in the European philosophical vision that defines the Asian as a figure of nature, a negative characterization when seen through comparison to the ideal of Western subjectivity. In the Yellow-Peril fiction of the United States and England of the early twentieth century, the West is "the site within which the true essence of the human finds realization" (Button 2006, 427). This Eurocentric belief is closely tied to the Christian concept of progress toward a paradisiacal future and a world free from suffering and sin. Such a concept of progress necessarily sets up contesting notions by which the upright goal is underscored by its opposite, which is also its opponent. The presence of an enemy, therefore, lends vitality to the Euro-Christian worldview. Running parallel to the Euro-Christian vision of universal progress is the ideology of eighteenth-century Enlightenment thinking that posits perfectibility as achievable through intellectual reason. The iconic zombie of contemporary imagination stands as an extreme example of the human devoid of intellectual capabilities, and therefore lacking in any of the qualities that define what is human.

Respect for the human based on intellect and the mind shaped the political philosophies of Enlightenment thinkers such as Voltaire, Montesquieu, Hume, Locke, Kant, and Jefferson, all of whom developed liberal and egalitarian ideals concerning "the rights of man" (see Baum 2006, 42; West 2002, 105). And yet, argues Cornel West, these same political philosophers of the Enlightenment were also profoundly influenced by French physician Francois Bernier's 1684 publication, *New Division of the Earth*, which attempted a classification of the human species according to racial qualifications. Bernier placed the white European at the top of his hierarchy of races, basing his ranking on ideals borrowed from the classical Greek notions of beauty and form (see West 2002, 99; McGary 2002, 434).[3] West credits Bernier as the first Enlightenment scientist to give intellectual legitimacy to the idea of white supremacy: "This legitimacy can be illustrated by the extent to which racism permeated the writings of the major figures of the Enlightenment" (2002, 105).[4]

As noted previously, the primary standard against which races were judged was the ability to engage the human intellect toward rational thought resulting in progress. In this intellectual contest, the white European stood alone as a figure ennobled by the use of reason to achieve progress across all realms, including the establishment of governments, the enlargement of capital markets, and the development of laws that uphold standards of ethical and moral behavior—attitudes that still resonate to this day.[5] By the standard of human reason, then, the human species could be categorized along racial lines, with human races ranked according to degrees of "humanness" (see Baum 2006, 43). Building upon these standards, Enlightenment philosophers saw the Asian as only slightly better than the African, who was positioned at the bottom of the hierarchy of humanity. The Asian was viewed as animate but animal, so deeply embedded in nature that any possible chance of achieving a "truly human life" could not emerge (Button 2006, 430).[6] This certainly was the philosophical underpinning of the Yellow Peril as manifest in the anti-immigrant nativist movement that so strongly dominated economic and political discourse in the United States of the late nineteenth and early twentieth centuries.

As Europe moved from one world war to the next, the political and business elite in the United States reformed the notion of biologically based difference to notions of social and cultural difference (see Tolentino 2001, 5). This enabled a new element of discrimination to be brought into play by the American nativist movement, namely the notion of "benevolent assimilation" (7). Unable to legally stop the flow of unwelcome immigrants from Eastern Europe or Ireland, the nativist movement comforted itself with the notion that at least these "white" arrivals could potentially "reproduce Anglo-European values and settlement practices" (8).

Asian immigrants were labeled by the nativist movement as essentially "unassimilable" aliens on American soil (11). This notion of Asians as foreigners whose loyalties remain outside US borders helped fuel the notion of "danger" that has played an important part of the Yellow-Peril discourse. Chinese laborers bore the brunt of the anger and paranoia fueled by the nativist movement (see Olivas 1995, 13). The anti-Asian antagonism toward "the dreaded and unpopular Chinese" soon shifted to other immigrant communities, especially the Japanese, who were characterized as disloyal and dangerous (14). Nativist politicians campaigned on an anti-immigration platform that denounced the "tricky and unscrupulous" Japanese as being even more "aggressive and warlike" than the Chinese (Lee 2003, 46). Organizations such as the Asian Exclusion League referred to Asian immigration as "The Silent Invasion" (47) by "Asiatic hordes" intent on "insurrection" (50–51).

Asian immigrants were seen not only as a danger to national security, but as a threat to the moral status of the nation as well. Notions of the Asian as immoral suggest a philosophical worldview tainted by white supremacy that perceives Asians as animals whose behavior is universally predictable as a result of animalistic drives or instincts. In some way, this racist view of the Asian is similar to the contemporary figure of the fictional zombie, an uncanny being in motion only to satisfy an animalistic drive for prey. Most certainly the original, early Western iconic zombie was inseparable from the racist view of the African slave and closely connected to anxieties about possible slave uprisings on white plantations. It was Victor Halperin's 1932 Hollywood film *White Zombie* that frightened Americans with "the true horror" of the possibility of a white person, a "Westerner," becoming "dominated, subjugated, symbolically raped, and effectively 'colonized' by pagan representatives" (Bishop 2010, 66), or Africans. Halperin's Haitian voodoo zombie, which Kyle Bishop describes as "a new monster for a new world," was able to incite fear in white American audiences "because of its direct ties to the racial dichotomies of colonialism" (69). At the tail end of the colonial period, white viewers most likely saw in *White Zombie* the realization of "the greatest fear of the colonizers—that the natives will rise up and become the dominating force" (80). Interestingly, for Americans living during in the years of the US occupation of Haiti (1915–33), Haiti was understood by many to be "the West's East": "Conjured by Orientalist fears, the 'Voodoo zombie' genre arose," helping to spur Hollywood movie producers and audiences toward an "interest" in zombies (see Hamako 2011, 108).

Belief in the Asian as dangerous and immoral found its way into various cultural productions in both North America and England throughout the late nineteenth and early twentieth centuries. Among these were novels by noted authors such as Jack London, whose 1914 short story *The Unparalleled Invasion* describes the takeover of the world by Chinese hordes. Published just two years later was J. Allen Dunne's novel *The Peril of the Pacific*, which narrated the colonization of the United States by Japanese forces. The science-fiction figure of Buck Rogers first appeared in Philip Francis Nowlan's 1928 novel *Armageddon 2419 A.D.*, a work that also portrayed the United States being colonized by Chinese invaders. Less dramatic in plot were the representations by novelists and journalists throughout the 1930s and 1940s of Chinese family lives, narratives that clearly advanced the notion of Asians as dangerous and immoral aliens on American soil (see Keely 2007, 129). Such articulations of anti-Asian Yellow-Peril anxieties were familiar to British readers as well, courtesy of Sax Rohmer's highly successful Fu Manchu novels. For Rohmer, the fear of the foreigner, or more specifically, the anxiety about the Asian within the English imperial homeland, was "the raison d'être and organizing principle of the Fu Manchu titles" (Shih 2009, 307). Equally relevant is Rohmer's project of defining English masculinity in accordance with European notions of reason and evolution. As David Shih argues, English masculinity in the Fu Manchu series is dependent upon the British man's ability to "maintain his civilized appearance while in the midst of the foreign presence" (308). This proximity is suggested as infectious and dangerous to the "rational" English Victorian subject, both at the individual and national levels. In his first novel, the villainous Fu Manchu poisons a policeman, who then lapses into animal-like behavior, suggesting Rohmer's fear of degeneracy, decay, and decadence at the hands of the Asian interloper. This reduction toward animal-like behavior can be seen as a precursor of the contemporary viral zombie fiction's portrayal of rational humans being transformed into irrational creatures motivated only by the drive to feed.

The suggestion of viral malevolence is stronger in Rohmer's second Fu Manchu novel, in which a Chinese national has murdered a white American and successfully assumed his identity in order to infiltrate England. This incident of "passing" betrays anxieties over miscegenation, the forbidden love that would bring the threat of infection even to the English bloodline itself, giving birth to barbarism and incivility within the center of British civilization (see Shih 2009, 314). Whatever form it may take, Yellow-Peril anxiety perceives the Asian as being essentially an infectious agent whose presence disrupts the West's grand narrative of progress and civilization. The similarities between the destruction of "civilization" by the agents of the Yellow Peril in early twentieth-century fiction and the ruination of civilization portrayed in contemporary postapocalyptic zombie fiction are striking. Ruth Mayer's descriptive list of Yellow-Peril assumptions about the Chinese could easily be applied to the modern zombie: "(T)he Chinese entered the Western world in the form of a uniform, robotic 'invasion' or 'flood': faceless, impervious to pain and hardship, enduring, impassionate, and infectious" (2014, 22).

That the anxieties surrounding the Yellow-Peril discourse might continue to be effective in US society cannot be surprising to scholars of critical race studies, who recognize continuing elements of the nativist movement in contemporary anti-immigration campaigns. Economic claims of illegal immigration undercutting employment opportunities for US citizens serve only to thinly veil actual racist anxieties; Aihwa Ong suggests that "racial hierarchies and polarities continue to inform Western notions of cultural difference" (1999, 286–87). "I maintain," says Ong, "that the white-black polarities emerging out of the history of European-American imperialism continue to shape attitudes and encode discourses directed at immigrants from the rest of the world that are associated with racial and cultural inferiority" (287). Like Ong, Joe Feagin notes, "[A]s in the past, most of the new American nativists wish to keep the nation predominantly white and European" (1999, 348).

YELLOW-PERIL CONTAGION

The notion of Western civilization being disrupted is central to Brooks's *World War Z*. This fictional oral history, which details the global spread of a viral zombie infection and the American-led battle to reclaim mass geographies lost to the cannibalistic undead, begins in China. With overtones similar to discussions of the introduction of HIV/AIDS into Europe and North America, the zombie pandemic of *World War Z* begins similarly with a "Patient Zero," a child who becomes infected while looting from the underwater ruins of his family village of Dachang.[7] The village had been buried some years before by what in the novel is represented as the grossly negligent and poorly conceived Three Gorges Dam construction project. It is this viral origin that serves as an initial indication that *World War Z* portrays elements of Yellow-Peril anxiety. Brooks betrays what could arguably be called an anti-Chinese attitude in his novel, a political stance that may easily be understood as arising from contemporary rhetoric accompanying an ongoing global competition between the United States and the People's Republic of China (see O'Sullivan 2000, 28). However, it is the presence of negative stereotypes typically attached to "Orientals" that validates the suggestion that *World War Z* contains rudiments of Yellow-Peril anxiety.

In Brooks's novel, the Chinese Communist bureaucracy is seen as corrupt, self-serving, and ignorant. To hide the spread of the zombie plague from prying Western eyes, Beijing makes aggressive moves toward invading democratic Taiwan as a diversionary tactic to refocus global attention. "And it worked!" exclaims a postwar CIA director. "If suddenly . . . one day the ChiComs show up at your front door with an eviction notice in one hand and a Molotov cocktail in the other, then the last thing you're going to do is look over his shoulder for a walking corpse. . . . It was deception, a fake out" (2006, 47). Meanwhile, the People's Liberation Army performs poorly in its task of controlling the zombie outbreak. "The army, arrogant bastards that they were, kept insisting that they had the problem under control" (234), says one Chinese naval informant: "Those generals, sick, twisted old criminals sitting safely in their bunker and ordering wave after wave of conscripted teenagers into battle" (235).

As China is overwhelmed by the zombie plague, the army wastes time, energy, and lives fighting an unnecessary civil war. Brooks's Chinese informant, an officer aboard the nation's last fully equipped nuclear-weapons submarine, blames the infighting on the Politburo, "those hated old men who had caused so much misery already" (253). Still in control of at least half of the nation's ground forces, the party politicians "would never surrender. . . . If the civil war dragged on any longer, the only being left in China would be the living dead" (234). To end the civil war, the submarine's commander sides with the rebels and launches a nuclear-missile strike against his former political bosses in their secured bunkers.

Beyond such easily recognizable nationalist-encouraged rhetoric about an incompetent and corrupt Chinese Communist Party leadership, *World War Z* also contains further disturbingly stereotypical references suggestive of Yellow-Peril thinking. One of these is the belief that the Asian lacks the capability for reasoning and rational thought—in other words, the Asian is incapable of thinking beyond immediate satisfaction. This is the image of the Chinese presented in Brooks's novel by a corrupt but clever Russian human trafficker, Yuri Televadi, whose description of the human-smuggling business places blame for the international spread of the zombie virus on the Chinese. Televadi points a finger at a number of officials who participated in human smuggling across borders: border guards, bureaucrats, police, and elected officials (see Brooks 2006, 13). Officials from Central Asian and other Third-World nations were also identified as guilty in their collusion with international human smugglers.

As Televadi relates, human traffickers were often hired by wealthy Chinese businessmen and bureaucrats trying to flee the country. Unwilling to leave their seemingly "alive" loved ones behind, these wealthy illegal migrants often brought their zombified relatives with them—bound and gagged—not realizing the potential danger of contagion their reanimated loved ones posed should they escape their confinements. Televadi also speaks of infected travelers who would board flights out of China with only mild symptoms of disease, and arrive at their overseas destinations as raging zombies. Televadi shows sympathy for those he calls "refugees," sympathizing with their desire to try to bring their loved ones out of China for medical treatment and save themselves from China's "treatment" of the illness (14). Still, Televadi acknowledges that it may well have been a smuggled Chinese migrant—a living man already infected with the virus—who introduced the zombie plague to Paris. "He had been bitten," Televadi explains. The infected man and his wife checked into a hotel in Paris "just as he began to collapse" (14). Ordering his wife to abandon him rather than call a doctor and risk deportation back to China, the man died and reanimated in the room. It was only after "two days of groans and commotion" that the hotel staff broke into the room. "I'm not sure if that is how the Paris outbreak started, though it would make sense," Televadi says (14).

Another stereotype generated by Yellow-Peril thinking is the notion that Asians are unethical and immoral. In this racist context, Asia is "as opposite morally from the West as it is geographically," says Frank Chin (1991, 8). "The highest and lowest minds of the nineteenth and early twentieth century described Asian culture as being stagnant, morally inferior, irrelevant, or nonexistent," Chin states (10). And much like the viral zombie, with whom close contact engenders the risk of one becoming similarly undead, those who come in close contact with Asians are similarly at risk of being infected and becoming unethical. This was certainly suggested in Rohmer's first Fu Manchu novel, as cited by Shih (2009, 309) earlier in this chapter.

In Brooks's novel, unethical Asian behavior is depicted in the Chinese human-organ trade, a practice that began in China but that spread its unethicality to those in the West who were intimately involved in medical-organ transplants.[8] Fernando Oliveira, too closely involved with Asian organ traders, is infected by their corruption, and therefore fails to maintain so-called Western ethical standards and thereby contributes to the spread of the zombie plague outside of China. Oliveira is a Brazilian doctor specializing in illegal organ transplants. Hearts, kidneys, livers, and other necessary organs are "found" in China—the government of which in the real world has been accused of turning a blind eye toward illegal organ removals from executed prisoners for sale on the medical black market (see Coonan and McNeill 2006, online).[9] Oliveira is aware that he is colluding with Chinese agents in an illegal undertaking, but he justifies his unlawful behavior by seeing the ends as outweighing the means: his is a life-saving undertaking. Of note is the Brazilian surgeon's defensiveness about his involvement in the illegal organ trade, his adoption of a stance that echoes contemporary self-defensive arguments put forth by Beijing-based defenders of China's negative human-rights record who refute criticism by pointing to the history of discrimination in Western nations.[10] He sees himself as better than those from "the self-righteous, hypocritical North" who would point fingers at him (Brooks 2006, 22). Despite his defensive self-justification, Oliveira is engaged in an unethical and illegal act. In the context of the Yellow-Peril stereotype of the Asian as an agent of infection, Oliveira has been corrupted through his close relationship with his Chinese broker in Macau. He trusts his broker to supply clean organs: "I took him at his word; I had to" (22), Oliveira says. The mistake of trusting his broker becomes evident when an infected Chinese heart transplanted into an Austrian patient in Oliveira's Brazilian clinic leads to the recipient's death and reanimation. Thus infected through his close contacts with Chinese organ traders, Oliveira goes on to contaminate his fellow nationals, bribing the local police who then go on to ineptly dispose of a bitten hospital worker's body—this being the possible source of the zombie outbreak in Sao Paulo.

For Oliveira to place his trust in a Macau-based broker is a violation of Yellow-Peril logic that would indicate that no Asian can be trusted to do the right thing. Oliveira acknowledges his own awareness that the Chinese army—"you want to talk about immoral," he says—had "been making millions on organs from executed political prisoners" (27). Oliveira is not so much corrupt as corrupted, a victim of close interactions with the unethical Asian. His Chinese-influenced corruption and that of other surgeons like him around the world contributes to the spread of the zombie plague across the globe. "By the time I realized the danger," Oliveira says, "it was scratching at my front door" (28).

One of the more popular scenes in Brooks's novel is the interview with Kondo Tatsumi, who recalls his teenage experience of escaping from his nineteenth-floor apartment in Kyoto while zombie crowds struggled to break down his front door. Tatsumi's story displays several Yellow-Peril stereotypes, one being Asians as lacking in reasoning or critical-thinking skills. The Japanese educational system is blamed: "Prewar Japanese children were not taught to think, we were taught to memorize" (Brooks 2006, 205). The Japanese educational system prepares Tatsumi for a life dedicated to Internet surfing, "a world of information without context, where status was determined on its acquisition and possession" (205). Japanese students were trained to memorize information, facts that "had no moral component, no social context, no human connection to the outside world," Tatsumi says (204). When the zombie plague strikes Japan, Tatsumi and his fellow Internet friends went into full information-gathering mode: "I memorized everything from the size of the Japanese merchant fleet, to how many rounds the army's Type 89 assault rifle held. No fact was too small or obscure" (205). Not until the undead are banging on his door does Tatsumi's survival instinct kick in: he makes the leap from knowledge acquisition to knowledge application, and this in the simplest of ways as he fashions bedsheets into an escape ladder.

An even more troubling example in Brooks's novel of a stereotype contributive to Yellow-Peril anxiety is the portrayal of Tatsumi's overall disregard for his parents, a fitting application of an anti-Japanese World War II stereotype that saw the enemy as so completely "different in the nature of their humanity" as to be inhuman (Walker 2004, 32–33). The stereotype of the Asian as animal-like suggests the Japanese parent as being incapable of normal familial relationships, the family unit being based on instinctual responsibility for reproduction of the species rather than notions of parental-filial love. Indeed, in *World War Z*, Tatsumi throughout his narration displays no powerful emotional concern for his parents: "We lived in the same apartment," he says, "but I never really conversed with them" (Brooks 2006, 207). When his parents go missing, Tatsumi is more annoyed than worried, for their absence means he has to prepare his own food: "The only reason I cared was because of the precious minutes I was wasting having to feed myself" (207), time that would otherwise be dedicated to the Internet. "I hated those feelings, hunger or fatigue or, the worst, sexual desire," Tatsumi says, "Those were physical distractions" (207). In this regard, Tatsumi displays to a lesser degree the stereotyped qualities that Frank Chin ascribes to the villainous Fu Manchu: he is "intelligent, brilliant and perverse" (1991, 9).

The narration by Tomonaga Ijiro divulges yet another stereotype typical of Yellow-Peril thinking, that of the mystical and inscrutable Asian, which sees the Asian male as a product of a culture built upon Zen-like mysticism (see Ijiro 9). Ijiro displays just such perverse brilliance of intellect arising from obscure mysticism. He is a blind survivor of the Nagasaki atomic bombing who, when the zombie plague strikes, flees unaided to the forested isolation of the Hidden Mountains national parkland. Ijiro turns out to have an exceptional and intimate understanding of traditional Japanese Shinto gods, of nature, and of martial arts. Like a shogun in classic Japanese cinema, the blind warrior lives in the woods with his personal weapon and dispatches the hordes of zombies that assault him. His narrative, because of the mystical nature of the telling, moves beyond the classic shogun adventure into the realm of the supernatural, as Ijiro fights alongside "the gods" and practices ritualistic burial of the zombies he kills (see Brooks 2006, 225). When he matches up with Tatsumi as his disciple, Ijiro comes to see himself as a servant of divinities that would introduce the rise of a new Japan: "I told (Tatsumi) that we might be facing fifty million monsters, but those monsters would be facing the gods" (227).

THE FUTURE WAR STORY

Given the presence of Yellow-Peril anxieties in *World War Z*, it is easy to identify the novel as belonging to a specific style of similar fictions that Patrick Sharp (2000) identifies as the "future war story." This subgenre within the field of science fiction was born with the 1871 publication of George Tomkyns Chesney's "The Battle of Dorking" in *Blackwoods Magazine*. H. G. Wells's 1898 *War of the Worlds* is perhaps the most popular example of a future war story. Works classified as future war stories arise from the Victorian-era reader's need to make sense of new technologies, and associated with this goal are a host of anxieties (see Sharp 2000, 434). Future war stories typically meditate upon the dangers of allowing an enemy to become more technologically advanced than you are. Both "The Battle of Dorking" and *War of the Worlds* are narrated by "everyman" citizens who witness mass destruction and strive to survive the carnage. These narrators reflect a total loathing of a cruel enemy that has invaded and unjustly ravaged the homeland.

In the early twentieth century, American authors wrote within the future war story subgenre, creating works such as the popular Buck Rogers and Flash Gordon serializations. One of the most notable future war story texts is Jack London's 1910 novella *The Unparalleled Invasion,* which makes an Asian invasion and a biological retribution part of its central plot (see Sharp 2000, 437). Throughout World War II, in both Buck Rogers and Flash Gordon, American readers saw a number of Yellow-Peril anxieties, this time focused on the Japanese, who were consistently represented within the US news media as an unquestioning, malicious, and single-minded "herd" in service to the Japanese imperial vision of worldwide conquest (see Sharp 2000, 438).

World War Z, as a story of a global viral spread, the victims of which are nicknamed "Zack" by the book's fictional military figures, can unquestionably be seen as a future war story. Among the most important narrations in the novel is the so-called Battle for Yonkers, in which the American military takes a stand against the hordes of hungry zombies coming from Manhattan. Despite superior weaponry—MLRS bombs that scatter to create a "steel rain" on the enemy, high-explosive HE 155 bombs that cause bodies to burst, tanks, mortars, missiles, grenade-firing machine guns, helicopter gunships, and armor-piercing uranium darts—the military is unable to defeat the shambling zombie hordes. The zombies have a stronger advantage, perhaps not technological but biological: they can only be killed by a carefully targeted head shot. Eventually, at great cost of lives, the world is overrun. The solution to reclaiming the land from the zombie masses is reliance upon strategy and simple weaponry, and a very slow advance through zombie-infested lands. The war takes years to complete, and even at the narrative time of the novel, it is not fully accomplished.

The zombie plague as described in Brooks's novel betrays further Yellow-Peril anxieties: the fear of miscegenation and the near-paranoid suspicion of an enemy within. Indeed, one of the "most potent aspects" of Yellow-Peril anxiety, argues Gina Marchetti, is the fear of racial impurity through sexual contact, most likely by means of rape. In the American experience, worries about racial purity in the face of increased immigration eventually metastasized into a fear about the physical presence of the Asian, leading to impurity of what the Euro-American perceived as the national culture (1993, 4).

In Brooks's zombie novel, the Yellow-Peril anxiety about miscegenation is tied closely to the contemporary fear of sexually transmitted diseases. For the viral zombie, the biological act of infection results from a transmission of bodily fluids, through the bite-transmitted saliva or blood of a zombie. This is not the exchange of bodily fluids through a romantic encounter, nor is it the playful nibbling of foreplay—this is the hostile and aggressive bite of a creature intent on consumption without any regard for the victim. Nevertheless, the infection through bodily fluids crossing the lips suggests a sexual element. And if the virus is understood as originating in China, and therefore as being a Chinese virus, this is an invasion via oral transmission of body fluids infected with Chinese viral agents. This is miscegenation at the cellular level, with a Chinese virus symbolically penetrating a non-Chinese cell. Here, too, the general discourse of disease reveals elements of Yellow-Peril fear of miscegenation as a form of social destruction. In her study of disease narratives, Priscilla Wald notes how in some "less subtle outbreak narratives" the germs "overtly challenge Americanism rather than humanity" (2008, 63). Wald notes that in some films, the infected are no longer considered Americans, but have become unwelcome immigrants, former citizens who have been "thirdworldized" (61).

The alteration, both physical and behavioral, resulting from this viral invasion at the cellular level displays a terror of the enemy within. The zombie that now seeks to viciously consume was once a beloved family member, a trusted friend, a reliable neighbor. Frighteningly, in World War Z one can be, at least temporarily, a viral carrier displaying few symptoms of infection. Indeed, this inability to distinguish friend from foe among the newly infected is reflected in the novel's fictional narration by Jesika Hendricks. She speaks of a hitchhiker trying to hide what Hendricks's parents assume to be a bite wound: "She saw that we saw and suddenly looked nervous" (Brooks 2006, 124). Another example is from the narration of Bohdan Taras Kondratiuk, who describes the Russian military's failed attempts to check for infected people during the civilian population's flight from Kiev. As Kondratiuk laments, "How are you supposed to check for infection without [sniffer] dogs? What are you supposed to do, visually inspect each refugee . . . strip them naked to examine every centimeter of skin?" (118). For the infected individual, the enemy is within, with its presence depicted as a form of viral rape leading to unwelcome miscegenation at the cellular level.

For those in proximity to the infected living individual, the enemy is already within the confines of home, threatening danger within the boundaries of what could be considered a safe zone. Once the infected individual dies, she or he will reanimate as the foreigner, the frightening other, the enemy—the zombie. Until that moment of death and reanimation, however, the infected individual is essentially a hybrid of viral and nonviral organisms. The infected are already altered, yet they continue to mimic their former noninfected selves until the moment of their full conversion, whereupon they attack. The infected person is, suggests Wald, potentially "queer" in the sense of the straight-acting closeted homosexual's potential for bringing about "a disruption of normative institutions" (2008, 197) through his or her very presence, with the closeted gay individual, like an infected person, representing a potential threat to the norm: The virus "comes from without and corrupts, creating an enemy within" (197).[11] This comparison serves to further recognition of another stereotype, that of Asian males as "queer . . . sexually repugnant, comically effeminate yellow men" (Chin 1991, 10).

RECLAIMING HUMANITY

What does the recognition of Yellow-Peril anxieties within a popular narrative such as *World War Z* suggest about the social and political context that might have influenced the author in his writing of the novel? Brooks researched and wrote the novel in the early years of the Bush administration, during which the United States was engaged in a dual-front contest in the "war on terror" following the terrorist attacks of September 11, 2001. As a New York resident who identifies himself as "a fanatical patriot" (Brooks 2010a, online), Brooks has argued that the zombie serves as an icon through which individuals can make sense of the various crises that shape individual and national destinies: "I think zombies are safe. Zombies are manageable. You can't shoot the Gulf oil spill in the head. I think some of these problems are too big and too tough to understand. What does the global financial meltdown of 2008 mean? I can't explain it, and I sure know you can't shoot it in the head" (2010b, online).

The viral zombie also serves as a catchall figure for the virtual display and perhaps cathartic dismissal of actual anxieties arising from the experience of 9/11 and the pervasive "fear campaign" put into play by the Bush administration. A primary factor in the administration's political platform of fear was the less-than-subtle message that the greatest threats to domestic safety come from outside the national borders, just as the terrorists who piloted civilian aircraft into Manhattan and Washington, DC, were considered "outsiders" despite the fact that many of them had lived in the United States for what could be thought of as considerable amounts of time (see Simpson 2006, 7). Such a political approach to domestic security serves to "violently reinscribe on the world fundamental moral and political metaphysical distinctions between inside and outside, friend and foe, good and bad . . . and security and insecurity" (George 2009, 35).

In a similar fashion, the Yellow-Peril anxiety unleased by the Japanese attack upon Pearl Harbor led to an identification of "the enemy" as being outside the American nation's national borders, and resulted in the besmirching of US citizens of Japanese ancestry as internal agents in the service of this foreign adversary. Likewise, in the aftermath of the 9/11 attacks, US citizens of the Islamic faith or of Middle Eastern appearance were targeted for racist assaults. This tendency to paint fellow citizens in foreign colors reveals, perhaps, the anxiety about the inability to distinguish insider from outsider, friend from foe; thus, the zombie—an obvious foe and outsider— offers a momentary relief from a continual stream of anxiety-inducing factors. When confronted with the zombies of *World War Z*, the reader can gratefully identify the threat. This occasional release may prove cathartic to the average American who is, more than a decade after the event, still affected by a ceaseless flow of unease arising from the perception of the 9/11 attacks, eliciting a very powerful sense of the pending apocalypse/postapocalypse. Indeed, argues René Girard, the fall of the World Trade Center was certainly "a seminal event" representative of "a revolutionary threat, a global threat" that can best be conceived of through "the apocalyptic dimension of Christianity" (Doran 2009, 20–21). Further, as James Berger suggests: "Postapocalyptic representations are simultaneously symptoms of historical traumas and attempts to work through them" (1999, 19). Therefore, the sense of impending apocalypse is served well by the contemporary zombie figure. Zombies, says Brooks, are fundamentally apocalyptic. "I think that's why people love them, because we're living in . . . fear of the apocalyptic times" (2010b, online). Zombie fiction is "a safe vessel for the end of the world" (2010b, online).[12] After the cathartic experience of a zombie work of fiction, readers or viewers can set aside their worries, knowing that zombies are ultimately not real.

It is the very unreality of the popular zombie icon that makes it so dangerous, however. In her critique of the political responses to 9/11 by the Bush administration and the influence of the "war on terror" upon the American psyche, Judith Butler suggests that a period of mourning following a catastrophic event may serve to unify a nation. Grief, says Butler, "furnishes a sense of political community of a complex order, and it does this first of all by bringing to the fore the relational ties that have implications for theorizing fundamental dependency and ethical responsibility" (2004, 22). The rush toward vengeance via martial incursions into both Afghanistan and Iraq has denied the American nation an appropriate period of mourning, and subsequent public discourse has tended to dehumanize the thousands who die in these conflicts.[13] Not only does this dehumanization prohibit proper mourning, Butler maintains, but it also prevents true unity, empathy, and the building of bonds across differences:

> Violence against those who are already not quite living . . . leaves a mark that is no mark. . . . If there is a "discourse," it is a silent and melancholic one in which there have been no lives, and no losses; there has been no common bodily condition, no vulnerability that serves as the basis for an apprehension of our commonality; and there has been no sundering of that commonality. (2004, 36)

While zombie fiction may therefore provide a sense of catharsis, it does not ultimately encourage the individual consumer of these cultural products toward positive actions that will strengthen their communities. Despite Gayle Baldwin's positive reading of *World War Z* as a warning bell for the citizens of a US society fractured along various lines of difference—because "in Zack's world, none of these differences matter" (2007, 419)—the novel may contribute very little by the way of resolution and restitution to a readership wounded by the traumas of not only the 9/11 attacks and the retributive "war on terror," but of other national crises as well. In fact, if Brooks's novel portrays elements of Yellow-Peril anxiety, these racist features may well serve only to encourage divisions within society rather than to heal them. The private reaction to the reading of *World War Z* may be similar to the public reaction arising from the "policy of fear" put forth by the Bush administration. As Butler says, the inexplicit warnings of the many "terror alerts"–which have continued throughout the Obama administration—have helped encourage "an amorphous racism" rationalized by the claim of self-defense (2004, 39). Even in the latter years of the Obama presidency, the social atmosphere remains permeated by what Henry A. Giroux identifies as "a discourse of security and a culture of fear" that encourages "a rampant nationalism, hatred of immigrants, and a bunker politics organized around an 'us-versus-them' mentality" (2011, 154). Certainly, Brooks's *World War Z* may merely express what might be the author's personal perceptions of China and Japan, but through its uncritical representation of anti-Asian stereotypes based on Yellow-Peril anxiety, this best-selling work of modern horror fiction gives voice and vent to racist discourse and strengthens the shuffling, reanimated corpses of bias and hatred in an already divided America.

NOTES

1. Although the film's release led to a reissue of *World War Z*, Max Brooks disavowed the film as having nothing to do with his novel other than the title. He even went so far as to lobby his publisher against using Brad Pitt's image on the cover of the paperback tie-in, arguing that the character played by Pitt in the film appears nowhere in the novel. "I was very clear with Random House that while I would not lead a boycott against the movie, I was just crazy enough to boycott my own book," Brooks said (Brodesser-Akner 2013, online). Despite Brooks's public disavowal of the Hollywood production, director Marc Forster's "loose adaptation" of *World War Z* went on to earn an impressive global box-office intake of $502 million (US) ("'World War Z' Is Brad Pitt's Career High" 2013, online). Buoyed by this success, Brad Pitt publicly expressed support for a sequel (see Child 2013, online).

2. See, for example, Terkel, *The Good War* (1984).

3. West does not mention the German anthropologist Johann Friedrich Blumenbach, whose 1775 doctoral thesis, *On the Natural Variety of Mankind*, was the scientist's first in what would be a series of works that would popularize the notion of consolidating the human species into five distinct races—Caucasian (white), Mongolian (yellow), Ethiopian (black), American (red), and Malay (brown). Blumenbach's categorization, based in large part upon his comparative study of cranial structures, was highly influential on subsequent generations of scientists (see Gossett 1963, 37). Nevertheless, Blumenbach spoke against those who thought races were superior or inferior, and he was "especially irritated" by those who chose to rank the races in order of their beauty (see Gossett 1963, 39).

4. Even John Locke, who argued that all men are "equal and independent" and was generally against slave ownership, was a shareholder in a slave-trading enterprise and justified the trade as saving pagan Africans from both barbarism and eternal damnation. Thomas Jefferson, while noting that "all men are created equal," also insisted that some were nevertheless "'racially' deficient" (Baum 2006, 43).

5. With the concept of racial categorization deemed acceptable by scientists and philosophers alike, race became a marker of moral and social distinctions (see McGary 2002, 434).

6. Despite the development of ancient world civilizations, Asians were—according to French novelist and intellectual Comte Arthur de Gobineau, writing in the mid-nineteenth century—incapable of forming a bourgeoisie society and imbuing it with intelligence, beauty, or achievement. De Gobineau suggests that Asians "have little scope of imagination" and "display neither great stamina nor capacity for anything great and exalted" (de Gobineau 1856, 195).

7. In separate interviews, Brooks has made comparisons between the HIV/AIDS pandemic and a fictional zombie plague, which is "like being attacked by walking AIDS" (Ullrich 2008, online).

8. The Yellow-Peril suggestion here is that the Western man must struggle to remain civilized in the presence of the Asian man whose contaminated morality may be infectious.

9. Allegations of Asian and European complicity in the organ trade have taken a macabre turn with the legal exploits of Dr. Gunther von Hagens, founder of the Body Worlds exhibition of plastinated human corpses. Von Hagens was investigated and cleared of allegations that he had illegally received and plastinated several hundred corpses from prisons, psychiatric institutions, and hospitals in Kyrgyzstan. A year later, *Der Spiegel* magazine alleged that von Hagens obtained the corpses of executed prisoners in China, an accusation that the magazine later retracted (see Baker 2007, online). Von Hagens oversees plastination centers in both Kyrgyzstan and China; the latter now only deals with animal carcasses (see Preston 2008, online).

10. State defenders of the Chinese Communist Party continue to take refuge behind the adage that those who live in glass houses should not throw stones. In August 2014, for example, China's Xinhua News Agency used the racially motivated riots in Ferguson, Missouri, to criticize the United States' stance as a human-rights advocate: "Obviously, what the United States needs to do is to concentrate on solving its own problems rather than always pointing fingers at others" (Li 2014, online).

11. Wald offers these insights in her reading of Albert Finney's novel and two subsequent film versions of *The Body Snatchers* (see 2008, 191).

12. Although Glenn Kay suggests that the popularity of zombie films had already peaked by 2005 according to "weakened responses from audiences and shrinking profit margins" caused by the release of "far too many zombie films" (2008, 300), media studies blogger Jennifer Palmer, writing in 2008, suggests that "the zombie trend" will continue for quite some time thanks to the uncanny ghostly presence of 9/11: "So much death—so little closure!" (2008, online). Indeed, according to New Zealand blogger M. A. Williams, at least four hundred zombie-themed films were released by largely American and British filmmakers between 2000 and 2010, with the serious rise in numbers starting in 2003 and exponentially increasing ever since, "not unlike the zombie hordes they are portraying" (2011, online). Annalee Newitz in 2008 posted online her findings of a correspondence between horror-film releases and traumatic social events such as war or economic recession (see 2008, online). My own count from the Wikipedia listing of global productions suggests totals at almost seven hundred entries (see Wikipedia 2012, online). The website's "list of zombie films" ranges from 1919 to 2012, but almost 450 of the films listed were released from 2001 to 2012 (see Wikipedia 2012, online). The inclusion in the list of independent films and short works suggests a grass-roots advancement of the zombie icon; it also contains international films, works produced for television, short films, and documentaries.

13. A disturbing example of this discourse of dehumanization can be found in a short piece posted at the *GlobalPost* website and picked up by *CBS News* that notes that US soldiers in Afghanistan are fans of Max Brooks's *World War Z* (see Brody 2010, online). The piece compares Afghan insurgents to zombies: "The problems of war against the undead have parallels with the problems soldiers face daily in Afghanistan. A zombie needs no food, water or equipment and pursues the living with implacable determination. For soldiers trying to defend a million dollar vehicle against a malnourished, illiterate man wielding a $40 roadside bomb, the similarity must be chilling" (Brody 2010, online).

WORKS CITED

Baker, Mark. 2007. "Body Sensations." *Register-Guard.* June 17. Accessed January 14, 2012. http://www.thefreelibrary.com/Body+sensations.-a0165339958.

Baldwin, Gayle R. 2007. "*World War Z* and the End of Religion as we Know It." *Cross Currents* 57 (3): 412–25.

Baum, Bruce. 2006. *Rise and Fall of the Caucasian Race: A Political History of Racial Identity.* New York: New York University Press.

Berger, James. 1999. *After the End: Representations of Post-Apocalypse.* Minneapolis: University of Minnesota Press.

"Best Sellers: October 16, 2006." 2006. *New York Times.* October 16. Accessed September 3, 2010. http://query.nytimes.com/gst/fullpage.html?res= 9C0DEEDA1530F936A25753C1 A9609C8B63.

Bishop, Kyle. 2010. *American Zombie Gothic: The Rise and Fall (and Rise) of the Walking Dead in Popular Culture.* Jefferson, NC: McFarland.

Brodesser-Akner, Taffy. 2013. "Max Brooks Is Not Kidding about the Zombie Apocalypse." *New York Times Magazine*. June 21. Accessed October 21, 2014. http://www.nytimes .com/2013/06/23/magazine/max-brooks-is-not-kidding-about-the-zombie-apocalypse .html?pagewanted=all.

Brody, Ben. 2010. "Hunting Zombies in Afghanistan." GlobalPost.com. August 20. Accessed September 11, 2010. http://dispatches.globalpost.com/2010/08/20/hunting-zombies-in -afghanistan.

Brooks, Max. 2006. *World War Z: An Oral History of the Zombie War*. New York: Crown.

———. 2010a. "Exclusive Interview: Max Brooks on *World War Z*." *Eatmybrains.com*. October 20, 2006. Accessed: September 11, 2010. http://www.eatmybrains.com /show feature.php?id=55.

———. 2010b. "Zombie-Survival Expert Max Brooks." Interviewed by Allie Townsend. *Time*. July 26, 2010. Accessed September 11, 2010. http://www.time.com/time/arts/ article/0,8599,2006405,00.html.

Butler, Judith. 2004. *Precarious Life: The Powers of Mourning and Violence*. London: Verso.

Button, Peter. 2006. "(Para-)humanity, Yellow Peril and the Postcolonial (Arche-)type." *Postcolonial Studies* 9 (4): 421–47.

Child, Ben. 2013. "World War Z Earns Sequel after Gobbling Up Global Box Office." *TheGuardian.com*. June 24. Accessed October 21, 2014. http://www.theguardian.com/ film/2013/jun/24/world-war-z-sequel-brad-pitt.

Chin, Frank. 1991. "Come All Ye Asian American Writers of the Real and the Fake." In *The Big Aiiieeeee! An Anthology of Chinese American and Japanese American Literature*, edited by Jeffery Paul Chan, Frank Chin, Lawson Fusao Inada, and Shawn Wong, 1–92. New York: Meridian.

Coonan, Clifford, and David McNeill. 2006. "Japan's Rich Buy Organs from Executed Chinese Prisoners." *The Independent*. March 21. Accessed: September 10, 2010. http:// www.independent.co.uk/news/world/asia/japans-rich-buy-organs-from-executed -chinese-prisoners-470719.html.

de Gobineau, Comte Arthur. 1856. *The Moral and Intellectual Diversity of Races*. Translated by Henry Hotze. Philadelphia: J. B. Lippincott.

Deutsch, Linda. 2013. "Book Buzz: Brad Pitt Movie Boosts 'WWZ' Sales." *USA Today*. Online. June 27. Accessed March 22, 2014. http://www.usatoday.com/story/life/books/ 2013/06/27/book-buzz/2464199/.

Doran, Robert. 2009. "Apocalyptic Thinking after 9/11: An Interview with René Girard." *SubStance* 37 (1): 20–32.

Essed, Philomena, and David Theo Goldberg. 2002. *Race Critical Theories: Text and Context*. Malden, MA: Blackwell.

Feagin, Joe R. 1997. "Old Poison in New Bottles: The Deep Roots of Modern Nativism." In *Critical White Studies: Looking Behind the Mirror*, edited by Richard Delgado and Jean Stefancic, 348–53. Philadelphia: Temple University Press.

George, Larry N. 2009. "American Insecurities and the Ontopolitics of U.S. Pharmacotic Wars." In *The Geopolitics of American Insecurity: Terror, Power and Foreign Policy*, edited by Francois Debrix and Mark Lacy, 34–53. London: Routledge.

Giroux, Henry A. 2011. *Zombie Politics and Culture in the Age of Casino Capitalism*. New York: Peter Lang.

Gossett, Thomas F. 1963. *The History of an Idea in America*. Dallas, TX: Southern Methodist University Press.

Hamako, Eric. 2011. "Zombie Orientals Ate My Brain! Orientalism in Contemporary Zombie Film and Fiction." In *Race, Oppression and the Zombie: Essays on Cross-Cultural Appropriations of the Caribbean Tradition*, edited by C. Rushton and C. Mormon, 107–23. Jefferson, NC: McFarland.

Kay, Glenn. 2008. *Zombie Movies: The Ultimate Guide*. Chicago: Chicago Review Press.

Keely, Karen A. 2007. "Sexual Slavery in San Francisco's Chinatown: 'Yellow Peril' and 'White Slavery' in Frank Norris's Early Fiction." *Studies in American Naturalism* 2 (2): 129–49.

Lee, Erika. 2003. *At America's Gates: Chinese Immigration during the Exclusion Era, 1882–1943*. Chapel Hill: University of North Carolina Press.

Li, Li. 2014. "Commentary: Ferguson Riot Reveals U.S. Racial Divide, Human Rights Flaw." *Xinhua: English News*. August 18. Accessed September 5, 2014. http://news.xinhuanet .com/english/indepth/2014-08/18/c_133564928.htm.

Marchetti, Gina. 1993. *Romance and the "Yellow Peril": Race, Sex, and Discursive Practices in Hollywood Fiction*. Berkeley: University of California Press.

Mayer, Ruth. 2014. *Serial Fu Manchu: The Chinese Supervillain and the Spread of Yellow Peril Ideology*. Philadelphia: Temple University Press.

McGary, Howard. 2002. "Reflections on 'A Genalogy of Modern Racism.'" In Essed and Goldberg, 433–36.

Newitz, Annalee. 2008. "War and Social Upheaval Cause Spikes in Zombie Movie Production." October 29. Accessed January 14, 2012. http://io9.com/5070243/war-and -social-upheaval-cause-spikes-in-zombie-movie-production.

Olivas, Michael A. 1995. "The Chronicles, My Grandfather's Stories, and Immigration Law: The Slave Traders Chronicle as Racial History." In *Critical Race Theory: The Cutting Edge*, edited by Richard Delgado, 9–20. Philadelphia: Temple University Press.

Ong, Aihwa. 1999. "Cultural Citizenship as Subject Making: Immigrants Negotiate Racial and Cultural Boundaries in the United States." In *Race, Identity, and Citizenship: A Reader*, edited by Rodolfo D. Torres et al., 262–93. Malden, MA: Blackwell.

O'Sullivan, John. 2000. "A Yellow Peril? No." *National Review* (May 2000): 28–30.

Palmer, Jennifer. 2008. "Zombie Apocalypse." February 8. *Reality Sandwich*. Accessed January 14, 2012. http://www.realitysandwich.com/zombie_apocalypse.

Preston, John. 2008. "Gunther von Hagens: A Man of Many Parts." *Telegraph* (London). October 15. Accessed January 14, 2012. http://www.telegraph.co.uk/culture/art/3562062/ Gunther-von-Hagens-a-man-of-many-parts.html.

Publishers Weekly. 2011. "Brooks's 'World War Z' Hits Sales Milestone." *Industry News*. November 10. Accessed January 13, 2012. http://www.publishersweekly.com/pw/by -topic/industry-news/publisher-news/article/49456-brooks-s-world-war-z-hits-sales -milestone-.html.

Sharp, Patrick B. 2000. "From Yellow Peril to Japanese Wasteland: John Hersey's 'Hiroshima.'" *Twentieth Century Literature* 46 (4): 434–52.

Shih, David. 2009. "The Color of Fu Manchu: Orientalist Method in the Novels of Sax Rohmer." *Journal of Popular Culture* 42 (2): 304–17.

Simpson, David. 2006. *9/11: The Culture of Commemoration*. Chicago: University of Chicago Press.

Terkel, Studs. [1984] 1991. *The Good War*. New York: Ballentine Books.

Tolentino, Cynthia Hocson. 2001. "The Liberal, the Sociologist, and the Novelist: Narratives of Race and National Development in African American and Asian American Fiction of the 1940s." PhD diss., Brown University.

Ullrich, Chris. 2008. "WWC Interview: 'World War Z' Writer Max Brooks." *ComicMix.com*. June 29. Accessed September 11, 2010. http://www.comicmix.com/news/2008/06/29/wwc-interview-world-war-z-writer-max-brooks/.

Wald, Priscilla. 2008. *Contagious: Cultures, Carriers, and the Outbreak Narrative*. Durham, NC: Duke University Press.

Walker, J. Samuel. 2004. *Prompt and Utter Destruction: Truman and the Use of the Atomic Bomb against Japan*. Chapel Hill: University of North Carolina Press.

West, Cornel. 2002. "A Genealogy of Modern Racism." In Essed and Goldberg, 90–112.

Wikipedia. 2012. "List of Zombie Films." Accessed January 14, 2012. http://en.wikipedia.org/wiki/List_of_zombie_films.

Williams, M. A. 2011. "10 Years of Zombies—Zombie Movie List: 2000–2010." *Hub Pages*. Accessed January 14, 2012.

"'World War Z' Is Brad Pitt's Career High Box Office Winner." 2013. *HuffPost Entertainment*. October 12. Accessed October 21, 2014. http://www.huffingtonpost.com/2013/08/12/world-war-z-brad-pitt-box-office_n_3743597.html.

PART 4

CIRCULATING TECHNOLOGIES

"DOCTOR! I'M LOSING BLOOD!" "NONSENSE! YOUR BLOOD IS RIGHT HERE"

The Vampirism of Carl Theodor Dreyer's Film Vampyr

JOHANNES WEBER

"If it's not in frame, it doesn't exist."[1]

Since John Polidori in 1819 made a vampire the eponymous hero of his Romantic tale "The Vampyre," vampires have never disappeared from the pages of collections of supernatural tales, penny dreadfuls, or horror novels. They soon migrated to theater stages and movie screens, and more recently from the pages of serialized novels to weekly episodes on television. As cultural icons, vampires are the subject matter of an impressive body of academic writing. In his study *Metamorphoses of the Vampire in Literature and Film*, Erik Butler sums up:

> *Representations of vampires in literature, film, and the visual arts are many and contradictory. Sometimes these creatures are suave and urbane. Sometimes they are rustic and crude. There are male and female vampires. Yet all vampires share one trait: the power to move between and undo borders otherwise holding identities in place. (2010, 1)*

This is a creature a world apart from contemporary images of the vampire, as found in aristocratic figures such as Lord Ruthven or Count Dracula, nostalgic dandies such as Lestat and Louis in Anne Rice's works, or the suicidal vampire Adam in *Only Lovers Left Alive* (2013). Shape-shifting vampires materialize in the most unexpected guises. Cultural critics such as Nina Auerbach have long established the notion of vampire fashions: exploring the ways in which historically specific readings are generated, one can identify Lord Ruthven as a Byronic hero, Dracula as the epitome of a Victorian monster, and Edward Cullen as a globally marketable Romantic hero of the more recognizable kind. Similarly, Max Schreck's *Nosferatu* (1922) has been given his place among other German Expressionist monsters as the harbinger of upcoming terror (see Eisner [1952] 1969, 95), while Christopher Lee's *Dracula* (1958) has been praised as a Technicolor liberator of female sexuality in the wake of the sexual revolution. Meanwhile, *Bram Stoker's Dracula* (1992) serves as a work of metafiction by not only attempting to adhere more closely to the plot of Bram Stoker's 1897 novel, but also by commenting upon and placing itself within a century of cinematic bloodsuckers through the incorporation of multiple references to earlier vampire films. Present now for two hundred years, the culturally processed vampire seems to lend himself to writers of both literary and film history.[2]

In this essay, I position Carl Theodor Dreyer's *Vampyr* (1931)[3] within this larger context of the vampire film. Although *Vampyr* is commonly believed to be an adaptation of J. Sheridan Le Fanu's 1872 tale of a lesbian vampire, "Carmilla," the film is less an adaptation of this Gothic tale than an appropriation of certain modes of narrative representation surrounding earlier vampires. In the opening credits, the film explicitly names its source: Le Fanu's *In a Glass Darkly*. This collection contains not only "Carmilla," but four other stories as well. As I show, Dreyer uses one of them, "The Room in the Dragon Volant," as the model for the most iconic sequence in *Vampyr* in which a man meets his own corpse and faces the horror of being buried alive. Further, I claim that Dreyer thus turns the representation of this experience into a depiction of the filmic condition per se. At the threshold between the silent and the sound film, *Vampyr* enters into a unique relationship with those narrative modes that have previously surrounded literary and film vampires, appropriating them for its own medium. *Vampyr* thus goes well beyond conventional views of adaptation and ultimately represents film as itself a vampiric medium.

THE MOST CONFUSING OF ALL FILMS?

For a long time, biographers had considered *Vampyr* to be Dreyer's weakest film and therefore paid considerably less attention to it than to his consistently highly acclaimed films *Le Passion de Jeanne d'Arc* (1928), *Ordet* (1954), and *Gertrud* (1964). Although, in contrast, Alfred Hitchcock declared *Vampyr* to be the only film worth seeing twice, film historian Kirk Bond has summed up the negative attitude of viewers and critics: "To say that *Vampyr* is the most confusing of the Dreyer films would be an understatement. It might well be the most confusing of all films" (1965, 34). It was not until 1981 that film neoformalist David Bordwell in *The Films of Carl-Theodor Dreyer* discussed *Vampyr* as a systematic subversion of the contemporary viewers' cinematic storytelling expectations.

Asked why he made the movie, Dreyer said: "Vampires were the fashionable thing at the time" (quoted in Tybjerg 2008, DVD documentary). *Vampyr* was filmed the same year Tod Browning made *Dracula* for Universal Studios (1930). While Bela Lugosi's *Dracula* has hardly anything in common with Stoker's villain, Lugosi's portrayal—more than that of any other film star—has influenced our idea of what a vampire "should" look like. The script of Browning's *Dracula* is based on Hamilton Deane and John Balderston's hugely successful theatrical dramatization of Stoker's novel. This stage version, which enjoyed a five-year run on Broadway between 1927 and 1931, is a drawing-room melodrama that relies on the revelation of Count Dracula's true nature fairly late in the play. Dracula is described in the script as a "tall, mysterious man. Polished and distinguished. Continental in appearance and manner. Aged fifty" (Deane and Balderston [1927] 1960, 5). The stage directions require the actor playing Dracula to wear "full evening dress" (90), a costume note that Browning adapted as part of the many touches that would lend a unique look to his film.[4] Despite the freedom available through film technology, Browning's *Dracula* remains relatively stage bound and thus rather conventional in terms of its storytelling techniques. And by the late 1920s, the "classical style" of continuity editing had been established and was widely practiced (see Thompson 1985, 245).

Although Browning's *Dracula* was made to be easily followed by mass audiences, watching—and trying to comprehend—Dreyer's *Vampyr* was surely a frustrating experience for many contemporary viewers. Rather than in an establishing shot presenting the protagonist's arrival at the village of Courtempierre, the first frame portrays Allan Gray coming up from a river bank. The angle of the camera suggests that he is virtually rising from the water. After having taken a rest in his hotel room, Gray is visited by an old man who later turns out to be the father of Léone and Gisèle. The cinematic presentation of this confrontation, however, is disconcerting. The father and Allan are never in the same frame together and there are no over-shoulder shots. Furthermore, Gray never says a word. The viewer wonders: are these men really in the same room at the same time? When the father finally turns toward the camera and addresses it directly, the scene is shot in the subjective mode, a breach with the illusionistic credo of the continuity system. Very early in the film, the viewer thus has the impression of following Gray into a dreamworld where nothing can be taken as reality.

In his discussion of *Vampyr*, Bordwell argues that the film systematically "ruptures Bazinian phenomenal continuity" and the reliance upon the representation of a spatiotemporal continuum. Courtempierre is made up of "contradictory spaces" (1981, 97); characters move upstairs even though they were previously shown already on the top floor of a building; they leave frames to the left and reenter them seconds later from the right; both the château and the factory appear to be labyrinths. Although the camera follows Gray and the others through the rooms and presents elaborate long tracking and 360-degree shots, the viewer never really has a sense of a coherent space. According to André Bazin ([1967] 2005), the necessary impression of reality is only perfect if the nonvisible space is included in the filmic representation; in *Vampyr*, however, the viewer becomes skeptical of both what he sees on the screen and what is beyond the frame. Designed to be disquieting, *Vampyr* frustrates by subverting all those conventions that usually serve to make it easier to comprehend cinematic representation.

The construction of story time is equally enigmatic: the first intertitle announces that Gray arrives at Courtempierre "one late evening," and he is shown approaching the inn at dusk. However, while the framing implies that everything happens at night, in all those shots that show windows from within, the light seems to come from the outside. The audience has followed Gray into a liminal state between day and night, between waking and dreaming. Indeed, from the moment he enters the inn, it is hard to tell how (much) time passes. This is due to the elliptic editing of the film: by crosscutting different strands of the action within scenes, the film produces ellipses (see Bordwell 1981, 96). None of the crucial story events is rendered in its complete duration: "The only order of time that we can trust is the time it takes for the film to be seen" (Grant 2003, 148).

Further, *Vampyr* succeeds in frustrating yet another expectation that contemporary audiences had just developed: the one of hearing diegetic sound. Dreyer's first sound film was released in the year that followed the introduction of sound in Hollywood films. Together with *Frankenstein* (1931), *Dracula* was the first major sound film for Universal Studios. In the years before, Hollywood studios had carefully prepared their transition to "the talkies." According to Robert Spadoni, it was no coincidence that Universal chose to produce these two films with sound: "[W]ith *Dracula* and *Frankenstein* film critics and marketers started referring explicitly to 'horror pictures,' and producers started making films with this appellation in mind" (2007, 12).[5] One of the trademarks of these early horror films was the use of diegetic sound to create suspense. *Dracula* prominently features creaking doors, off-screen screams, and the sound a stake makes when driven through a vampire's chest. Indeed, this film virtually establishes a definition of diegetic sound when Dracula, for example, refers to the howling of wolves outside the door: "Listen to them! The children of the night! What music they make!" While Browning thus succeeds in exploiting diegetic sound for the newly emerging commercial genre of the horror film, Carl Dreyer uses sound quite differently. The few short sentences exchanged between characters are no more than small talk and are never functional for the development of the plot. During one of Gray's trips through the house, the barking of dogs is audible. In the hallway Gray meets the doctor:

DOCTOR. Did you hear that?
GRAY. Yes—the child.
DOCTOR. The child? There's no child here.
GRAY. But the dogs!
DOCTOR. There are no children or dogs here.

In this scene, Dreyer subverts any expectation of diegetic sound viewers might have developed. The sound track of the film contains the barking. Gray seems to have heard dogs and a child. The doctor has obviously heard neither dogs nor a child but rather something else that neither the film audience nor Gray has heard. The viewer is completely at a loss, with the use of sound here in the service of creating even more ambiguity. In this film, neither the visual representation nor the representation of sound can be trusted; narrative logic seems to be abandoned. In deliberate opposition to the continuity storytelling of its time, *Vampyr* thus even transcends the tradition of the Expressionist vampire film *Nosferatu*, to which it has been frequently compared.[6]

TRACES OF VAMPIRES

While it receives applause as an artistic venture, Dreyer's *Vampyr* is disappointing to those viewers who approach it expecting a "vampire film." The pursuit and elimination of the vampire by a band of hunters—a key focus of vampire narratives from the early days of folktales to more modern literary works—is only marginal to the plot. Throughout the film there is one vampire attack only, and the attack is more suggested than explicitly shown; no blood is spilled apart from a tiny puddle beneath the carriage when a dead coachman arrives at the château. The vampire in Dreyer's film, Marguerite Chopin, is neither alluring nor supernaturally gifted. She is not an attractive aristocrat like Lord Ruthven or Carmilla, and does not possess the sort of supernatural strengths attributed to Stoker's Dracula. Quite to the contrary, Chopin needs a cane and in one scene even has to be supported by the doctor. Indeed, the only clearly recognizable vampire story element is the vampire's final staking and her metamorphosis from fresh corpse to skeleton.

Some obligatory features of earlier vampire stories appear in the film but these are either irrelevant or are subverted.[7] In narratives such as "Carmilla" and *Dracula*, paternal figures are the main agents of destruction of the vampire. Certainly, there are patriarchal figures in this film, such as the father and the doctor, yet the former figure is mysteriously shot by a shadow some twenty minutes into the film, and the latter turns out to be the vampire's accomplice. Both the title and various story elements thus encourage viewers to make connections to earlier versions of vampire stories, only to realize that familiar patterns of signification cannot be applied here.

While on the story level *Vampyr* does not seem to take the literary vampire legacy very seriously, on the discourse level there are various similarities to earlier vampire narratives. First, Dreyer's Gray is reminiscent of the "young gentleman," Aubrey, in Polidori's "The Vampyre." Aubrey's distorted perception of Lord Ruthven as the "hero of a romance" not only brings him misery but casts doubt upon his whole narrative:

> *Attached as he was to the romance of his solitary hours, he was startled at finding, that . . . there was no foundation in real life for any of that congeries of pleasing pictures and descriptions contained in those volumes, from which he had formed his study. ([1819] 2008, 4–5)*

Aubrey is described as a bookish dreamer, as is Allan Gray in the first intertitle of *Vampyr*:

> *This is the story of the strange adventures of young Allan Gray, who immersed himself in the study of devil worship and vampires. Preoccupied with superstition of centuries past, he became a dreamer for whom the line between the real and the supernatural became blurred.*

Although Aubrey is looking for "the hero of a romance" and finds a Byronic hero, Gray is looking for vampires and is rewarded by finding Marguerite Chopin. To a significant degree, Gray and his blurred perception of reality echo the oversensitive Aubrey of Polidori's tale.

The use of intertitles leads to the second vampire narrative that Dreyer refers to. Although *Vampyr* is a sound film, intertitles are used in the first

third of the film. Indeed, with the confusion centered on Allan, these intertitles seem to be the single believable source of information for viewers.
However, the intertitles disappear the moment Allan unwraps the package
containing the book *The Strange Story of the Vampire*, which he has been
given by his father. About two-thirds of the way through the film, Gray is
portrayed reading from the book, pages of which are shown to the viewer
in subjective shots. Using a book on vampire lore as narrative agent is not
Dreyer's invention: in Murnau's *Nosferatu*, Ellen Hutter[8] finds the crucial
information on the lethal effect of sunlight on vampires in a book. Hutter,
however, lacks Gray's earlier background of studying literature on vampire
lore. For Gray, the man who perceives his reality in relation to what he has
read about "devil worship and vampires," a book on vampire lore is useful as
a reinforcement of what he already knows or thinks he knows.

The book leads Gray toward the vampire's identity and provides information on how to destroy her. Similarly, the book in *Nosferatu* is in-
strumental as a guide to the vampire's destruction, while in Stoker's novel
Dracula, various journal entries, letters, and medical reports are used to
authenticate and organize knowledge about the monster (see Wicke 1992,
467). In *Vampyr*, however, the book is part of Allan's dreamworld. At one
level, it is not Allan but his manservant who finds the necessary information on the vampire's identity in the book and thereby the means by which
to eliminate the supernatural villain.[9] However, the manservant's reading
about the vampire forcing her victims into suicide is crosscut with the shot
of Allan lying in an armchair; he is recovering from the drawing of blood
and has his first dream about a skeletal hand holding a vial labeled with a
skull. The film thus suggests that Allan already knows what the manservant
learns about the vampire. Similarly, while sitting down on the bench before
the onset of his second dream,[10] the manservant is shown reading how the
vampire can be destroyed: her grave must be opened and the corpse must
be staked.

In Murnau's film, the book is a narrative agent that tells both Ellen and
her viewers how to tackle the vampire. It therefore signifies *Nosferatu*'s literary origins. *Vampyr* begins similarly, using both a book on vampire lore and
intertitles to refer back to the silent-film tradition and earlier literary modes
of representing the vampire. However, these textual traces disappear in the
course of the film and make way for an exclusively filmic representation of
Allan's dreamworld, of which the book has been but a part rather than the
whole. Thus, the film technique locates the vampiric not only in the filmic
character but also in the film technology itself. The transition from print
medium to film becomes far more significant than the fact that the Danish

filmmaker Dreyer based his film on English pretexts taken from outside of his own culture.

The opening credits of *Vampyr* mention the film's source: "Frei nach dem Roman" (a free adaptation of the novel) *In a Glass Darkly* von (by) J. Sheridan Le Fanu."[11] Le Fanu's *In a Glass Darkly* (1872), however, is not a novel in the strict sense, but rather a collection of five tales—and only one of them features a female vampire. This story, "Carmilla," is most often referred to in secondary literature on *Vampyr* as the sole source material for the film. Le Fanu's "Carmilla" itself has been read by critics as the story of a Victorian monster that infiltrates the private sphere of the bourgeois household and corrupts the family's precious daughter, Laura, who is forced into a fatally intimate friendship with the vampire Carmilla. The vampire seeks not only prey to satisfy her thirst, but longs for a lover as well. Indeed, theorists of the Gothic have found "Carmilla" an ideal composite of fear and desire: Laura's admiration for Carmilla's beauty, and especially her repression of a childhood dream in which the beautiful vampire had announced herself, have made "Carmilla" a casebook example for Freud's theory of "the uncanny" (see Gelder 1994, 42–64). While Carmilla's homosexuality certainly contributed to her otherness and exoticism for Victorian readers, it also added to the literary vampire's eroticization: "the element of sexual delight in sucking is here almost uncensored" (Twitchell 1981, 130).

Unsurprisingly, "Carmilla" served filmmakers of the postsexual revolution era for presenting some exceptionally gory lesbian lovers.[12] The female vampire in Dreyer's *Vampyr*, however, is not an eternally young, seductively beautiful aristocrat; she is instead an old village criminal. By removing the eroticism of the original tale, Dreyer subverts yet another expectation that would be met later that same year with Browning's staging of the seductively "weird sisters" in *Dracula*. Dreyer's portrayal of the vampire challenges not only readers' expectations, but contributes to the realization that *Vampyr* is not merely an adaptation of Le Fanu's short story but should rather be contextualized within Dreyer's larger perception of Le Fanu's writing.

Referring to the notion of *Vampyr* as an uncommitted adaptation of "Carmilla," David Rudkin emphasizes that there is hardly anything left of Le Fanu's story in the film. Rudkin argues that "all that Dreyer [has] 'really' taken from Le Fanu is a vampire and a castle" (2005, 20). Others do not consider the film to be an adaptation at all: "Rather than from any particular literary basis, the film seems more to have developed from its settings" (Harrington 1952, 197). By explicitly naming *In a Glass Darkly* as his immediate source, the director both appropriates "Carmilla" and draws attention to the other four tales (none of them featuring vampires). Furthermore, he calls attention to the narrative frame that surrounds the five stories. It is therefore necessary to consider the collection and its narrative representation as a whole, the first step being a closer look at the handful of important voices that make themselves heard within Le Fanu's collection: most notably Dr. Martin Hesselius (who appears as a protagonist in the short story "Green Tea"), his unnamed assistant turned editor whose narration links the five tales, and Laura, the young narrator of "Carmilla."

LE FANU'S DARKENING GLASS

All five tales comprising *In a Glass Darkly* had been previously published.[13] In the collection, the stories are newly framed by the prologues and editorial notes of an unnamed author, who claims to be the editor of the papers of Dr. Martin Hesselius. This metaphysician has collected hundreds of accounts of people who claim to have seen ghosts. He distinguishes between two classes of such sightings: hallucinations created by a "diseased brain or nerves" and those that are the workings of actual "spiritual agencies." However, sometimes, there is a third class: "[S]ufferings to a mixed condition. The interior sense, it is true, is opened; but it has been, and continues open, by the action of disease" (Le Fanu [1872] 2008, 40–41). Men beset by this affliction are not able to close their "inner eye" and are unable to remove themselves from the liminal zone between reality and the supernatural.

Most of the cases mentioned by Dr. Hesselius fall into this third category. Interestingly, in none of them can he help the sufferers—they all die. Indeed, Hesselius is personally consulted only in one case, which is related in the tale of "Green Tea." In this short story, Rev. Jennings feels haunted by a little, mean-spirited monkey. While the patient reports the apparition is "urging me to crimes, to injure others, or myself," and claims that the "situation is urgent" (Le Fanu [1872] 2008, 32), Hesselius does not stay with him but takes rooms in an inn, "a very quiet and comfortable house, with good thick walls" (34). While Jennings sends his servant with pleas for help to Dr. Hesselius's home address, the doctor enjoys the quietude of his hotel lodgings, "without the possibility of intrusion or distraction, in my comfortable sitting-room" (34). Thus, he learns too late about Jennings having swallowed a razor blade. Unaware of his own shortcomings, Hesselius sums up the case in an instructive tone: "Poor Mr. Jennings I cannot call a patient of mine, for I had not even begun to treat his case, and he had not yet given me, I am convinced, his full and unreserved confidence" (40). Although the supernatural quality of the apparition remains an open question, Hesselius turns out to be a fairly unreliable narrator of events.

The glass we read through is further darkened by the attitude of the nameless editor. He straightforwardly claims that the choice of cases presented has been made to "amuse or horrify a lay reader." Although he admits that he has "here and there" omitted or shortened passages and disguised names, he insists: "I have interpolated nothing" (6). However, the few personal details that the editor discloses are enough to cast doubt on his claim of being "faithful." Trained as a surgeon, the editor falls ill after having cut and lost two of his fingers. No longer able to work in his profession, he finds himself forced to travel, "seldom [being] twelve months together in the same place." It is in this situation that he meets "a wanderer like myself," a "metaphysical doctor" under whose influence the former surgeon falls: "In Dr. Martin Hesselius, I found my master" (5). A young man under the spell of an older man[14] with whom he travels around and whom he views as his mentor—a constellation found in both Polidori's and Byron's contributions to the notorious ghost-story competition at Lake Geneva.[15]

In "The Vampyre," the young gentleman, Aubrey, falls under the spell of Lord Ruthven, whom "he soon formed . . . into the hero of a romance, and determined to observe the offspring of his fancy, rather than the person before him" (Polidori [1819] 2008, 5). In Byron's fragment, the first-person narrator travels with Augustus Darvell, whom he considers "a being of no common order" (Byron [1819] 2008, 246). Clearly, Hesselius is not a vampire. However, the editor claims that the bond between himself and Hesselius goes well beyond the grave: "My admiration has stood the test of time and survived the separation of death" (Le Fanu [1872] 2008, 5). Thus, the editor's interest may well lie in being "faithful" not to the facts that he might derive from the narratives at hand but to his adherence to both the memory of his mentor and his methods. His view of events is as "blurred" as Allan Gray's vision of Courtempierre in Dreyer's *Vampyr.*

In his "prologue" to "Carmilla," the by-then suspicious editor describes Laura as a "clever and careful informant," her report described as "a conscientious particularity" (243). However, in the course of the story she tells, Laura turns out to be neither clever nor trustworthy. Very early in her tale, she describes herself as a young woman who conceals her childhood obsession with Carmilla, claiming that "no one suspected of what I was thinking" (259). In the eight years following Carmilla's initial nightly visit, Laura's sleep has to be guarded by servants set up in the nursery (see 247). For cognitive narratologists, this might hint more at traumatization than at infantile timidity. At various points, Laura displays memory gaps[16] and emphasizes the state of loneliness Carmilla found her in: "My life was . . . a rather solitary one, I can assure you" (245); "I was a little shy, as lonely people are" (259). Of course, Carmilla confesses her love to Laura only when there is no witness present: "'I have been in love with no one, and never shall,' [Carmilla] whispered, 'unless it should be with you'" (273). Is it possible that Laura is merely imagining things? At least at one point crucial to the narrative she does contradict herself: while the whole Carmilla episode could not have taken more than a few months, Laura simultaneously claims that "[e]ight years have passed since then" (245) and that "I now write, after an interval of more than ten years, with a trembling hand" (264). Not until the closing pages of her account is the reader told that the tale is offered by one who was actually bitten by a vampire. Laura herself concedes: "The narcotic of an unsuspected influence was acting upon me, and my perceptions were benumbed" (283). If Laura has really had contact with a vampire, how might her having been bitten be disturbing her memory? Carmilla is finally found out and staked. This information, however, is only quoted by Laura from official documents. From a narratological perspective, Laura's biased perception of Carmilla as both "the writhing fiend" and the "playful, languid, beautiful girl" (319) casts doubt upon her entire account.

With "Carmilla," Le Fanu became best known for having introduced the first female to the canon of literary vampires. Critics thus conventionally read "Carmilla" in relation to her "own kind." However, *In a Glass Darkly* is constructed like a Russian nesting doll: before reaching Laura's account of the vampire, readers have to pass through the accounts of a considerable number of suspicious narrators. Dispensing with the sexual undertones that have made "Carmilla" so popular among both readers and cultural theorists, Dreyer appears to translate these instances of narrative uncertainty into his own medium: As shown previously, the camera eye, which silent-film viewers had just learned to rely on, cannot be trusted in this film. In its defiance of continuity editing, *Vampyr* confuses film space and time much like Laura mixes up both cause and effect and dates connected to the vampire. Even more so, the sound track of this early talkie is as dubious as Laura's and the editor's voice in "Carmilla" and *In a Glass Darkly*. Using distinctively filmic means, Dreyer experiments with reconstructing the disconcerting effect of Le Fanu's tale evoked by its narrative ambiguities.

BURIED ALIVE

The longest of the stories collected for *In a Glass Darkly*, "The Room in the Dragon Volant," has a special place within the framework established by the unidentified editor. This "case" had been chosen by Dr. Hesselius as a complementary piece illustrating points made in *Mortis Imago*, his "Essay upon the drugs of the Dark and the Middle Ages." The fictitious editor is straightforward about the essay being "very curiously enriched by citations, in great abundance, from medieval verse and prose romance" ([1872] 2008, 119). The doctor's intertextual method of using literary models to reinforce his theses can also be found within the tale. Almost to its denouement, "The Room in the Dragon Volant" appears to be the most traditionally supernatural tale in the collection. The narrator Richard Beckett's account is brimful of Gothic imagery: stories of mysterious disappearances, talks of revenants (see 141, 168), deserted places evoking "the gloom of fallen grandeur" (165), secret rooms and hidden passageways, a rendezvous on a moonlit graveyard, and the Count's manor—a location as "black as a clump of gigantic hearse-plumes" (193) and reminiscent of Manfred's castle at Otranto. Richard can be so easily deceived by Eugenie, posing as the damsel in distress who must be saved from her greedy husband, because his idea of romantic love is constructed through his literary imagination. When Eugenie calls Richard "my hero," he has already portrayed himself as a chivalric knight, rescuing his beloved from the broken carriage and a frantic Colonel. Beckett himself reveals: "My heroics were, unconsciously, I daresay, founded upon my ideal of the French school of lovemaking" (224). Richard's account is highly subjective, as are those of his predecessors. When he sneaks up to Eugenie in her private room at the inn, he catches a glimpse of her face in a mirror:

> [S]he placed herself before a little cabriole-table, which stood against the wall, from which rose a tall mirror, in a tarnished frame. I might, indeed, have mistaken it for a picture; for it now reflected a half-length portrait of a singularly beautiful woman. . . . I never saw a living form so motionless—I gazed on a tinted statue. (122)

Beckett stages seeing "my dulcinea" (219) unveiled in an exceedingly artificial manner. In the lover's account, the object of desire turns into a representation of idealized beauty. Reflected through a mirror, the "living form [is] so motionless" that Beckett mistakes her "for a picture" (122). Significantly, Beckett's experience is reminiscent of Alfred Tennyson's "The Lady of Shalott" (1833/1842). Sitting in a tower and endlessly weaving, the Lady dies the moment she leaves her loom and the mirror through which she is intended to perceive the world. While the poem does not reveal whether the Lady can be seen by those outside the tower looking up to the mirror, she is known to be the "fairy Lady of Shalott" (Tennyson [1833] 2000, 195–96). She abandons her double status as artwork and artist (the Lady weaves "the mirror's magic sights" of the court of Camelot)[17] when she attempts to approach the knight whose chivalry she is expected to display in her tapestry—a victim of the idealization that surrounded the "damsel in distress" in Romance literature. Similarly, Beckett becomes a victim of his own idealizing Eugenie in terms of his romantic ideals. However, while the Lady arrives at Camelot as a corpse (in a boat on which she has written her name in her last act of autonomy), Beckett faces being buried alive under a false name.

Not until Beckett is poisoned by Eugenie and falls into catalepsy does he realize that he has been tricked. The moment his "romantic curiosity" turns into the realization that he has been given a paralyzing drug, the tale significantly stops being fantastic. It is now clear to Beckett and his readers that he shall be robbed, buried alive, and experience "a death the most horrible that imagination can conceive" (Le Fanu [1872] 2008, 233). *Taphephobia*, the fear of premature burial,[18] was exploited in many horror tales of Le Fanu's time. Edgar Allan Poe described the fascination the literary representation of this fear held for writers: "It may be asserted, without hesitation, that no event is so terribly well adapted to inspire the supremeness of bodily and of mental distress, as is burial before death. . . . And thus all narratives upon this topic have an interest profound" (Poe [1844] 1990, 312).[19]

Le Fanu's tale is another such narrative "upon this topic": just before his being boxed up in the coffin, the paralyzed Richard Beckett sees what is going on before him visualized as a fundamentally filmic experience:

I had not the power of turning the eyes this way or that, the smallest fraction of hair's breadth. But let any one, placed as I was at the end of a room, ascertain for himself by experiment how wide is the field of sight, without the slightest alteration in the line of vision, he will find that it takes in the breadth of a large room, and that up to a very short distance before him. . . . Next to nothing that passed in the room, therefore, was hidden from me. (228)

Although he is still able to perceive what is happening before his eyes, Beckett can no longer communicate. Eugenie and her accomplice, the Count, talk to each other about him, but no longer to him. The protagonist is reduced to a passive recipient of images and sounds. Like a viewer in a cinema, Beckett can only see what is shown to him. His field of vision resembles the frame within a static medium-long shot of a room, the standard frame of early film.[20]

It is this scene from "The Room in the Dragon Volant" that Dreyer chooses to transpose into his vampire film. In recent years, Hollywood films have shown a growing interest in presenting premature burials from within the grave[21]; however, the manner in which Dreyer stages the preparations for Gray's burial remains unmatched. Much more than just the primal human fear of premature burial is represented in the most iconic scene of the film: *Vampyr* here negotiates the alienating encounter with the filmic apparatus itself already anticipated in Le Fanu's tale.

Still exhausted from the blood transfusion, Allan Gray sits down on a bench and falls asleep. In a double exposure, a "secondary" Gray splits from the sleeping body and walks into the factory. There he discovers a third Gray lying in the coffin with his eyes wide open. Having seen his own corpse, the secondary Gray hides under a trapdoor, never to return. Having shown the doctor giving commands to his servants, the camera enters the coffin in order to stay with the third Gray. For the first time in the film, the viewer is presented with unequivocally subjective shots and shares Gray's point of view exclusively. During the few minutes of this scene, "a new orthodoxy in the film language" (Rayns 2008, DVD audio commentary) is presented. While shots have hitherto disquietingly failed to match each other, suddenly the angles fit together and create a coherent representation of the experience of one's own burial from within the coffin. Narratively framed as a dream within a dream, this union between Gray and the viewer abandons all previous inconsistencies. From within, the corpse/viewer witnesses the lid being screwed to the coffin. Here, Dreyer exhibits the process of adaptation from Le Fanu's literary text to the film most explicitly. While Beckett, lying in his closed coffin, can only listen to "these vulgar sounds" (Le Fanu [1872] 2008, 234) of the screwdriver, Gray hears *and* sees the screwdriver through the glass panel in the lid at the height of his face—diegetic sound and vision become one (figure 9.1).

Watching a film has been theorized as a primarily bodily experience. According to somatic film studies, movie images first have an impact on the human body, before the viewer is able to mentally process what he or she is shown.[22] For Steven Shaviro, watching a film is "radically passive, the suffering of a violence perpetrating against the eye. Images themselves are immaterial, but their effect is all the more physical and corporeal" (1993, 51). Thus, while Gray lives through the primal fear of being buried alive, the film viewer is not offered but forced to identify with him. The first subjective

9.1 *VAMPYR*, 1931

shots from within the coffin present a framed view: like Allan the corpse, the viewer sees the frame of the glass panel. The movie theater has turned into a coffin.

In his discussion of instances of "the uncanny," Freud explicitly refers to the fear of premature burial:

> *To some people the idea of being buried alive by mistake is the most uncanny thing of all. And yet psycho-analysis has taught us that this terrifying phantasy is only a transformation of another phantasy which had originally nothing terrifying about it at all, but was qualified by a certain lasciviousness—the phantasy, I mean, of intra-uterine existence. ([1919] 1985, 366–67)*

Representing (the dream of) premature burial in a vampire film,[23] Dreyer draws attention to the fact that, for a vampire, being buried indeed is the beginning of a new existence—for a vampire, lying in a coffin is an intra-uterine experience. Accordingly, Gray does not (only) dream his death but dreams of becoming a vampire. This is already suggested when the secondary Gray lifts the shroud and discovers his own fresh corpse with eyes wide open. The scene is reminiscent of Jonathan Harker's discovery of Dracula's resting place, complete with occupant: "There, in one of the great boxes . . . lay the Count. He was either dead or asleep, I could not say which—for the eyes were open and stony, but without the glassiness of death" (Stoker [1897] 1997, 50).

By forcing his viewer to identify so closely with this vampire/corpse/ Gray, Dreyer makes him experience both the primal fear of being buried alive and the act of turning into a vampire. Looking through his glass panel, Gray/the viewer sees a man lighting a candle and putting it down on the glass. Marguerite Chopin, the vampire, shows up in front of the window, takes the candle, and looks into the coffin/auditorium. Her sudden appearance from beyond the window/film frame once again shows that the vampire controls film space: Through the small window of the coffin, the frame for Gray's and the film viewer's vision, Dreyer exhibits the status of cinema as a "window onto the world" (Bazin [1967] 2005, 111), as Bordwell has noted (see 1981, 108). Like the paralyzed Richard Beckett in Le Fanu's tale, the film viewer is radically forced to realize the passive role he is assigned in this configuration. Thus, Dreyer does not only translate Beckett's paradigmatically uncanny experience of being buried alive into film, but uses this motif for addressing the medium—film itself—and negotiating the phenomenological effect it has on the audience: while the literary figure Beckett has to fear for both his life and his account to come to a violent end, the film figure Gray here mirrors our experience of film viewing.

However, this scene is only the final point in a continuous process of bodily alienation that Gray experiences. *Vampyr* stands in a long filmic tradition of negotiating the anthropocentric dimension of cinema. In contrast to the theater stage, where the human body is always completely presented, cinematic space is created by bodies that move within, into, or out of the frame. Early film was preoccupied with the fear of destroying the integrity of the human body by showing it in close-ups and thus fragmenting it.[24] Using sources from Gothic literature, German Expressionist directors then introduced characters meeting their own mirror images or shadows.[25] Freud himself used many examples from Gothic literature to reinforce his theses on "the uncanny," exemplars being "[d]ismembered limbs, a severed head, a hand cut off at the wrist . . . all these have something peculiarly uncanny about them, especially when, as in the last instance, they prove capable of independent activity in addition" (Freud [1919] 1985, 366). Already before the burial scene discussed previously, Gray and the viewers share this paradigmatically uncanny experience, when observing shadows climbing up ladders, dancing a polka, and even shooting a man. After the blood transfusion, Gray for the first time perceives the fragmentation of his own body. Sitting down to recover, he calls for the doctor:

GRAY. Doctor! I'm losing blood!
DOCTOR. Nonsense! Your blood is right here!

In the screenplay to the film, Dreyer's production notes suggest: "His blood is speaking to him from the other room" (quoted in Rayns 2008, DVD audio commentary). As if his dream within the dream intensifies Gray's filmic experience, he perceives himself as a fragmented body. Like a vampire having sucked his blood, Dreyer seems to suggest that the film deconstructs Gray's body. In this respect, the casting of the film amateur Nicolas von Gunzburg as Allan Gray is fitting: through his clumsy, passive acting style, Gunzburg literally appears to be a man who accidentally got lost in a film.[26]

In conclusion, we can see that the title of the film denotes different vampires. Of course, it can refer directly to Marguerite Chopin, the film's vampire protagonist; however, the name *Vampyr* also signifies the transgressive qualities of this film as well. Dreyer preys on our expectations of how a film should be told, how an adaptation of "Carmilla" is constructed, and which effect intertextual references to other vampire narratives have. Displaying the "power to move between and undo borders otherwise holding identities in place" (Butler 2010, 1), *Vampyr* is not only a vampire film but also a vampiric film. In contrast to the popular American film *Dracula* and the vampire films that have followed, *Vampyr* is extremely self-reflexive, negotiating while simultaneously juxtaposing various literary and filmic modes of representation. The vampire here is, as in Murnau's film, a hybrid of the literary and the filmic. By having Gray hear his own blood talking to him from the other room and meeting his own corpse, Dreyer introduces film as a vampiric medium that is able to deconstruct but simultaneously revitalize the human body. By appropriating Richard Beckett's burial scene for his film, Dreyer boxes up both Gray and the viewer in a coffin. By having his audience immediately participate in Gray's dream of becoming a vampire, Dreyer exhibits the ultimately "dangerously mimetic" (Shaviro 1993, 258) force of film.

NOTES

1. The character of Friedrich W. Murnau in *Shadow of the Vampire* (2000).

2. Already in 1994, Ken Gelder calculated that "[a]round 3,000 vampire or vampire-related films have been made so far" (86). The number of literary texts prominently featuring vampires is considerably larger and equally impossible to determine.

3. My analysis is based on the 2008 Criterion DVD edition that uses a German version restored in 1998. *Vampyr* was filmed and released in three different languages: German, French, and English; all English copies, however, have been lost. Film quotes are taken from the English subtitles to the German version.

4. For a book-length discussion of Dracula's transition "from novel to stage to screen," see David Skal's *Hollywood Gothic* (2004).

5. Another difference between *Dracula* and *Vampyr* is worth mentioning here. Although *Dracula* was released with one of the major Hollywood studios, *Vampyr* was financed privately. Dreyer's benefactor Nicolas von Gunzburg, an aristocratic Dutch cinephile, demanded that he play the lead role (see Rudkin 2005, 117).

6. See Paul Schrader's assessment of the film: "*Vampyr* is Dreyer's only exclusively expressionistic film. . . . Gray's vampire world is rife with familiar expressionist visual fetishes: an obsession with darkened staircases, arching doorways, and vanishing corridors" (1972, 117).

7. For example, there are various displays of religious symbols, such as a statue in the hallway of the château, the nun attending Léone, or the rosary in her bedchamber. These symbols, however, have no significance for the chain of events; there is no indication that the vampire may be afraid of them.

8. Note the phonetic and aural similarity between the given names of Dreyer and Murnau's protagonists: Allan and Helen.

9. The servant reads the book as Gray rests after having donated blood. Blood transfusions meant to keep a vampire's victim alive first appear in *Dracula*: "[Van Helsing:] 'There is not time to be lost. She will die for sheer want of blood to keep the heart's action as it should be. There must be a transfusion of blood at once. Is it you or me?' [Dr. Seward:] 'I am younger and stronger, Professor. It must be me!'" (1997, 312). Correspondingly, Allan subjects himself to a blood transfusion in *Vampyr*: "[Allan:] 'Can't she be saved?' [Doctor:] 'Perhaps. But she needs blood. It must be human blood. Are you willing to give her your own?'"

10. Seated on a bench outside, Gray falls asleep and splits into two. His second self goes to an abandoned factory, where he discovers himself lying in a coffin. The Gray within the coffin sees the vampire Marguerite Chopin gazing upon him as the casket is carried to the graveyard. As the coffin passes the sleeping Gray on the bench, he awakens and heads to the graveyard, arriving just in time to witness the staking of the vampire by the manservant.

11. "Adapted from the novel *In a Glass Darkly* by Sheridan Le Fanu" (my translation).

12. There have been memorable comebacks in literature and film. The lesbian vampire, for example, achieved some public notoriety with Whitley Strieber's 1981 novel *The Hunger* and Tony Scott's 1983 film adaptation of the book, both of which portray a relatively eroticized relationship between a female vampire and her female victim. Of late, however, the exclusively lesbian vampire seems to have lost her lure. While Alan Ball's highly sexualized television series *True Blood* (from 2008) features vampires with various sexual appetites, there is no character especially reminiscent of Carmilla. Ironically, in *True Blood*, "Carmilla" is the name of a hotel in Dallas designed for a vampire clientele, with lightproof windows and room-service selections that include a variety of human "snacks" of all blood types.

13. "Green Tea" and "Mr. Justice Harbottle," along with the two longer texts "The Room in the Dragon Volant" and "Carmilla," had appeared in literary magazines between 1869 and 1872. "The Familiar" is a slightly revised version of a story that originally appeared in *Ghost Stories and Tales of Mystery* (1851).

14. "He was an old man when I first saw him; nearly five-and-thirty years my senior" (5).

15. In "The Author's Introduction to the Standard Novels Edition" of *Frankenstein* (1831, Mary Shelley remembers: "'We will each write a ghost story,' said Lord Byron. . . . Poor

Polidori had some terrible idea about a skull-headed lady who was so punished for peeping through a keyhole" (355). While Byron's tale "Augustus Darvell" remained a fragment, Polidori's final contribution "The Vampyre" was published as "[A] Tale by Lord Byron" in April 1819. For the accusation of plagiarism surrounding "The Vampyre" and Polidori's disturbed relationship with Byron and his circles, see David Macdonald's *Poor Polidori* (1991).

16. "At this distance of time I cannot tell you, or even understand, how I overcame my horror so effectually as to lie alone in my room that night" (280).

17. Very popular among Le Fanu's contemporaries, Tennyson's "The Lady of Shalott" (1833/1842) negotiates modes of textual and visual representation. It inspired various Pre-Raphaelite paintings.

18. For a sociohistorical discussion of this fear from the seventeenth century onward, see Philippe Ariès's *L'homme devant la mort* (1975).

19. Tales by Poe featuring premature burial are "Berenice" (1835), "The Fall of the House of Usher" (1839), "The Premature Burial" (1844), and "The Cask of Amontillado" (1846).

20. There is another harbinger of film in Beckett's story: after he has been rescued, the police look for previous victims, but their bodies are already decomposed beyond recognition. However, one of them can still be identified: He had a glass eye that "remained in the socket, slightly displaced, of course, but recognizable" (239). This prosthesis, reminiscent of a camera lens, serves to authenticate the plot that has just been revealed to the reader by Beckett.

21. The Dutch filmmaker George Sluizer directed *Spoorloos* (1988) and its US remake *The Vanishing* (1993). In Quentin Tarantino's *Kill Bill 2* (2004), "the bride" has to rely on her martial arts skills in order to escape coffin and grave. In 2005, Tarantino directed a feature-length double episode of the TV series *CSI: Crime Scene Investigation*; the CSI team has to find a colleague who has been buried alive by a psychopath in a Perspex coffin ("Grave Danger," 2005). The thriller *Buried* (2010) presents the point of view of an intentionally prematurely buried truck driver.

22. This perspective allows for classifying films according to the degree to which they physically affect the viewer. Linda Williams introduced the term *body genres* for horror films, melodramas and porn films (see Williams 1991, 6–9). See also Abbott (2004) and Warner (2006).

23. The second premature burial in *Vampyr* is similarly iconic: at the end of the film, the evil doctor flees to a mill, is magically trapped in a cage, and suffocated by flour falling down on him. The more flour that pours down on him, the whiter the screen gets until finally the camera light passes the celluloid filmstrip nearly undisturbed: the filmic representation of the doctor has disappeared.

24. See Méliès's films *Dislocations mystérieuses* (1901) and *Le bourreau turc* (1904). Another famous example closer to Dreyer's time is Luis Buñuel and Salvador Dali's surreal film *Un chien Andalou* (1929), which features a razor blade cutting through an eye.

25. See *Der Student von Prag* (1913). In Stellan Rye and Paul Wegener's film, the student Balduin sells his mirror image to a charlatan.

26. Indeed, the only professional actress in the whole cast is Sybille Schmitz. She plays Léone, the woman bitten by the vampire.

WORKS CITED

Abbott, Stacey. 2004. "Spectral Vampires: *Nosferatu* in the Light of New Technology." In *Horror Film: Creating and Marketing Fear*, edited by Steffen Hantke, 3–20. Jackson: University Press of Mississippi.

Ariès, Philippe. 1975. *L'homme devant la mort*. Paris: Seuil.

Bazin, André. [1967] 2005. Vol. 1 of *What Is Cinema?* Translated by Hugh Gray. Berkeley: University of California Press.

Bond, Kirk. 1965. "The World of Carl Dreyer." *Film Quarterly* 19 (1): 26–38.

Bordwell, David. 1981. *The Films of Carl-Theodor Dreyer*. Berkeley: University of California Press.

Le bourreau turc. 1904. Directed by Georges Méliès. Perf. Georges Méliès. Produced by Georges Méliès.

Bram Stoker's Dracula. 1992. Directed by Francis F. Coppola. Perf. Gary Oldman, Winona Ryder, Keanu Reeves, Anthony Hopkins. Columbia Pictures.

Butler, Erik. 2010. *Metamorphoses of the Vampire in Literature and Film: Cultural Transformations in Europe, 1732–1933*. Rochester, NY: Camden House.

Buried. 2010. Directed by Rodrigo Cortés. Perf. Ryan Reynolds. Versus Entertainment.

Byron, George Gordon, Lord. [1819] 2008. "Augustus Darvell." In *The Vampyre and Other Tales of the Macabre*, edited by Robert Morrison and Chris Baldick, 26–52. Oxford: Oxford University Press.

Un chien Andalou. 1929. Directed by Luis Buñuel. Perf. Pierre Batcheff, Simone Mareuil, Salvador Dali. Produced by Luis Buñuel.

Deane, Hamilton, and John L. Balderston. [1927] 1960. *Dracula: The Vampire Play in Three Acts*. New York: Samuel French.

Dislocations mystérieuses. 1901. Directed by Georges Méliès. Perf. André Deed. Produced by Georges Méliès.

Dracula. 1931. Directed by Tod Browning. Perf. Bela Lugosi, Helen Chandler, David Manners. Produced by Tod Browning and Carl Laemmle Jr.

Dracula. 1958. Directed by Terence Fisher. Perf. Christopher Lee, Peter Cushing, Michael Gough. Produced by Anthony Hinds.

Eisner, Lotte. [1952] 1969. *The Haunted Screen: Expressionism in the German Cinema and the Influence of Max Reinhardt*. Berkeley: University of California Press.

Frankenstein. 1931. Directed by James Whale. Perf. Boris Karloff. Produced by Carl Laemmle Jr.

Freud, Sigmund. [1919] 1985. "The Uncanny." In *Art and Literature*, Vol. 14 of *The Pelican Freud Library*, edited by Albert Dickson and translated by James Strachey, 335–76. Harmondsworth, UK: Penguin.

Gelder, Ken. 1994. *Reading the Vampire*. London: Routledge.

Grant, Michael. 2003. "Fulci's Waste Land: Cinema, Horror, and the Abominations of Hell." In *The Couch and the Silver Screen: Psychoanalytic Reflections on European Cinema*, edited by Andrea Sabbadini, 145–56. New York: Routledge.

"Grave Danger." 2005. *CSI: Crime Scene Investigation*. May 19. Directed by Quentin Tarantino. Produced for CBS.

Harrington, Curtis. 1952. "Ghoulies and Ghosties." *Quarterly of Film Radio and Television* 7 (2): 191–202.

The Hunger. 1983. Directed by Tony Scott. Perf. Catherine Deneuve, David Bowie, Susan Sarandon. Produced by Richard Shepherd.

Kill Bill 2. 2004. Directed by Quentin Tarantino. Perf. Uma Thurman, David Caradine, Michael Madsen, Daryl Hannah. Miramax Films.

Le Fanu, J. Sheridan. [1872] 2008. *In a Glass Darkly.* Edited by Robert Tracy. Oxford: Oxford University Press.

Macdonald, David L. 1991. *Poor Polidori: A Critical Biography of the Author of "The Vampyre."* Toronto: University of Toronto Press.

Nosferatu. 1922. Directed by Friedrich W. Murnau. Perf. Max Schreck, Gustav von Wangenheim, Gerda Schröder, Alexander Granach. Produced by Enrico Dieckmann and Albin Grau.

Only Lovers Left Alive. 2013. Directed by Jim Jarmusch. Perf. Tom Hiddleston, Tilda Swinton, John Hurt. Produced by Jeremy Thomas and Reinhard Brundig.

Poe, Edgar Allan. [1844] 1990. *The Short Fiction.* Edited by Susan and Stuart Levine. Urbana: University of Illinois Press.

Polidori, John. "The Vampyre." [1819] 2008. In *The Vampyre and Other Tales of the Macabre,* edited by Robert Morrison and Chris Baldick, 3–23. Oxford: Oxford University Press.

Rayns, Tony. 2008. Audio commentary featured on the Criterion DVD edition of *Vampyr.*

Rudkin, David. 2005. *Vampyr.* London: BFI.

Schrader, Paul. 1972. *Transcendental Style in Film: Ozu, Bresson, Dreyer.* Berkeley: University of California Press.

Shadow of the Vampire. 2000. Directed by E. Elias Merhige. Perf. John Malkovich, Willem Dafoe. Produced by Nicholas Cage and Jeff Levine.

Shaviro, Steven. 1993. *The Cinematic Body.* Minneapolis: University of Minnesota Press.

Shelley, Mary. [1831] 1999. *Frankenstein; or, The Modern Prometheus.* Edited by D. L. Macdonald and Kathleen Scherf. Peterborough, ON: Broadview.

Skal, David J. 2004. *Hollywood Gothic: The Tangled Web of "Dracula" from Novel to Stage to Screen.* New York: Faber and Faber.

Spadoni, Robert. 2007. *Uncanny Bodies: The Coming of Sound Film and the Origins of the Horror Genre.* Berkeley: University of California Press.

Spoorloos. 1988. Directed by George Sluizer. Perf. Bernard-Pierre Donnadieu, Johanna Tersteege. Produced by Anne Lordon and George Sluizer.

Strieber, Whitley. 1981. *The Hunger.* New York: William Morrow.

Stoker, Bram. [1897] 1997. *Dracula.* Edited by Nina Auerbach and David J. Skal. New York: Norton.

Der Student von Prag. 1913. Directed by Hanns Heinz Ewers and Stellan Rye. Perf. Paul Wegener, Lyda Salmonova. Produced for Deutsche Bioscop.

Tennyson, Alfred, Lord. [1833/1842] 2000. "The Lady of Shalott," reprinted in *The Victorians: An Anthology of Poetry and Poetics,* 195–96. Edited by Valentine Cunningham. Oxford: Blackwell.

Thompson, Kristin. 1985. "The Formulation of the Classical Style, 1909–1928." In *The Classical Hollywood: Film Style and Mode of Production to 1960*, edited by David Bordwell et al., 245–472. London: Routledge.

True Blood. 2008–present. Written by Alan Ball. Produced for HBO.

Twitchell, James B. 1981. *The Living Dead: A Study of the Vampire in Romantic Literature*. Durham, NC: Duke University Press.

Tybjerg, Casper. 2008. "The Rise of the Vampire: A Visual Essay." Documentary featured on the Criterion DVD edition of *Vampyr*.

Vampyr. [1931] 2008. Directed by Carl Theodor Dreyer. Perf. Nicolas von Gunzburg, Sybille Schmitz, Julian West, Maurice Schutz, Rena Mandel. DVD. New York: Criterion.

The Vanishing. 1993. Directed by George Sluizer. Perf. Jeff Bridges, Kiefer Sutherland, Sandra Bullock. Produced by Larry Brezner and Pieter Jan Brugge.

Warner, Marina. 2006. *Phantasmagoria: Spirit Visions, Metaphors, and Media into the Twenty-First Century*. Oxford: Oxford University Press.

Wicke, Jennifer. 1992. "Vampiric Typewriting: Dracula and Its Media." *ELH* 59:467–93.

Williams, Linda. 1991. "Film Bodies: Gender, Genre, and Excess." *Film Quarterly* 44 (4): 2–13.

DISRUPTIVE CORPSES

Tales of the Living Dead in Horror Comics of the 1950s and Beyond

RICHARD J. HAND

In his foreword to the zombie comic collection *Fleshrot: Tales from the Dead* (vol. 1) (2003), George A. Romero states that the anthology reminds him of the days when "I smuggled *Tales from the Crypt* into the house and chuckled, under the bedspread with a small flashlight casting dim light on the pages. The drawings in this book made me chuckle again. This is balls-out-what-it's-all-about stuff" (2003, 4). In this statement, Romero, the director whose name is most frequently associated with zombie movies, gives us an insight into one of his earliest influences: the horror comics of the 1950s, the epitome of which is *Tales from the Crypt,* published by EC (Entertaining Comics). Romero emphasizes that the effect of reading these often gruesome comic books is laughter, and that "chuckle" has an important place in the reception of popular horror. There is also, arguably, something masculine and adolescent in this perception. Romero says that he "grew up on EC comics" (4), a phrase that connotes a rite of passage. Horror is something taboo that must be smuggled into the house and read beneath the sheets, not dissimilar to pornography. Even today, the horror graphic narrative can be "balls-out" and stimulate laughter. Not only did 1950s horror comics explore the twin taboos of death (blatantly) and sexuality (latently), but in the context of their production, they were also perceived as a palpable danger.

The horror comics so influential on Romero's oeuvre and remembered by him so fondly some fifty years later, existed for a mere five years before they were, as it were, shot in the head by the forces of censorship. Even crueler in this annihilation is the fact that the horror comics were forced to destroy themselves by introducing the self-regulatory system of the Comics Magazine Association of America Comics Code Authority (CCA) in 1954 in order to preempt the far worse prospect of official legislative intervention. This marks, as Walter Kendrick argues, "the first large-scale censorship of any medium on grounds of violence rather than sex" (1991, 247), although, as we shall see, sexuality nonetheless often provides an important subtext. Prior to the establishment of the code, horror comics were violent, grotesque, and explicit. They were also inventive, adventurous, and enjoyed a popularity that was the envy of other forms of popular horror culture, with distribution in the multimillions to a consumer base comprised of not only adolescent boys, but "a surprising number of girls" and "a significant adult readership" (Sabin 1993, 154) as well. The horror comics of the pre-code era may have been short-lived but they nonetheless remain an astonishing and prolific body of work.

The fully realized horror comic began to come into being in the late 1940s—with a one-off example like *Eerie* (January 1947) testing the water—but they are predominantly an early 1950s phenomenon. When 1950s horror culture is subjected to critical analysis, emphasis is usually placed on the social anxieties reflected in the Red Peril or atomic age zeitgeist, whereby themes of enemies within, bodily invasion, or horrific mutation become thinly veiled metaphors for anticommunism or technophobia. Such terrors are present in horror comics and their affiliated science-fiction titles, but there is one iconic figure in the pre-code horror comic that is hard to explain away so conveniently: the zombie. Indeed, the 1950s zombie's refusal to be compartmentalized into a convenient interpretative tomb reflects its abiding potency. Before they were banned, the living-dead stories were not only some of the most resolutely shocking works in horror fiction, but also some of the most distinctive and iconic creations in the history of the comic-book medium. Even if we consider only the cover art, for example, as good as the covers were in their depiction of Transylvanian monsters or acts of homicidal violence, the most disturbing and paradigmatic covers were those that featured animated skeletons dressed in clumps of rotting flesh.

Although pre-code horror comics are evidently from a particular historical period in their style and substance, I illustrate that they continue to cast a long shadow over subsequent popular horror culture, not least movies. As we shall see, the slow, staggering living corpse inhabited horror comics a generation before George A. Romero's seminal *Night of the Living Dead* (1968). In addition, although the living dead depicted in the comics may be a repulsive and abject spectacle, this does not mean that the reader does not have any empathy for these creatures: as in some of the most sophisticated examples of zombie culture, we realize that the worst monster of all is the living, breathing human being. An implication to this is the potency of the zombie: many creators, from graphic artists and writers to filmmakers such as Romero himself, have found in their narratives of the living dead a vehicle for sociopolitical comment.

DISTURBING VAULTS: COMICS OF THE LIVING DEAD IN THE 1950S

In an article in the February 1954 issue of *Writer's Digest*, EC editor William Gaines calls for new writers and artists, and divulges what his creative team is interested in:

> *You should know this about our horror books: we have no ghosts, devils, goblins or the like. We tolerate vampires and werewolves, if they follow tradition and behave the way respectable vampires and werewolves should. We love walking corpse stories. We'll accept the occasional zombie or mummy.* (Gaines quoted in Bernewitz and Geissman 2000, 192)

This playful statement gives a fascinating insight to the horror comic of the period. It is clear that its development draws on the golden age of horror in the form of the Universal movies of the 1930s (no doubt the adolescent influence on many of the horror creators of the 1950s), and deliberately shifts away from the ghosts, goblins, and devils of the nineteenth-century tradition of horror and the supernatural. Indeed, the vampires and other Transylvanian monstrosities in the horror comics are more obviously popular Hollywood than literary Gothic. Also striking is Gaines's acceptance of the "occasional zombie." The voodoo zombie does indeed creep into a number of EC's stories and, exactly like the mummy Gaines twins it with, has a clear, albeit purely fantastical (if not downright xenophobic), ethnographical treatment. But what is most impressive in Gaines's call is his expression of "love" for the walking corpse.

Unsurprisingly, the living dead are a favorite in the EC opus, occurring in numerous stories and covers and in its advertising. The titles of EC's two most famous comic books say it all: when readers opened *Tales from the Crypt* or *The Vault of Horror*, they were peering into and unleashing terrors from the grave. This elucidates the fact that like virtually all horror culture, a central impetus of the horror comic is to present us with displays of death in order to explore our fundamental *todesangst*, our fear of death. The implications of this are clear in Martin Barker's argument that the pre-code horror comics function in terms of a "dare-relationship" whereby they "proffer a social relationship with their readers based on the logic of testing our limits" (1992, 112): the horror comic challenges us to discover how much we dare to *see* and *contemplate*.

While EC was certainly a major player in the horror comic-book industry, it is important to take heed of Stephen Sennitt's reminder that "there's more to horror comics than EC" (1999, 61). EC was neither the first nor the most prolific of the many publishers that began to produce horror titles at an extraordinary rate in the early 1950s. EC remains the most famous company because of the devoted fan base it nurtured in its heyday, which has resulted in its full corpus continuing to be resurrected in reprints, film adaptations, and the long-running HBO television series *Tales from the Crypt* (1989–1996). This has helped ensure that EC's reanimated corpses live on as the name *EC* becomes synonymous with the genre. It would be a mistake, however, to think that the walking corpse was a phenomenon peculiar to EC.

In the vast body of pre-code horror comics, zombies and the living dead are ubiquitous. Some stories are contextualized within the origins of zombie folklore and are set in Haiti, some tales of the living dead rely upon distinctly historical or neo-Gothic settings, while in other stories the zombies crawl from the grave seeking revenge or retribution in a contemporary setting, most noticeably America. Whatever the scenario, the story is always the same, for as David Skal states: "In the horror comics view of America, morality was a state of grace attainable only by the living dead and the murderously insane. The world was made right only when a fetid corpse crawled out of its grave to revenge itself on the living" (2001, 231).

The quintessential drive and function of the zombie in EC is vengeance, making these figures of the living dead more like the revenants of European folktales than the zombie of Haitian legend. Furthermore, retribution has a biblical connotation whereas vengeance is a key feature in classical European drama. Indeed, if we regard comics as a form of media drama and performance (in other words, the animation of script into visual narrative), the links with a theatrical tradition are compelling. The 1950s zombies stagger, within their narratives, somewhere between the Furies in the Greek tragedy *The Oresteia* (458 BCE) and the vengeful ghosts of the Elizabethan-Jacobean stage such as Hamlet's father (1602).

EC was also influenced by more recent performance traditions. There are examples of EC material that has an intertextual relationship with the Théâtre du Grand-Guignol (1897–1962), the legendary "Theatre of Horror" in Paris. Several story lines and images in the comics are reminiscent of the theater's plots and visual iconography of its posters and photographic documentation (Hand and Wilson 2012, 301–19). Similarly, another unmistakable influence on EC is to be found in US horror radio of the 1930s to the 1950s. Part of a popular genre, horror radio shows such as *The Witch's Tale* (1931–1938) and *Inner Sanctum Mysteries* (1941–1952) had a formula of mordantly humorous character hosts framing self-contained tales of terror, including an identifiable subgenre of zombie narratives (Hand 2011, 39–49). The radio plays can be surprisingly nihilistic and gruesome compared with the screen media of the day, but they are extremely similar to the unsettling narratives of pre-code comics. Evidently, the remembered or contemporaneous horror plays broadcast on the airwaves were an influence on the EC creative team.

In terms of the classical graphic tradition, Skal persuasively locates a connection between pre-code horror comics and Hans Holbein's *The Dance of Death*, a sequence of engravings from 1534 (2001, 230–31). We could also draw parallels with other sixteenth-century art such as Hans Baldung Grien's "The Three Ages of Man and Death" and "The Three Ages of Woman and Death," both of which feature animated corpse-like figures beside images of living beauty. The 1950s horror comics also allude to the darker images of Goya, such as "The Disasters of War" (1810–1814) or "Saturn Devouring His Sons," created in the 1820s. Of course, pre-code horror comics find particular resonance in the art of the nineteenth-century popular press, such as the often gruesomely illustrated tabloids such as the *Illustrated Police News* (London) or *Le Petit Journal* (Paris).

As well as drawing on such theatrical and graphic ancestry, the 1950s horror comics belong to the vernacular tradition of folktales and fairy tales, not least because they are always snappy and self-contained and are never "to be continued." These are moral tales in which the wicked perpetrate an illegal or immoral act for personal gain but eventually get their comeuppance. This is not to imply that EC stories are as timeless as folktales: indeed, it is possible to see a materialist dimension to the genre where stories look at the corruption of capitalism in the postwar wonder years of unprecedented economic expansion. As well as presenting the eons-old archetypes of adultery and murder, pre-code horror sometimes presents stories in which corrupt businessmen and slanderers who have directly or indirectly driven undeserving victims to the grave through penury or humiliation are visited by shambling corpses who give the perpetrators their just deserts. In "The Death Wagon!" (*The Vault of Horror* 24, April 1952), a group of men, women, and children killed in automobile accidents rise from the grave and dismember the greedy and exploitative used-car salesmen who knowingly sold faulty vehicles. Such a story is a powerful cautionary tale about the unacceptable side of capitalism, touching on the conscience of the nation as a kind of horror-comic equivalent to Arthur Miller's play about industrial corruption, *All My Sons* (1947).

Although for Stephen King the "horror comics of the fifties still sum up . . . the epitome of horror," he sees their power to horrify as "less fine" than the concept of terror "because it is not entirely of the mind" (1981, 36). Here, King is most likely singing the praises of his principal craft: fiction.

However, one of the great achievements of the pre-code horror comics was their graphic portrayals of the forbidden, their revelation of disturbing images that abide in the mind. As Kendrick writes, "Few American children in 1954 had entered a crypt or a burial vault; fewer yet had seen a rotting corpse" (1991, 244). In contrast to their young readers, many of the writers and artists of early 1950s comics had served in the Second World War and seen human bodies in various forms of corporeal devastation. Certainly, the range of decay presented in the comic books—putrid tissue falling off the bone, slimy in some cases, flaky in others; colors of flesh ranging from brown, green, yellow, or blue and bored into by worms, chewed by rats, or pickled in formaldehyde—has an almost medical or forensic textbook verisimilitude. For these creators of tales of the living dead, synthetic cadavers are inadequate: their corpses may not behave like authentic corpses, but they unquestionably look like them. Perhaps the realism of the graphic work reflects the shock of war: there is something posttraumatic in the artists creating corpses who, in the stories, have always died before they should have or needed to. Certainly, Digby Diehl argues, these horror comics appealed to people who were "trying to cope" (1996, 28) with the reality of the recent slaughter of the concentration camps and atomic bomb sites of World War II, not to mention the contemporaneous war in Korea. The grisly zombies in horror comics explore the abject horror of the fetid. In analyzing the concept of horror, Jonathan Lake Crane contends: "We are literally filled with shit. The rotting corpse, the fetid stool, and the worrisome symptoms of disintegration that accompany any illness are the clearest signs of what and who we really are" (1994, 32). The zombies in horror comics represent everything that is fetid. Rather than being flushed away, they resurface from subconscious anxiety or historical guilt and fascinate as much as haunt us.

The covers of many horror comics feature variations on a classic motif not just of pre-code horror but also zombie culture more generally: the birth of zombies. The (un)birth of the living dead is compelled by a motivation for revenge that even death cannot quash. As a concept and as an image it is subversive in its irrationality and in its defiance of the "natural order of things." The grave is a kind of womb (one is reminded of the prehistoric practice of burying corpses in the fetal position), but that represents a journey into, as it were, Mother Earth, not back into the surface of the living. On EC covers we have multiple births with zombies climbing out of coffins, out of the earth, out of wells, and even out of alligator pits. On more than one occasion, the covers present us with the quintessential image of zombie birth: a pair of decaying hands emerging from the ground. Do these hands bloom with the tentative movements familiar in Hammer Films' *Plague of the Zombies* (John Gilling, 1965) and the Romero archetype? Or do they spring up with the ferocity of the eponymous character at the finale of *Carrie* (Brian de Palma, 1976) and the living dead in movies following *28 Days Later* (Danny Boyle, 2002)? The narrative accounts are less ambiguous when it comes to the movements of the living dead. In "Poetic Justice" (*The Haunt of Fear* 12, April 1952), for example, we find this description: "The thing . . . got to its feet, swaying uncertainly. . . . Then it stumbled off toward town! Crawling clods of grave mud fell away as it tottered along!" (8).

The descriptive words here—"swaying uncertainly," "stumbled," and "tottered"—make it clear that the 1950s comic zombies are precursors to the monsters in Romero's late 1960s *Night of the Living Dead*. Stephen King recalls a 1950s living-dead comic in which the slow movements of the zombie are not merely explained, but are apologized for by the creature itself: "I am coming . . . but I have to come slowly . . . because little pieces of me keep falling off" (1981, 37). Indeed, while this self-awareness of the living dead occurs elsewhere, as a whole, the levels of consciousness of zombies varies: some are able to talk and think, while others are driven by an unutterable, one-track motivation.

It is not clear if the zombies in EC are destructible: certainly no clear Romeroesque "shoot 'em in the head" rule seems to apply. Indeed, "Horror! Head . . . It Off!" (*Tales from the Crypt* 11, December 1951) is set in revolutionary France and concerns a fleeing aristocrat who is betrayed and condemned to the guillotine. He returns as a headless zombie and exacts his revenge by decapitating the man who sold him to the authorities. The scenario is reworked in "The Sliceman Cometh" (*Tales from the Crypt* 44, October 1954) in which another guillotine victim returns, this time to reclaim his severed head. Such zombies would seem to be indestructible, but most 1950s comic-book zombies seek placation, after which they slip into the oblivion of soil. The placation they seek is usually personal revenge, but sometimes this is more broadly a moral justification. In "None but the Lonely Heart" (*Tales from the Crypt* 17, December 1952), we are presented with Howard King, a serial killer who preys on rich widows through lonely-hearts advertisements. Howard receives a photograph, albeit a couple of years old, of a beautiful woman with a letter describing a home surrounded by vast, opulent grounds, and he hurries to exploit his next victim. The directions in her letter lead him to a cemetery where a zombie drags him into a coffin with her and closes the lid, murmuring, "It's been so lonely here" (8). By slaying the serial killer, this zombie achieves revenge for the ruined brides but also acts as moral executioner on society's behalf. This tale is not an isolated example, being a reworking of the scenario in the revenge tale "Madame

Bluebeard" (*Tales from the Crypt* 11, December 1951) in which a female serial killer, Teresa, is surrounded and destroyed by the seven zombies of her previous husbands when she takes wreaths to their tombs in the cemetery. The story ends with eight graves in a row instead of seven, with the new grave festooned with all seven wreaths.

These stories are just two examples in an oeuvre that frequently explores the taboo and angst of sexual horror. The group murder of Teresa and the "laying" of her into the ground is a hideously symbolic violation, as is the closing image of the one grave, grotesquely verdant with plants and red flowers—an ironically fertile *vagina dentata*—next to the seven stark phallic-looking tombstones. The trapping of Howard King in the tomb is another blatantly symbolic moment of sexual horror. His crimes against womankind are suitably punished by squeezing him into a female's coffin where a zombie is "spewing its foul-smelling breath" (8). A broadly similar scenario occurs in "Marriage Vow" (*The Haunt of Fear* 26, July 1954) in which a husband murders his wife only to have her return from the grave to live with him, taking the "Till death do us part" vow as meaning when they *both* die. The cover of this issue has an ironic image of domesticity with the undead wife bringing her living husband his slippers. The content of the story itself is robustly sexual. In the final section of the story we see Eva, the living dead wife, undressing and coaxing her husband into bed: "She stands over you, grinning down at you with her stained, tarnished, decayed teeth, and you smell her fetid breath as she whispers . . . 'It's time for *bed*, Martin!'" (7).

Our sustained reluctance, as the narrative forces the reader into adopting the vantage point of the murderous husband Martin, is greeted by Eva's ironic "I never *used* to have this *trouble* with you" (7). The final frame of the story is an ironic version of the "Death and the Maiden" theme in art, although it is a half-naked female cadaver with gaping wounds in her back embracing the choking man and whispering to him: "Come to bed!" (8). In "None but the Lonely Heart" and "Marriage Vow," the reader, constructed as male regardless of his or her actual gender, is presented with a horror worse than a *vagina dentata*: an undead *vagina dentata*. In fact, such images of the abject permeate the EC oeuvre: on a number of covers we have zombies clasping onto terrified, living victims with vice-like grips, even including an undead matador and zombie bull (*The Haunt of Fear* 10, December 1951). These are powerful images of Thanatos and Eros in the tradition of the "Death and the Maiden" archetype: the dead *embrace* the living quite resolutely and, inevitably, they smile as they do it, beaming the broadest smile humanly possible with the exposed teeth of a skull. Indeed, nothing in pre-code horror is without comedy, and even in fetid abjection there is sardonic humor. Certainly, EC deploys sick humor on many layers throughout its repertoire: the titles of its stories frequently exploit puns; its dialogue is full of irony; and its plotlines revel in schadenfreude.

The 1954 Comics Code declared that scenes dealing with "the walking dead . . . are prohibited" (Sabin 1993, 252), and this, in a phrase, annihilated both the rich narratives and the graphic images that together constructed the 1950s horror-comic zombie tales. The obliteration of the pre-code horror comics was unfortunate, although some critics suggest that the medium was already approaching the end of its tether. These critics note that horror comics were reaching a breaking point insofar as having grotesquely attempted to top the excesses of their previous stories and those of their rivals. Arguably, examples of sadism, misogyny, and mutilation seem to flourish with less finesse in art or irony, created with a rapidity of production necessary to meet the demands of a booming but competitive market. As Ron Goulart argues, the sheer level of proliferation was itself a problem because too many of the comics were simply "dreadful and frightening only in their lack of merit and restraint" (1986, 89). Nevertheless, the ascendant hegemony prevented us from ever seeing what the horror comics may have evolved into.

POST-CRYPT: THE COMICS THAT WON'T GO AWAY

After the demise of the horror titles, comics concentrated on superheroes, science-fiction stories, and the like while EC itself was forced to abandon comics altogether and rebuild their fortunes by inventing *MAD* magazine. Pre-code horror comics now seem somewhat quaint. Contemporary readers may even, at their peril, patronize the past and underestimate not just the impact of explicit comic-book horror (more graphic than anything Hollywood or television of the 1950s would have dared to display) but also the conscious playfulness and humor of the comics. The legend and achievement of these comics seems to stand as a precursor to everything in horror comics that has followed. Like a zombie from the grave, the horror comics began to return a decade later, most notably with Warren Publishing. Although it began with popular film magazines such as *Famous Monsters of Filmland* (1958–1983), Warren Publishing carefully ventured into the horror comic void left by the purge of the Comics Code Authority. Warren published titles such as *Creepy* (1964–1983) and *Eerie* (1966–1983), clearly adhering to the formula of EC, with playful host characters presenting anthologies of self-contained tales of terror, and even recruited veteran artists from EC such as Joe Orlando and Jack Davis. However, in a brilliant coup, Warren's horror comics were published only in a black-and-white format of a certain size and evaded the strictures of the code because they were legally classified as "magazines" rather than "comics." The fact that the Warren horror magazines were allowed to publish uninterrupted for two decades was not simply because of its shrewd use of publication category; it also succeeded because of changes in social concerns. This was not necessarily because society became less anxious and proscriptive but because graphic narratives suddenly seemed naive and harmless in light of the perceived dangers of television, Hollywood in the wake of Alfred Hitchcock's *Psycho* (1960) and every other subsequent cultural and technological development. There is a rich vein to mine in looking at the renaissance of the American horror comic, but what follows in this essay is a look at examples of the zombie in various countercultural and postmodern comic books.

Tales from the Fridge 1 (Kitchen Sink, 1973) is an example of an underground comic that directly pastiches the EC horror comics in format and style. The creative team of Russ Jones and Bhob Stewart produced an anthology of horror tales related to issues of food anxiety, from personal anxieties over weight gain to larger worries related to the fast-food industry. Inevitably, the zombie motif finds its way into *Tales from the Fridge* in the story of Rod Usher, an unscrupulous businessman who pushes Global McBlimp, the obese and gullible inventor of the "Globalburger," to eat himself to death in order to take control of the industry. Soon after McBlimp's death, a new Globalburger restaurant opens next to the cemetery where he is buried. Closely following the 1950s zombie-comics formula, under a moonlit sky McBlimp's grave stirs as a decaying corpse—"a nightmarish creature of loathsome rot" (21)—comes to life. If in EC the zombie usually has an obvious and unspoken desire for revenge, in this *Tales from the Fridge* example, Jones and Stewart present a different motivation. Thought clouds explain that the emaciated zombie of the once-obese McBlimp is driven by the quintessential *mortal* desire: "*Food . . . Must have food . . .*" (21). It is only when the zombie discovers that any food he ingests spews out onto the floor that he decides to exact revenge on Usher. In a decision that makes it clear that *Tales from the Fridge* is part of the American countercultural comic-book tradition most popularly associated with the artistry of Robert Crumb, the vengeful path of the zombie is interrupted when he encounters a prostitute. This encounter explores taboos in a manner worthy of the grotesque humor of Crumb, and is a startlingly literal moment of eroticism and death. To the zombie's horror, his penis has "rotted off" (24) but the prostitute mistakes his distended intestines for "the longest I've ever seen" (24). While she achieves orgasm with McBlimp's decaying colon in her vagina, the zombie rips off the intestinal slack so that he can move on to annihilate Usher. The final tableau reveals Usher half-eaten on a spit and the placated, and therefore inanimate, corpse of McBlimp in the corner: "A hideous and foetid travesty of what had once been a human being" (26).

The story is a respectful pastiche of the pre-code zombie comic book and succeeds in being a humorous exploitation of politics and the taboo with its double attack on the immorality of capitalism and the dietary implications of fast food, laced with a "shocking" sexual subplot. If the style is 1950s, the content, target, and message are very 1970s. This last point is hammered home in the final line of the comic strip. The "Fridge-Keeper" narrator (identical to EC's Vault-Keeper storyteller) informs us that although Rod Usher endured a terrible fate, he would have "suffered an even *worse* fate if he'd been born a Vietnamese peasant!" (26). If the living dead in 1950s comics reflected the guilt and anxieties of World War II and Korea, the zombie in the countercultural comic is used to make a blatant condemnation of then-contemporary US foreign policy. The fact that a flesh-eating zombie is not as bad as what the United States was doing in Vietnam is redolent of what Noël Carroll calls "sympathy for the devil" (1990, 143). This feature is evident in Romero's zombie movies from the scene of first dawn in *Night of the Living Dead* when the undead suddenly seem pathetic and vulnerable. This sense of sympathy can be traced back to the moral justification of the 1950s zombies and the purity of their vengeance. The zombie may be terrifying, unsettling, and disruptive, but it is never as evil as the living. The worst monster is the fiend lurking within the average living person.

Tales from the Fridge is emblematic of the underground comic movement of the 1960s and 1970s and seems, with historical perspective, inventive, vibrant, and provocative. The influence of these comics on subsequent countercultural and postmodern comics is profound. Yet the fact that these comic artists and writers made use of the pre-code horror comics demonstrates the significance of those pioneering works. Moreover, the fact that the 1950s horror comics were forced to self-regulate themselves out of existence reflects their own status as victims of political and "moral" circumstance, and their disappearance will always be a milestone in the history of censorship. In the light of this, it is worth emphasizing the homage, rather than the pastiche, that later works and artists pay to the 1950s horror comic books. Among these is Frank Miller, a major doyen of the postmodern comic-book industry, whose *Tales to Offend* 1 (Dark Horse Comics, July 1997) is a deliberately provocative work that supports the Comic Book Legal Defense Fund's campaign to defend the First Amendment rights of comic books and their creators. Miller's cover for the comic book is unambiguously 1950s in style. It is not "retro," but rather it pays homage to a generation of artists whose careers were martyred by the code. The later, more contemporary comic-book creators do not just allude to the iconography of the pre-code era; they also adopt its provocative and subversive potential. As Peter Normanton argues, as "the genre entered the 1990s, comics gradually became more daring than they had been in almost forty years" (2008, 268).

Death is the great leveler, as biological realities dictate that every living individual will someday become a homogenous corpse obedient to the natural laws of physical disintegration. In light of this, it is easy to envision the zombie as a revolutionary symbol, an undead everyman inexorably setting right the injustices of mortal hegemonies. But what of those politically provocative works in which the living dead have recognizable identities? One of the most interesting examples of the political use of the zombie in the countercultural and postmodern comic books is the portrayal of Uncle Sam. The front cover of *Rip Off Comix* 30 (Rip Off Press, 1991) features Dave Meraz's drawing of a skeletal Uncle Sam with money in his pockets, the flames of hell behind him, and a revolver aimed at the reader. With no story inside the comic book specifically featuring this image of zombie imperialism, Meraz's cover serves on its own as a powerful emblem offering overall support for those pieces within the issue that grotesquely or earnestly attack US imperialism and militarism. Similarly, *Route 666* 1:19 (Crossgen, February 2004) and *Raise the Dead* 1 (Dynamite, April 2007) make use of an Uncle Sam zombie even though no stories within the books refers to such a character. Arthur Suydam's *Raise the Dead* cover has a one-eyed and one-armed Uncle Sam leering at the reader with an undead vulture posing, like an eagle, on the patriot's shoulder. Karl Moline, Drew Geraci, and James Rochelle's *Route 666* cover has a similar rendering of Uncle Sam "wanting you," except that the left third of his body is skeletal. Once again, the cover is striking and subversive, capturing the mood of a story that revolves around a conspiracy of monsters in human disguise endeavoring to infiltrate international politics.

A precursor adopting the same principle is Garth Ennis's *John Constantine, Hellblazer: Damnation's Flame* (DC, 1999), published as a series of comics in 1994. One of the issues within the series features an Uncle Sam zombie leering malevolently at the reader, the image serving as a fitting emblem for a story about a journey through a benighted America. The hero, Constantine, is condemned to witch-walk through an infernal and eternally twilighted United States. The unfortunate inhabitants are in a state of limbo: "I was dead and not dead and was kept from moving on" (77), as one character puts it. Constantine himself finds that he is able to insert his fingers into his slit jugular. On his journey he becomes the companion of John F. Kennedy, who is walking back to Washington, DC, constantly holding his shattered head together and in denial about his assassination: "It hurt like hell keeping his brains crammed in there but he ignored the pain as best he could; that way he didn't have to face up to what had happened" (33).

The JFK zombie is unusual both for being sentient of pain and for being motivated not by revenge but a desire to usurp the zombie Abraham Lincoln from the White House. In this living dead world, Lincoln is a president whose "term of office never ends" (101). Lincoln asks JFK to "give me your hands" (101), and in the final scene of the story it becomes evident that this is not an act of reconciliation but a literal demand: we see JFK with his arms severed, his "memories dimmed" (109), and his language disintegrating while a trail of blood and brain tissue stretches down the road behind him. The work suggests that only the mythologizing of JFK by the living has kept him in limbo and denied him the chance to accept the events of November 1963 and end his term of office. In a confession to Constantine, JFK admits that his aims as president amounted to nothing nobler than "immediate political survival, and regular extramarital sex" (66). However, the idolatry lavished on JFK by contemporary American officialdom means that he is obliged to forever stagger back to the Oval Office.

Although the walking dead that prowled through the popular comics of the 1950s were nullified by censorship, they found a forum in "magazines" and countercultural publications from the 1960s onward. In recent years, however, the zombie has become increasingly an icon of mainstream culture, a fact that is reflected in the contemporary comics industry. The most prominent example of this is Robert Kirkman's long-running comic-book series *The Walking Dead* (2003–), which rejects the portmanteau approach of short stories and has developed a genuinely epic saga with complex plots, subplots, and realistic characterization. Although the zombies are ubiquitous, they are almost tangential to the saga, and the narrative focuses instead on the psychological state of the survivors and their interrelationships. The sustained dramatic potential of *The Walking Dead* has led to it being adapted into a television series (2010–) which is one of the most-watched dramas in the history of US broadcasting. Consequently, the franchise has enjoyed a success as virulent as a zombie epidemic, the official brand now encompassing digital games, board games, action toys, and costumes.

Robert Kirkman is also behind the creation of another highly successful zombie comic-book franchise, the *Marvel Zombies* (2005–2006 with continuing sequels). While *The Walking Dead* is characterized by gritty realism, *Marvel Zombies* presents an undead pandemic within the Marvel universe. The infected superheroes devour most of the human race, after which ensues a bitter and gruesome struggle for domination against each other. While it has brought commercial success for the comic-book publisher, the *Marvel Zombies* series is nonetheless a radical and even subversive reimagining of the superhero genre. In this universe, the superheroes usually charged with defending civilization have become its indestructible and abject nemesis. They are capable of the unthinkable, as when the undead Spider-Man devours his beloved Mary Jane and Aunt May. Playful and darkly comic, *Marvel Zombies* can nevertheless be a demonstration that the zombies' voracious appetite for human flesh remains a disruptive taboo and provocation.

GRAPHIC TALES OF TERROR AND COMFORT

Classic and contemporary zombie comics continue to have a huge influence on subsequent popular culture in all forms, from cinema and television through digital gaming to zombie fashion. This impact has been financial and iconographic, reaching consumers who have never even purchased a comic book. Although an "invisible" source, zombie comics have been pioneering and even iconoclastic. The achievements of pre-code horror should not be overlooked because they remain an indelible moment in 1950s American cultural history that had far-reaching consequences. The anti-comics crusade saw the medium as corrupting the nation's youth into delinquency, amorality, and anti-Americanism. By the time of the last pre-code horror comics, however, the damage had already been done. At least, that would seem to be the case with George A. Romero, Stephen King, and other horror creators who, in childhood or adolescence, habitually devoured explicit tales of graphic terror only to have them vanish, almost overnight. Although Romero and King were most vocal in their unabashed homage to the EC horror comic books with their collaborative film project *Creepshow* (1982), the 1950s titles cast a long shadow of influence over a large number of contemporary artists working within the horror genre. Through them, the now-classic horror comic is experiencing a renaissance of sorts as comic book collaborative teams rediscover a market for explicit gore that provides the commercial interest that in turn enables them to pay conscious and open homage to the industry's pre-code predecessors. This is not just a technical and stylistic issue. The fate of the 1950s horror comics, censored into oblivion, stands as proof of the graphic medium's potency for later generations of comic creators who perceived their chosen form to be not innocuous but a veritable force, with the zombie frequently eating away at the heart of subsequent graphic horror. Certainly this is the aspiration of an artist such as Romero, who sees in the zombie genre the potential for political resistance and social activism. "I don't consider my flicks, especially *Dawn* [*of the Dead*], to be "fright-flicks," Romero says. "My flicks are meant to be more like *Bowling for Columbine*" (2003, 4).

We can look at a number of comics of the living dead in the same light. John Pearson, the editor and creative force behind *Fleshrot* (2003), suggests: "Because the zombie can be used in any political setting, the artist and author can use them to make his own statements on government, society and religion" (John Pearson, e-mail to author, March 19, 2004). Romero may call them "fun-dark" (2003, 4), but we should never regard them as "funny papers." Neither can they be accused of presenting gore for gore's sake. Rather, their power to frighten and offend distinguishes them as socially disruptive and provocative, whether they are displaying the universal everyman as zombie or offering an iconoclastic revision of a political emblem such as a living dead Uncle Sam. The horror comic can be classically allusive one moment, bitingly satirical the next. There is a curious mixture of terror and comfort in reading zombie comics, although to combine these two attitudes seems a conceit as oxymoronic as "living dead." There is a terrifying memento mori that we will all one day resemble zombies, albeit in tragic stillness. At the same time there is comfort in imagining the possibility that all the injustices and loose ends of our lived existences can be resolved from beyond the grave. And beneath all else is the comfort of assuming that despite what everyone may feel, living death is far preferable to the ultimate *todesangst* horror of the senseless and sense-less negation of life by death.

WORKS CITED

Barker, Martin. 1992. *A Haunt of Fears: The Strange History of the British Horror Comics Campaign*. Jackson: University Press of Mississippi.

Bernewitz, Fred von, and Grant Geissman. 2000. *Tales of Terror! The EC Companion*. Seattle: Fantagraphics.

Bowling for Columbine. 2002. Directed by Michael Moore. Perf. Michael Moore. United Artists.

Carrie. 1976. Directed by Brian de Palma. Perf. Sissy Spacek, Amy Irving, William Katt. MGM.

Carroll, Noël. 1990. *The Philosophy of Horror*. London: Routledge.

Crane, Jonathan Lake. 1994. *Terror and Everyday Life: Singular Moments in the History of the Horror Film*. Thousand Oaks, CA: Sage.

Creepshow. 1982. Directed by George A. Romero. Perf. Ted Danson, Leslie Nielsen, Hal Holbrook. Warner Brothers.

Creepy. 1964–1983. Philadelphia: Warren.

Diehl, Digby. 1996. *Tales from the Crypt.* New York: St. Martin's Press.

Eerie. 1947. 1. New York: Avon Periodicals.

Eerie. 1966–1983. Philadelphia: Warren.

Ennis, Garth. 1999. *John Constantine, Hellblazer: Damnation's Flame.* New York: DC Comics.

Famous Monsters of Filmland. 1958–1983. Philadelphia: Warren.

Goulart, Ron. 1986. "Comics." In *The Penguin Encyclopedia of Horror and the Supernatural,* edited by Jack Sullivan, 86–90. Harmondsworth, UK: Penguin.

Hand, Richard J. 2011. "Undead Radio: Zombies and the Living Dead on Live American Radio Drama in the 1930–40s." In *Better Off Dead: The Evolution of the Zombie as Post-Human in Film, Literature, Art and Culture,* edited by Sarah Juliet Lauro and Deborah Christie, 39–49. Bronx, NY: Fordham University Press.

Hand, Richard J., and Michael Wilson. 2012. "Transatlantic Terror: French Horror Theatre and American Pre-Code Comics." *Journal of Popular Culture* 45 (2): 301–19.

The Haunt of Fear. 1950–1954. New York: EC Comics.

Kendrick, Walter. 1991. *The Thrill of Fear: 250 Years of Scary Entertainment.* New York: Grove Press.

King, Stephen. 1981. *Danse Macabre: The Anatomy of Horror.* London: Futura.

Kirkman, Robert. 2003–present. *The Walking Dead.* Berkeley, CA: Image Comics.

Kirkman, Robert. 2005–2006. *Marvel Zombies.* New York: Marvel Comics.

Night of the Living Dead. 1968. Directed by George A. Romero. Perf. Duane Jones, Judith O'Dea, Karl Hardman. Image Ten.

Normanton, Peter, ed. 2008. *The Mammoth Book of Best Horror Comics.* London: Robinson.

Plague of the Zombies. 1965. Directed by John Gilling. Perf. André Morell, John Carson, Jacqueline Pearce. Hammer Films.

Raise the Dead. 2007. 1. Runnemede, NJ: Dynamite Entertainment.

Rip Off Comix. 1991. 30. Auburn, CA: Rip Off Press.

Romero, George A. 2003. "A Foreword." In *Fleshrot: Tales from the Dead.* Vol. 1, 3–4. Culver City, CA: Frightworld Studios.

Route 666. 2004. 1:19. Oldsmar, FL: Crossgen.

Sabin, Roger. 1993. *Adult Comics: An Introduction.* London: Routledge.

Sennitt, Stephen. 1999. *Ghastly Terror! The Horrible Story of the Horror Comics.* Manchester, UK: Critical Vision.

Skal, David J. 2001. *The Monster Show: A Cultural History of Horror.* New York: Faber and Faber.

Tales from the Crypt. 1950–1955. New York: EC Comics.

Tales from the Fridge. 1973. 1. Princeton, NJ: Kitchen Sink.

Tales to Offend. 1997. 1. Milwaukee, WI: Dark Horse Comics.

28 Days Later. 2002. Directed by Danny Boyle. Perf. Cillian Murphy, Naomie Harris, Christopher Eccleston. British Film Council.

The Vault of Horror. 1950–1955. New York: EC Comics.

UNDEAD AVATARS

The Zombie in Horror Video Games

EWAN KIRKLAND

D espite the monster's pervasive presence within the medium, academics writing about zombies in popular culture can have a somewhat smug attitude toward video games. There is often something slightly elitist in the attitude of theorists in their treatment of the video-game zombie as a lesser creature, a monstrous aberration in comparison to the true undead of cinema. Kyle Bishop's disparaging description of the first *Resident Evil* film as "an action-packed science fiction movie that is more video game than narrative" (2009, 19) resonates with Geoff King and Tanya Krzywinska's observation that, within the cultural hierarchy, comparing films to games represents a derogatory act, in contrast to the positive praise of identifying cinematic qualities in video games (see King and Krzywinska 2002, 16). The subject of video games also rarely features throughout Richard Greene and K. Silem Mohammad's (2010) edited collection on zombies and vampires and philosophic thought.

Hamish Thompson only indulges in the "research and development" of playing video games in what seems to be a patronizing afterthought when he recounts an anecdotal experience of "partial zombiehood" (35) involving compulsive behavior, dilution of temporal awareness, and a lapse in professional conduct. Whenever the *Resident Evil* franchise is cited in zombie studies, it is more often the films inspired by the games than the games themselves that are studied. While video games are blamed for desensitizing audiences to violence, requiring contemporary horror films to up the gore of their own offerings (see Bishop 2009, 21), Shaun's undead game-playing pal, symbolic of the optimistic zombie rehabilitation that ends *Shaun of the Dead*, is frequently mentioned. Less is made of the clear influence of zombie video games on the film itself. This was already evident in the presence of *Resident Evil* in British sitcom and *Shaun of the Dead* forerunner *Spaced*, with star and cowriter Simon Pegg's *Guardian* article of November 4, 2008, crediting the video-game series with effectively having rescued zombies from the camp theatricality of Michael Jackson's *Thriller* video.

While representing a patchy element throughout cinema history, zombies appear as a continual presence in video games. David Flint details many games that, from the 1980s onward, have featured these undead creatures, including the *Dungeons and Dragons*–inspired *Ghosts 'N' Goblins*, the comic *Zombies Ate My Neighbors*, the Japanese samurai bikini series *Onechanbara*, and genres such as shooting, pinball, beat 'em up, and typing games. Zombies appear in classic video-game series like *Monkey Island*, *Quake*, and *Doom*, through to contemporary horror games like *Dead Island*, *The Walking Dead*, and the ongoing *Resident Evil* series. The latter, Flint observes, from its original 1996 release on the Sony Playstation, "has gone on to achieve levels of commercial success that most moviemakers would envy," having "shifted over thirty-four million units to date" (2009, 171).

Throughout the evolution of the form, and in contrast to other horror archetypes such as vampires or werewolves, zombies have been a frequent presence in video games, suggesting a special relationship between the medium and this undead creature of horror culture. No matter where the game is geographically situated or culturally circulated, the fear of becoming a zombie oneself and the loss of potential interactivity, agency, and control are deeply rooted in these video games, making the zombie a potentially useful metaphor in understanding the processes of game play in general. Thus the cultural markers characterizing zombies in various locations are eradicated at the moment of game-play zombification, based on medial requirements. In this instance, transmediality takes precedence over transculturality.

Bishop acknowledges that "the terror and action of zombie movies translate[s] quite logically from the big screen to the video screen" (2009, 19). It is this logic that is examined here, exploring the fit between the zombie and the video-game medium, which many horror titles themselves interrogate. The suggestion of a correlation between supernatural phenomena and media technologies is not new. Something ghostly, spiritual, or uncanny in the photograph has long been recognized, as evident in Marina Warner's (2006) extensive study of the spectral dimensions perceived in representational technologies, from waxworks to film. In an essay on F. W. Murnau's 1922 film *Nosferatu*, Stacey Abbott similarly argues that there is something vampire-like about cinema. Pointing to the media technologies through which Stoker's Count Dracula emerges—the stenograph, the phonograph, the typewriter—Abbott argues that the vampire of this adaptation was the product of specifically cinematic special effects developed from the magic lantern, the phantasmagoria, and the trick film. Shadows, negative image, fast motion, and stop-motion photography, editing, dissolves, and superimposition are all incorporated into Murnau's cinematic depiction of the vampire's supernatural presence, its telepathy, transformations, and "secret affinities" between characters. For Abbott, *Nosferatu* "imbues its vampire with the filmic and photographic qualities of the cinema as a means of exploring the inherent vampirism of this new technology" (2004, 14). The myth of vampires disintegrating in sunlight, just like melting film stock, was an element introduced in this first vampire film, constructing a connection between the noble undead and cinema.

Just as photography can be associated with the ghost, and cinema with the vampire, so too a relationship can be demonstrated to exist between the video game and the zombie, a connection evoking a similar sense of ambiguity concerning the technology of the video-game apparatus, the experience of video-game play, and the ontology of the zombie. Horror is a genre long mobilized by games designers, and zombies provide ideal computer-controlled cannon fodder: lacking in (artificial) intelligence, capable of sustaining multiple attacks, while presenting players with no ethical concerns about slaughtering them in significant numbers. Further, the uncanny qualities of the zombie are indicative of unsettling aspects of playable and nonplayable avatars and characters within the game world. The process of video-game play might be considered as entailing an experience of zombification, as players identify the mathematical rules of the game, synchronize their actions with mechanical figures, and experience a disembodiment and reembodiment of the self. Considering these and other issues, this chapter examines the ways in which zombie video games and video-game zombies reflect upon the nature of the monster, and of the medium, in an attempt to explore and explain the persistence of the zombie within video-game cultures.

THE ZOMBIE IN THE VIDEO GAME

As noted by Richard Rouse III (2009), the horror genre has proved to be tremendously useful for games designers in servicing many aspects of the form. A supernatural or evil presence can justify extraordinary player powers. Generic fog, mist, and darkness function to reduce the amount of information on screen that must be rendered by computer or console technology. Horror plays to the medium's strengths in generating tension and fear while marginalizing emotions the video game has more difficulty producing.

When it comes to video-game zombies, Bishop observes that these creatures "do not think or speak—they simply act, relying on purely physical manifestations of terror" (2006, 197). This makes them suited to a visual medium that is, to a large extent, about action, functionality, and the simulation of physical dynamic systems rather than narrative or psychological complexity. As Thompson points out, the mindlessness of the zombie and its unreasonable behavior, aggression, and cannibalistic tendencies serve as justification for not affording these undead creatures the same right to life as the living, despite their outward appearance as human beings (see 2010, 27). Hence, when faced with objections to its players running over pedestrians, producers of the sci-fi driving game *Carmageddon* simply replaced the humans with zombies, thereby appeasing concerns that their product was excessively antisocial (see Krzywinska 2002, 220). In the more-recent Capcom action game *Zombie Apocalypse*, if players were tasked with mowing down in such high numbers any other category of humanoid subject—soldiers, policemen, even terrorists—the real-world parallels might be vaguely troubling. In addition, if nobody objects to players eradicating zombies in extravagant numbers, neither will anybody complain that the AI (artificial intelligence) of zombies is too low. Video-game zombies shuffle unflinchingly into gunfire, stumble around in pointless circles, and even bump into walls, and their unintelligence can simply be attributed to their rotting gray matter and corroding faculties.

Barry Atkins points to the significant relationship between video games and other kinds of popular culture, observing that "game-fictions rely on an extensive audience understanding of the conventions of a wide range of popular genre fictions" (2003, 56). Such knowledge assists not only players' understanding of the narrative context of their virtual actions, but also the rules of the game being played. Encountering a zombie in a video game, immediately identified by its shuffling gait, low moan, and decaying appearance, brings to mind a series of understandings—or to use Dan Pinchbeck's term, "media schema"—concerning the nature of the creatures, drawn from zombie films, television, and comic books, as well as other video games. It is the player's role to speculate, based on this zombie script, frame, or template, how the threat might function in a manner consistent with the aspects that characterize the zombie as a fictional being: "If it looks like a zombie, sounds like a zombie, and moves like a zombie," Pinchbeck writes, "then the zombie schema fire" (2009, 87). For example, players must work out that the zombies of *Quake* have to be blown up with explosives; if simply shot to death, they slowly reanimate, pull themselves together, and continue to fling clumps of their own rotting flesh at the player.

Zombies allow other important game-play dynamics to be worked into a game's diegesis. The fact that zombies simply emerge from the ground means an endless stream of creatures can materialize from the graveyards, subway stations, and gardens of *Onechanbara*. As a result of the zombie's unstable physicality, these creatures conveniently disintegrate upon defeat, excusing the game engine of having to track the piles of fallen bodies left in the player's wake. Additionally, the way in which a zombie progresses relentlessly toward its quarry, irrespective of the number of shots suffered by its disintegrating form, provides a video-game adversary who can receive multiple hits while remaining a credible threat. *Burn Zombie Burn* makes use of these tropes to pack the bounded game space with preposterous numbers of foes while capitalizing on the understanding that zombies' capabilities and sense of purpose are unaffected by being set on fire. The recent reimagining of zombies as running, screeching crazies is incorporated into the co-op shooter game *Left 4 Dead*. Here players escape from a series of derelict urban environments while being assailed by wave upon wave of screaming, fast-moving humanoids that have no intelligent objective or concern for their own safety. Consistent with much zombie cinema, a clean head shot is often the simplest method of dispatching zombies in countless action games, rewarding virtual marksmanship in a manner that is satisfyingly within the rules of the genre.

In his design-informed discussion of horror video games, Rouse cites the "uncanny valley" (2009, 19), the well-known dip in user pleasure, as artificial robots, avatars, or images increasingly approach realistic dimensions yet remain somehow eerily unnatural. The term derives from Sigmund Freud's famous essay in which, among other things, sensations of "the uncanny" result when "an inanimate object becomes too much like an animate one" (Freud [1919] 1990, 354). Similar to the sense of disgust and revulsion evoked by the zombie—a figure Bishop (2006) argues as exemplary of the uncanny—viewers, spectators, and players react with unease when confronted with figures that seem to exist somewhere on the threshold between life and death. Video-game play can, therefore, be considered a multiply uncanny experience. The avatar that players control is an uncanny figure, being both animate and inanimate, attracting the disturbing resonance of the walking dead even when operating under the player's instructions. This applies even more so to figures controlled by the computer or game console. NPCs (nonplayable characters) can evoke a disquieting sense of the uncanny, particularly when appearing to act with intelligence, autonomy, and agency. Revealing the zombie mechanics at their core, these figures' lifelessness is betrayed in robotic motions and looping actions, their repetitive dialogue, and machinelike mannerisms. In *Dead Island,* the player is sent on missions by various besieged vacationers—NPCs who remain rooted to the spot, repeating the same phrases and animation cycles—while the zombies outside are anything but inanimate, exhibiting more signs of life than the human characters. Both playable and nonplayable video-game figures therefore muddy the boundary between the dead and the living in a manner that, in the creepy context of horror video games, gains particular resonance.

While avatars and nonplayable characters confuse distinctions between the animate and inanimate, the relationship between player and game might also be considered an uncanny one. In an early scholarly discussion of video games, Ted Friedman attempts to identify the specific experience of interactivity in digital games as distinct from the pleasures offered by other forms of narrative or visual culture. Critically considering the sense of "communion" with the computer, the "flow" between game and player, the "trance-like" experience of absorption, as well as the time dilation that Thompson (2010) notes occurs when playing a video game, Friedman argues successful play is not about identifying with a role or with a character, but about internalizing processes, procedures, and the technological operation of the game's simulation (see 1995, 85). Friedman is among the first scholars to apply Donna Haraway's notion of the cyborg to video-game play, suggesting a merging of human and machine: "The computer comes to feel like an organic extension of one's consciousness, and the player may feel like an extension of the computer itself" (1995, 83). Such arguments are developed further by Jon Dovey and Helen Kennedy, who examine tensions between player and program as agents in the video-game experience, between the phenomenological flesh-and-blood user manipulating the technologies of the console and the disembodied gamer immersed in the virtual world, and between consciousness and embodiment. Such aspects, the authors argue, as a consequence of the Cartesian legacy, have been unproductively considered distinct and separate. Like Friedman, Dovey and Kennedy employ Haraway's concept of the cyborg in arguing that play involves a cybernetic rather than dualistic relationship, invoking what is referred to as a "collapse of boundary between the human and the machine" (2006, 109). The embodied player must adapt to the demands of the game and the physical machine it is played on, while also being reembodied in the game world through the avatar. This gradually disappears in the seamless feedback cycle of the player's input and the game's audiovisual and haptic output. Achieving the "preferred performance" (116) within such a formation, getting the perfect score, or finding the most economic route represents a similar cyborgian subjugation of player actions according to the apparatus of the game.

Evoking imagery more science fiction than Gothic horror, there is a sense of the uncanny in such critically informed theorizations of the processes of video-game play, particularly in the context of parallels Larry Hauser (2010) draws between the zombie and the robot. To suggest that video-game play represents a process of zombification carries undeniably negative associations, ironically mobilized in the final scenes of *Shaun of the Dead*, in which we see the video-game player as a barely sentient undead creature chained up in the shed at the bottom of the protagonist's garden, experiencing an existence strangely similar to the one they enjoyed while alive. However, what emerges from these analyses is a productive sense of organic players becoming machinelike at the same time as the mechanical becomes somehow sentient: a confusion of boundaries between live and not-alive, as well as between not-alive and live, a loss of self, accompanied by a sense of expansion beyond the limitations of the body. The presence of cyborgs within video games clearly represents a response to the cybernetic dimensions of video-game play. At the same time, many of these aspects resonate with philosophical, psychological, and psychoanalytic issues revolving around the zombie. It may well be this sometimes unsettling overlap that has kept the monster alive in video games for so long.

RESIDENT EVIL: ZOMBIES AND AVATAR

The zombie clearly accommodates a wide range of video-game genres, featuring in futuristic racing games, militaristic first-person shooters, action adventures, arcade games, the light-gun series *House of the Dead*, the tower-defense comedy *Plants vs. Zombies*, and the sandbox construction game *Minecraft*. Yet the most generically significant incarnation of the zombie, and the one that most often reflects upon the video-game medium and its zombie-like affinities, can be found within "survival horror." A comparatively well-established subgenre of the horror game, survival horror aims to create an experience of entrapment, persecution, tension, suspense, and discomfort. Traditionally, the protagonist of such games is an ordinary individual trapped in some isolated, monster-infested location. Players are tasked with aiding their escape through, as Pegg's character in *Spaced* puts it, "a subtle blend of lateral thinking and extreme violence" (Pegg and Stevenson 2001, DVD audio). Although *Hunt the Wumpus, Sweet Home,* and *Alone in the Dark* represent early examples of the genre, *Resident Evil* was the first to coin the term *survival horror,* and Richard J. Hand argues that the popularity of the franchise's first installment, with its innovative graphics, story, and atmosphere, means survival horror is generically synonymous with the Capcom series (see 2004, 118).

Although Bishop's claims that *Resident Evil* differs from Romero's films in requiring "more 'fight' than 'flight'" (2009, 19), consistent with the conventions of survival horror that the franchise went on to consolidate, the games emphasize evasion, ammunition conservation, and tactical use of resources over indiscriminate violence. For example, the opening level of *Resident Evil 2* requires players to make their way through a burning city filled with moaning undeads intent on their harm. There simply is not enough ammunition for all these monsters to be destroyed, meaning the majority must be evaded through careful navigation. Dropping players into this action set piece ensures that most arrive at their destination, an abandoned police station, limping and bleeding following inevitable zombie maulings. The level simulates the experience of desperation that characterizes the classic apocalyptic zombie scenario. Such is the argument developed by video-game scholar Matthew Weise, who applies the term "procedural adaptation" (2009, 238) in describing the process whereby themes and content from an established text or medium are translated into an interactive computer simulation. Weise discusses how the *Resident Evil* series follows the "rules" concerning zombie behavior—zombies attack humans, are slow and unintelligent, and cannot use tools—and the "survival dynamics" of the shrinking fortress. Adapting these rules must accommodate video-game conventions. Consequently, a single bite from a zombie does not turn the protagonist into a zombie, and the creatures can be felled with repeated bullet or knife wounds as well as through decapitation. Nevertheless, Weise argues that the experience of zombie combat, the tactical decisions players must make concerning use of resources, and the repeated emphasis on the head as a zombie's Achilles' heel, effectively models the zombie movie as an interactive experience.

Across the franchise, *Resident Evil* continues to evoke the iconography and feel of the zombie movie, exhibiting aspects of the genre that Bishop lists as complementing the presence of the zombies themselves. These include "a postapocalyptic backdrop, the collapse of societal infrastructures, the indulgence of survivalist fantasies, and the fear of other surviving humans" (2009, 20). Raccoon City, the recurring site of the game, is a maze of abandoned streets, buildings hemmed in by burning cars, and wreckage-strewn roads that offer no easy means of escape. Players are free to plunder what they find, which largely consists of ammunition for an increasingly effective range of weaponry designed to combat increasingly nasty monsters. The Umbrella Corporation, responsible for the t-Virus that turns people into cannibalistic undead, is often more dangerous than the zombies themselves. In contrast to the endless hordes of more action-oriented titles, the zombies in *Resident Evil*'s early games are comparatively sparse, requiring players to either dispatch them with bullets or knives, or to evade them and move on. The zombies often provide the backdrop to trickier, less humanoid creatures that are the further result of the Umbrella Corporation's biochemical experiments: monstrous insects, venomous reptiles, and genetic mutants that must be destroyed in order for the player to progress.

There is something zombie-like about the undead of *Resident Evil* that goes beyond their trademark moans, the thumping sound of their slow footfalls, and their disheveled appearances. The zombies encountered throughout the games, whose movements are the product of the computation of the console, are creatures of instinct, rules, procedures, and code rather than intelligence. Insofar as *Resident Evil*'s zombies automatically move toward the avatar with murderous intent, these creatures, as defined by Manuel Vargas, seem to be malevolently evil, having "a non-instrumental desire to damage the welfare of others" (2010, 48). This is in contrast with the playable protagonists—Chris Redfield, Jill Valentine, Claire Redfield, Leon Kennedy, et al.—who, when in play, share the gamer's human agency and intelligence through the cybernetic relay of the control system and represent a force for good within the game world. At the same time, there is also something zombie-like about the avatar. A trope of the zombie movie, from *Dawn* (Walker 2010, 83-84) to *Shaun of the Dead* (Edwards 2008), is a paralleling between zombies and human survivors. *Resident Evil* develops this aspect in a manner that reflects on the nature of the video-game medium. A paradox observed by James Newman is that players are often psychologically situated as the protagonist of a video game while simultaneously being visually situated outside the figure they control (2004, 139–40). Playing as Claire Redfield does not approach the phenomenology of the character's diegetic sensations: players do not see things through the avatar's eyes or hear only what their ears can register. "Being" Claire is more akin to an out-of-body experience. The avatar is fully visible on the screen in a third-person perspective, at odds with the sensation of corporeally inhabiting a body. The controls by which the avatar is manipulated often seem clumsy and counterintuitive: in early *Resident Evil* games, the system of movement involves rotating the avatar in the necessary direction, then moving forward in a straight line. It is possible to completely lose sight of the avatar in a swarm of zombies, and thus have no idea in which direction the protagonist is facing as she ineffectually fires precious rounds of ammunition into the surrounding walls. The avatar has no independent movement beyond the player's prompting, which, in the case of shooting architecture, it performs with unthinking diligence. In this respect the avatar might be understood as a zombie in the original Haitian voodoo sense, as a human evacuated of life or agency. Leave an avatar alone and it reverts to a zombie-like state: completely immobile, only swaying slightly to distinguish its pixels from the background, devoid of anything approaching intelligent life.

Further blurring of boundaries is facilitated by contemporary developments in game cultures and technologies. Recent *Resident Evil* games have included a companion to accompany the main protagonists on their quest through the zombie-infested landscape. This figure resembles the playable character, a militaristic humanoid running around, shooting, being mauled, and occasionally requiring the player to revive them. At times, in the confusion of battle when surrounded by creatures, or when glimpsed in the corner of the screen during a particularly tense and claustrophobic moment, it is not unusual to mistake the companion itself for a zombie. The uncanny zombie-like dimensions of the companion are enhanced by an online cooperative mode whereby the other avatar can be controlled by another player—a silent, invisible, and potentially unknown presence beyond the screen. In the actions of this remote-controlled avatar, players see their own behavior strangely reflected. Such uncanny experiences, in which figures previously controlled by the game apparatus become unsettlingly possessed by online human agents, are not limited to zombie titles, but have particularly uncanny resonance within games themed around the disintegration of divisions between the living and the dead.

Zombies across the *Resident Evil* games share discomforting visual and ontological similarities with the player's own representative within the game world. The goal of *Resident Evil* is to ward off a lifeless state, using constant intelligent and dexterous action as the player navigates mazes, solves riddles, and reduces zombies to twitching pools of blood. It is significant that the onset of death is marked by reduced mobility in the avatar itself. Suffering increasing zombie attacks, the avatar starts to limp and becomes slower, approaching the same awkward gait and shuffling pace of the zombies themselves. Greene's suggestion that the "badness" of the zombie is the threat that we might become undead like them (see 2010, 3) is reflected in the final shot of any game that ends with the player/avatar dying. Here we are presented with the dramatic sight of the avatar, reduced now to a rag-doll-like virtual corpse, unresponsive to the player's manipulation, being feasted upon by zombies that suddenly, by comparison, seen much more animated and alive. As such, while toying with the similarities between hero and zombie, *Resident Evil* dramatizes the fear of lifelessness that the walking dead symbolize.

FORBIDDEN SIREN: EYE ZOMBIE

The zombies of *Forbidden Siren* are markedly different creatures than those of *Resident Evil*. Whereas Capcom's "transnational" (Picard 2009, 100) franchise revolves around the North American town of Racoon City, the *Forbidden Siren* series is set in the Japanese village of Hanuda or the island of Yamijima. If *Resident Evil*'s shuffling, moaning undead recall a subgenre of Western horror cinema and comic books, *Forbidden Siren*'s Shibito, with their gurgling shrieks and bloodied eyes, seem more inspired by media traditions within the producers' and developers' electronic region of origin—Sony Computer Entertainment, Japan Studios. The zombies of *Forbidden Siren* are integral to game play in a manner unique to the series, which employs a mechanic known as "sight jacking." This permits characters to project themselves into the bodies of zombies patrolling the game space, a technique that is essential in navigating this treacherous landscape. In such moments the screen is filled with the optical perspective of the respective Shibito, and the audio track echoes with the sound of their moans, comparable to the unsettling sequence in a slasher movie where events are seen through the eyes of the serial killer. By mapping the creatures' visual point of view onto the game space, players can determine the position of snipers, sneak past a waiting creature while its back is turned, or track the repetitive circle of a patrolling zombie in order to avoid an encounter. In this way, the *Forbidden Siren* series reflects upon different aspects of the zombie creature and the processes of video-game play.

Through the sight-jacking device, *Forbidden Siren* shares horror culture and survival horror video games' generic preoccupation with issues of vision. Successful play is dependent on remaining unseen; for example, hiding in darkness, crouching behind obstructions, or switching off the protagonists' flashlight in order to avoid attracting attention. It also involves exploiting the vision of the very creatures the player must avoid being seen by. Sight jacking is often the only way the zombies can be accurately positioned; in other words, they cannot be seen by the player except through their own eyes. In creating tensions between looking, being looked at, and hiding from the look, *Forbidden Siren* explores themes identified by many horror film critics, including Carol J. Clover (1992), Jeffrey Sconce (1993), and Linda Williams (1996). By shifting between two dramatically different perspectives—first- and third-person game play—*Forbidden Siren* engages with two of the three main ways video games represent the game world and create a virtual presence for the player, effectively deconstructing the nature of vision in the digital medium (see King and Krzywinska 2006, 97). The game also alternates between two different means by which interactive media reproduce the experience of biological embodiment, as discussed by Andreas Gregersen and Torben Grodal (2009, 65). In a normal avatar state within *Forbidden Siren*, the mode is the traditional third-person perspective of survival horror. Although this does not approximate the sensory dimension of actual embodiment, players are afforded presence through the interactivity inherent in their ability to make the character move, pick up objects, solve puzzles, and progress through the game space. As in the nondigital world, the player has a degree of agency and control, and is subjected to the agency of others. While "playing" as the zombie, the first-person perspective more authentically reproduces the visual and auditory sensation of "being" the "character," but players can no longer interact with the environment, only observe their surroundings as passive spectators trapped in the skulls of the creatures they are jacking. Through the separation of these elements of virtual embodiment, the zombies in *Forbidden Siren* confront players with discomforting questions of corporeal inhabitation.

Sight jacking capitalizes on the "twofold terror" that Sarah Juliet Lauro and Karen Embry discuss as being represented by the zombie: being killed by a zombie and becoming a zombie oneself. As in many survival horror titles, the game constantly engages the player's terror of being physically destroyed. Equally disturbing is the fear of losing oneself by becoming part of the "monstrous horde" (2008, 89), a terror experienced with each sight jacking, when the player experiences the world through the eyes of the uncontrollable Shibito. One of the most chilling experiences of *Forbidden Siren* is the sight of the player's avatar, immobile and transfixed, not unlike the actual player in front of the video-game screen, as seen through the eyes of an approaching monster. This further highlights the series' manipulation of a central feature of the video game: the promise of interactivity, agency, and control. Writing about horror video games, Tanya Krzywinska argues that oscillation between being in control and losing control is central to suspense in horror. This is a feature of all video games, but it gains particular resonance in those of the horror genre, in which "supernatural forces act on, and regularly threaten, the sphere of human agency" (2002, 207). Insofar as horror video games can promise players a sense of control unavailable to the horror reader, spectator, or viewer, emotional and affective pleasures resulting from the sensation of having this taken away are comparatively enhanced. By requiring players to shift between active third-person avatar mode and passive zombie first-person perspective, *Forbidden Siren* exemplifies this dynamic.

When the player exists as a silent passenger in the Shibito's head, a sense is communicated of the zombie as empty vessel, denied conscience or agency as it sits with infinite patience waiting for a figure to cross its line of sight or as it retraces the same solitary path in endless circles. As a consequence, *Forbidden Siren*, more so than *Resident Evil*, conveys the sense of the zombie as a machine. More specifically, the zombie functions as a surveillance technology, mechanically patrolling the landscape in search of trespassers. This impression is enhanced by the interface through which sight jacking is achieved. Upon activating this function, the player is presented with a static-filled screen. By rotating the joypad analogue stick, various zombies inhabiting the landscape can be "tuned in" and assigned a button on the controller. Constructing telepathy as a technological process engages with notions of electronic media as somehow imbued with supernatural powers, connections between mental communication and broadcasting, and ideas of wireless reception allowing communication with spiritual or astral planes, all detailed in the historical accounts of Sconce (2000) and Warner (2006), and evident across a range of horror video games (see Kirkland 2009). Indeed, a similar sensation of spatial and corporeal disembodiment as experienced by early users of these technologies might also be the appeal of video games. In terms of zombie scholarship, representing the Shibito as electronic machines corresponds with the frequent interpretation of living dead figures as variously symbolizing the dehumanizing impact of capitalist forces upon the individual. Among others, Jen Webb and Sam Byrnand (2008) provide a Marxist interpretation of the zombie trope; Matthew Walker defines the mall-wandering zombies of Romero's cinema as "the ultimate consumers" within capitalist society (2010, 81), while Lauro and Embry's (2008) primary argument is succinctly summarized in the title of their essay: "A Zombie Manifesto: The Nonhuman Condition in the Era of Advanced Capitalism."

Diegetic surveillance technology features in a range of survival horror video games, such as *Obscure*, *The Thing*, and *The Suffering*, set respectively in a school, a military outpost, and a prison. Inherent in these games is a critique of the ways in which such apparatuses operate to control the bodies contained within these institutions. *Forbidden Siren* goes further, by embedding such technologies within the undead monsters in the landscape. If these creatures were once human, they have become completely automated, as evidenced by their unthinking behavior and the ways in which their very vision—the sense privileged as representing comprehension, intelligence, and consciousness—is depicted as a mechanized process. These mournful creatures have become the disciplined subjects of Foucault's panopticon, internalizing the regimes of surveillance imposed upon them.

The horror video game also develops the trope already observed in *Resident Evil* whereby discomforting parallels are drawn between the zombies and humans. If the Shibito are unliving creatures compelled by some unseen force to perform repetitive ritualistic actions, this situation is perversely close to that of both avatar and game player. *Forbidden Siren* is a highly structured game in which a single narrow route is often the only one available through the monster-stalked maze. Success involves performing a strict series of actions in an exact order, adhering to the infrastructure of the game, defined by Krzywinska as the "inexorable predetermined force" (2002, 211) or "occulted fate" (210) that channels game play. This is provided by a supernatural resonance in the horror video game, giving players the impression of being subjected to unknown forces that are at odds with the control promised by the medium's interactivity. Moreover, the narrow pathway of *Forbidden Siren* elicits a strange identification with the game's zombies by requiring players to not only adopt the optical perspective of the monsters, but also requiring them to synchronize the movements of the avatar with those of the patrolling creatures. In assuming a particularly "ritualised, mechanical response to events" (218) the player who performs most successfully is the one whose actions become most zombie-like.

This represents a perverse version of Friedman's positive perspective on video-game play (1995). Identification with the game apparatus of *Forbidden Siren* is a disquieting experience, given the game's oppressive and claustrophobic environment, its unforgiving game play, its constricting structure, and the inhuman patience the game demands of its players as they synchronize their actions with the mechanical routines of their would-be executioners. Inasmuch as video-game engagement involves a cybernetic sense of players becoming machinelike, responding to the electronic stimulation of the game, and identifying with the apparatus and its demands, the zombie figures of the Shibito confront the player with a disturbing mirror of themselves as dehumanized by the very game-playing process through which the monsters are realized.

Given the negative claims made about video games and their players, it may not be the most politic strategy for a scholar of the medium to suggest that both share zombie-like characteristics. Such parallels reinforce notions of play as a dumb and stupefying activity, of players as mindless dullards hypnotized by a violent and intellectually bereft screen culture, and of video games as a destructive virus eating away at the minds and souls of all who come under their contaminating influence. Nevertheless, the case studies in this chapter have illustrated various ways in which the zombie might be considered a useful metaphor to understand, in a more thoughtful and nuanced manner, processes of video-game play. The nature of nonplayable characters, the player's relationship to the avatar, and the experience of synchronizing with the mechanics of a game's apparatus might well be understood through the figure of the zombie—the great cultural equalizer in (un)death. It is for this reason that many horror video games, consistent with the self-reflexivity common throughout the horror genre, play with the figure of the zombie as a means of interrogating the video-game experience. Far from corrupting the zombie, the video-game form might afford the most complete representation or—to use the terminology of video-game scholarship—simulation (see Frasca 2003) of the monster: as a humanoid devoid of conscience, as a body operating purely on instinct, as an abject creature existing somewhere between life and death. Far from dismissing the contribution that video games make to our understanding of the zombie as a creature of philosophical inquiry, horror lore, and popular culture, scholars would do well to consider what the monster within this medium reflects about the nature of their object of study.

WORKS CITED

Abbott, Stacey. 2004. "Spectral Vampires: *Nosferatu* in the Light of New Technology." In Hantke, 3–20.

Atkins, Barry. 2003. *More Than a Game: The Computer Game as Fictional Form*. Manchester, UK: Manchester University Press.

Bishop, Kyle. 2006. "Raising the Dead: Unearthing the Nonliterary Origins of Zombie Cinema." *Journal of Popular Film and Television* 33 (4): 196–205.

———. 2009. "Dead Man *Still* Walking: Explaining the Zombie Renaissance." *Journal of Popular Film and Television* 37 (1): 17–25.

Clover, Carol J. 1992. *Men, Women and Chain Saws: Gender in the Modern Horror Film*. London: BFI.

Dovey, Jon, and Helen Kennedy. 2006. *Game Cultures: Computer Games as New Media*. Oxford: Open University Press.

Edwards, Kim. 2008. "Moribundity, Mundanity and Modernity: Shaun of the Dead." *Screen Education* 50:99–103.

Flint, David. 2009. *Zombie Holocaust: How the Living Dead Devoured Pop Culture*. London: Plexus.

Frasca, Gonzalo. 2003. "Simulation versus Narrative: Introduction to Ludology." In *The Video Game Theory Reader*, edited by Mark J. P. Wolf and Bernard Perron, 221–35. London: Routledge.

Freud, Sigmund. [1919] 1990. "The 'Uncanny.'" In vol. 5 of *The Penguin Freud Library*, edited by Albert Dickson and translated by James Strachey, 339–76. London: Penguin.

Friedman, Ted. 1995. "Making Sense of Software: Computer Games and Interactive Textuality." In *Cybersociety: Computer-Mediated Communication and Community*, edited by Steven G. Jones, 73–89. London: Sage.

Greene, Richard. 2010. "The Badness of Undeath." In Greene and Mohammad, 3–14.

Greene, Richard, and K. Silem Mohammad, eds. 2010. *Zombies, Vampires, and Philosophy: New Life for the Undead*. Chicago: Open Court Press.

Gregersen, Andreas, and Torben Grodal. 2009. "Embodiment and Interface." In *The Video Game Theory Reader 2*, edited by Bernard Perron and Mark J. P. Wolf, 65–83. London: Routledge.

Hand, Richard J. 2004. "Proliferating Horrors: Survival Horror and the *Resident Evil* Franchise." In Hantke, 117–34.

Hantke, Steffen, ed. 2004. *Horror Film: Creating and Marketing Fear*. Jackson: University Press of Mississippi.

Hauser, Larry. 2010. "Zombies, *Blade Runner*, and the Mind-Body Problem." In Greene and Mohammad, 53–66.

King, Geoff, and Tanya Krzywinska. 2002. *ScreenPlay: Cinema/Videogames/Interfaces*. London: Wallflower.

———. 2006. *Tomb Raiders and Space Invaders: Videogame Forms and Contexts*. London: I. B. Tauris.

Kirkland, Ewan. 2009. "*Resident Evil*'s Typewriter: Survival Horror and Its Remediations." *Games and Culture* 4 (2): 115–26.

Krzywinska, Tanya. 2002. "Hands-On-Horror." In King and Krzywinska, 206–23.

Lauro, Sarah Juliet, and Karen Embry. 2008. "A Zombie Manifesto: The Nonhuman Condition in the Era of Advanced Capitalism." *Boundary 2* 35 (1): 85–108.

Newman, James. 2004. *Videogames*. London: Routledge.

Pegg, Simon. 2008. "The Dead and the Quick." *Guardian*. November 4.

Pegg, Simon, and Jessica Stevenson. 2001. "Art." In *Spaced: The Complete First Series*. Directed by Edgar Wright. DVD. London: Video Collection International Ltd.

Perron, Bernard. 2009. "The Survival Horror: The Extended Body Genre." In Perron, 121–43.

Perron, Bernard, ed. 2009. *Horror Video Games: Essays on the Fusion of Fear and Play*. London: McFarland.

Picard, M. 2009. "Haunting Backgrounds: Transnationality and Intermediality in Japanese Survival Horror Video Games." In Perron, 95–120.

Pinchbeck, Dan. 2009. "Shock, Horror: First-Person Gaming, Horror and the Art of Ludic Manipulation." In Perron, 79–94.

Rouse, Richard, III. 2009. "Match Made in Hell: The Inevitable Success of the Horror Genre in Video Games." In Perron, 15–25.

Sconce, Jeffrey. 2000. *Haunted Media: Electronic Presence from Telegraphy to Television*. Durham, NC: Duke University Press.

Sconce, Jeffrey. 1993. "Spectacles of Death: Identification, Reflexivity, and Contemporary Horror." In *Film Theory Goes to the Movies*, edited by Jim Collins, Hilary Radner, and Ava Preacher Collins, 103–19. London: Routledge.

Thompson, Hamish. 2010. "'She's Not Your Mother Anymore, She's a Zombie!': Zombies, Value, and Personal Identity." In Greene and Mohammad, 27–37.

Vargas, Manuel. 2010. "Dead Serious: Evil and the Ontology of the Undead." In Greene and Mohammad, 39–52.

Walker, Matthew. 2010. "When There's No Room in Hell, the Dead Will Shop the Earth: Romero and Aristotle on Zombies, Happiness, and Consumption." In Greene and Mohammad, 81–89.

Warner, Marina. 2006. *Phantasmagoria: Spirit Visions, Metaphors, and Media into the Twenty-First Century.* Oxford: Oxford University Press.

Webb Jen, and Sam Byrnand. 2008. "Some Kind of Virus: The Zombie as Body and as Trope." *Body and Society* 14 (2): 83–98.

Weise, Matthew. 2009. "The Rules of Horror: Procedural Adaptation in *Clock Tower, Resident Evil,* and *Dead Rising.*" In Perron, 238–66.

Williams, Linda. 1996. "When the Woman Looks." In *The Dread of Difference: Gender and the Horror Film,* edited by Barry Keith Grant, 15–34. Austin: University of Texas Press.

CONTRIBUTORS

KATARZYNA ANCUTA is a lecturer at the Graduate School of English at Assumption University of Thailand. She is the author of *Where Angels Fear to Hover: Between the Gothic Disease and the Metaphysics of Horror* and more than thirty articles on contemporary cultural manifestations of the Gothic, East/Southeast Asian horror film, and supernatural anthropology. Her recent publications include contributions to *A New Companion to the Gothic, The Encyclopedia of the Gothic, The Cambridge Companion to the Modern Gothic,* and *Global Gothic,* as well as, with Mary J. Ainslie, the first-ever edited collection on Thai horror film, published in *Horror Studies.* She is also involved in a number of film-related projects in Southeast Asia.

DANIELLE BORGIA is a lecturer in American cultures and women's studies at Loyola Marymount University in Los Angeles. Her dissertation "Specters of the Woman Author: The Haunted Fictions of Anglo-American, Mexican-American, and Mexican Women" was completed at the University of California, Santa Barbara. Her most recent work was a white paper on recidivism and rehabilitation in women's prisons that was used to lobby the California state Congress.

DOROTHEA FISCHER-HORNUNG is retired senior lecturer in the English Department at the University of Heidelberg and the Heidelberg Center for American Studies in Germany. Among her publications are the coedited volumes *EmBODYing Liberation: The Black Body in American Dance* and *Sleuthing Ethnicity: The Detective in Multiethnic Crime Fiction.* Her latest publication is the coedited collection *Aesthetic Practices and Politics in Media, Music, and Art: Performing Migration.* She is the author of numerous publications in the fields of African American and Native American literature and culture, with an emphasis on performance studies. She is founding editor of the interdisciplinary peer-reviewed journal *Atlantic Studies: Global Currents.*

TIMOTHY R. FOX is an associate professor in the Department of Languages and Literatures at National Ilan University in Taiwan, where he teaches classes in horror literature, the Gothic novel, and the zombie narrative. His interest in the zombie as a political icon arose from his previous work in Asian American literature and the discovery of a partial film script by a prominent Chinese American dramatist that had been contracted for the second installment of the *Return of the Living Dead* film series. His current writing on horror fiction draws upon his previous focus on both Asian American and Native American literary studies. He has lived in Taiwan as an American expatriate for more than two decades.

RICHARD J. HAND is professor of theater and media drama at the University of South Wales, UK. He is the founding coeditor of the international peer-reviewed *Journal of Adaptation in Film and Performance,* and his interests include adaptation, translation, and interdisciplinarity in performance media (with a particular interest in historical forms of popular culture, especially horror) using critical and practical research methodologies. He is the coauthor of books on Grand-Guignol horror theater, radio drama, Joseph Conrad, and Graham Greene and has published translations of plays by Victor Hugo and Octave Mirbeau. He has coedited academic volumes on Conrad and horror film and radio. As a practitioner he has written and directed radio and stage plays in the United Kingdom and the United States.

EWAN KIRKLAND lectures in film and screen media at the University of Brighton. Specializing in the study of survival horror video games, he has written on video-game storytelling, genre, advertising, and representation of gender, race, and sexuality. He has published in *Games and Culture, Camera Obscura,* and *Convergence: The International Journal of Research into New Media.* In addition to his studies on video games, Kirkland also writes on children's media, popular culture, and the representations of whiteness in film and television.

SABINE METZGER teaches in the American Studies Department at the University of Stuttgart, Germany. She is the author of *Eros and Morbid Artistry,* which examines the interdependence of poiesis and existence in the oeuvre of John Hawkes. She has published articles on Gertrude Stein, Nathaniel Hawthorne, and Vladimir Nabokov.

MONIKA MUELLER is senior lecturer of American literature and culture at the University of Bochum, Germany. She has published monographs on major nineteenth-century literary figures (*Gender, Genre and Homoeroticism in Hawthorne's* The Blithedale Romance *and Melville's* Pierre [1996] and *George Eliot U.S.: Transatlantic Literary and Cultural Perspectives* [2005]) and has coedited volumes on the work of Harriet Beecher Stowe, on multiethnic detective fiction, and on disgust as a cultural phenomenon.

TIMOTHY M. ROBINSON is an associate professor of literature at Livingstone College in Salisbury, North Carolina. He is the author of several articles in journals and edited collections that reveal the intricacies of race and gender in science fiction and fantasy. He is currently working on a book that explores the history and representation of black superheroes in America.

CARMEN SERRANO is an assistant professor at the University at Albany, SUNY. She graduated with a PhD in Spanish with a specialization in Latin American literature from the University of California, Irvine. She is currently working on her book project *Monsters, Vampires, and Doppelgängers: Innovation and Transformation of Gothic Forms in Latin American Narratives*, which is broadly situated within the interdisciplinary field of cultural studies framed in a transatlantic context. In addition to writing on themes of the supernatural and the fantastic, she also writes about the novel of the Mexican Revolution and US Latino literature and cultural studies.

RASMUS R. SIMONSEN is an instructor in the Centre for American Studies and the Department of English and Writing Studies at Western University, Canada. Simonsen's primary area of research is nineteenth-century American literature, and his article, "Melville's Chimney: Queer Syntax and the Architecture of Rhetoric," was published in *Leviathan: A Journal of Melville Studies*. He is also interested in the points of intersection between ecocriticism and food studies, especially in relation to veganism and new advances in biotechnology such as in vitro meat. He examines this in detail in "Eating for the Future: Veganism and the Challenge of *In Vitro* Meat," in *Biopolitics and Utopia*, edited by Patricia Stapleton and Andrew Byers.

JOHANNES WEBER has just completed his PhD thesis on *The Proto-Filmic Monstrosity of Late-Victorian Literary Figures* at the University of Bamberg. In his research he focuses on English literature of the nineteenth and twentieth centuries and adaptation and queer theory, as well as the history and theory of film.

INDEX

CPSIA information can be obtained at www.ICGtesting.com
Printed in the USA
LVOW07*2137030316

477707LV00006B/30/P